D1358538

The Move to
Global War

EUNICE PRICE • DANIELA SENÉS

Supporting every learner across the IB continuum

Published by Pearson Education Limited, 80 Strand, London, WC2R 0RL.
www.pearsonglobalschools.com

Text © Pearson Education Limited 2016
Edited by Sze Kiu Yeung
Proofread by Sarah Nisbet
Designed by Astwood Design
Typeset by Phoenix Photosetting, Chatham, Kent
Original illustrations © Pearson Education 2016
Illustrated by Tech-Set Ltd and Phoenix Photosetting
Cover design by Pearson Education Limited

The rights of Eunice Price and Daniela Senés to be identified as authors of this work have been asserted by them in accordance with the Copyright, Designs and Patents Act 1988.

First published 2016

19 18 17 16
IMP 10 9 8 7 6 5 4 3 2 1

British Library Cataloguing in Publication Data
A catalogue record for this book is available from the British Library

ISBN 978 1 292 10259 7
eBook only ISBN 978 1 292 10260 3

Printed in Slovakia by Neografia

Acknowledgements
The authors and publisher would like to thank Tom Buchanan for his invaluable help with and feedback on this title, and Malcolm Price for his expert help in the structuring and writing of the Theory of Knowledge section in this book.

The publisher would like to thank the following for their kind permission to reproduce their photographs:

(Key: b-bottom; c-centre; l-left; r-right; t-top)

5 TopFoto: ullsteinbild. **6 Getty Images:** The Print Collector / Hulton Archive. **8 Getty Images:** Keystone / Stringer. **10 Getty Images:** Popperfoto. **11 Bridgeman Art Library Ltd:** Universal History Archive / UIG / Portrait of Meiji emperor. **14 Art Object Photograph © 2016 Museum of Fine Arts, Boston:** Migita Toshihide, Japanese, 1863–1925 / After the Fall of Weihaiwei the Commander of the Chinese Beiyang Fleet, Admiral Ding Ruchang, Surrenders (Ikaiei kanraku Hokuyō kantai teitoku Tei Jōshō kōfuku no zu). **15 The Kobal Collection:** The Art Archive / Kharbine-Tapabor / "The Yellow Peril: European Nightmare" postcard by T. Blanco, c. 1900. **16 The Kobal Collection:** The Art Archive / Collection IM / Kharbine-Tapabor / 'Roosevelt: Assez! Enough! Genug!' President Theodore Roosevelt (1858-1919) separates Russia and Japan, political cartoon by T. Bianco, French postcard, 1905. **20 Courtesy of the Ohara Institute for Social Research, Hosei University. 24 Getty Images:** ullstein bild. **25 Getty Images:** Walter Gircke / ullstein bild. **27 Getty Images:** Keystone-France / Gamma-Keystone. **28 Getty Images:** ullsteinbild. **32 Getty Images:** ullstein bild (b); The Asahi Shimbun (t). **35 Getty Images:** Hulton Archive. **36 Getty Images:** Illustration by Jim Heimann Collection. **37 Getty Images:** Mansell / The LIFE Picture Collection. **39 Getty Images:** ullstein bild. **41 Alamy Images:** Everett Collection Historical. **42 Punch Limited. 43 Fotolia.com:** Krasnevsky. **44 By permission of the Estate of Rollin Kirby Post:** Cartoon 'His St Helena' by Kirby, Rollin, 1875-1952, artist DLC / PP-1933:0067.35 / Library of Congress, Prints & Photographs Division. **47 Library of Congress, Prints & Photographs Division:** Up "Nordics" and at 'em!, Pease, Lute, 1869-1963, artist. LC-DIG-ppmsca-13602. **48**

Shutterstock.com: Chungking. **49 Getty Images:** Hulton Archive / Stringer. **51 Corbis:** Bettmann (t). **TopFoto:** ullstein bild (b). **53 Getty Images:** Keystone-France / Gamma-Keystone. **54 Getty Images:** PhotoQuest. **56 TopFoto:** ullsteinbild. **58 TopFoto:** ullstein bild (b); Roger-Viollet (t). **59 Getty Images:** ullstein bild. **60 Getty Images:** The Asahi Shimbun (l), **London Express / Stringer (r). 61 Getty Images:** The Asahi Shimbun. **62 Getty Images:** The Asahi Shimbun. **65 Getty Images:** Pix Inc. / THE LIFE Picture Collection (b); Dorothea Lange (t). **74 Library of Congress, Prints & Photographs Division:** Japan splashing Uncle Sam by Berryman, Clifford Kennedy, 1869-1949, artist. LC-USZ62-39874 / Special Collections Research Center, The George Washington University. **75 Getty Images:** Underwood Archives. **76 TopFoto:** ullstein bild. **78 Rex Shutterstock:** Universal History Archive\UIG / REX Shutterstock (t). **TopFoto:** ullstein bild (b). **79 Getty Images:** MPI / Archive Photos. **80 Library of Congress, Prints & Photographs Division:** The Old Daisy Game by Berryman, Clifford Kennedy, 1869-1949, artist. acd1996000414 / PP / Special Collections Research Center, The George Washington University. **88 Getty Images:** Keystone-France / Gamma-Keystone. **91 Getty Images:** Keystone-France. **93 TopFoto:** World History Archive. **96 TopFoto:** TopFoto.co.uk. **99 Punch Limited. 102 Shutterstock. com:** Irisphoto1. **103 Getty Images:** DEA Picture Library. **104 Getty Images:** De Agostini / C. Sappa. **107 Mary Evans Picture Library:** P. Rotger / Iberfoto. **108 Corbis:** Hulton-Deutsch Collection (t). **Getty Images:** Istituto Nazionale Luce / Alinari (b). **111 Getty Images:** Keystone-France / Gamma-Keystone. **114 Mary Evans Picture Library. 117 Mary Evans Picture Library:** Picture-Alliance / Dpa. **118 TopFoto:** ullstein bild. **119 Alamy Images:** Glasshouse Images (l); David Cole (r). **120 Corbis. 123 Alamy Images:** Glasshouse Images (b). **TopFoto:** ullstein bild (t). **124 Getty Images:** Popperfoto. **126 TopFoto:** The Image Works. **128 TopFoto:** Roger-Viollet. **130 TopFoto:** ullstein bild. **131 Corbis. 134 Getty Images:** ullstein bild. **137 Corbis:** Michael Nicholson (r); Hulton-Deutsch Collection (l). **140 Bridgeman Art Library Ltd:** Soviet poster depicting 'Western powers giving Hitler Czechoslovakia on a dish', Kukryniksy (20th Century) / Private Collection / Bridgeman Images. **141 Getty Images:** London Express / Stringer. **142 Corbis:** Michael Nicholson. **144 McCord Museum, Montreal:** Gift of Mr. John Collins - The Gazette. **145 McCord Museum, Montreal:** Gift of Mr. John Collins - The Gazette. **146 Punch Limited. 147 Punch Limited. 148 Alamy Images:** Interfoto. **149 Bridgeman Art Library Ltd:** Underwood Archives / UIG. **150 Punch Limited. 151 TopFoto:** ullstein bild. **152 Punch Limited. 160 ©2012 Regents of the University of California. All rights reserved.:** Seuss, Dr.. **161 Getty Images:** Yoshikazu Tsuno (r); Dirck Halstead (l). **162 Getty Images:** George F. Lee / AFP. **164 Getty Images:** George F. Lee. **xiv 123RF.com:** Stefanina Hill (tr). **Fotolia. com:** Pict Rider (tc); Elzloy (br). **Shutterstock.com:** Niyazz (bl); Dariush M (tl)

All other images © Pearson Education

Maps
Map on page 106 adapted from *Pearson Baccalaureate: History: A Comprehensive Guide to Paper 1 for the IB Diploma*, Pearson Education Ltd. (Mimmack, B., Daniela Senes, D., Price, E. 2009) p.87.

Tables
Table on page 129 republished with permission of Greenwood Press from *Why England Slept*, John F. Kennedy, 1981, permission conveyed through Copyright Clearance Center, Inc.

Text
Extracts on pages 7, 8, 11, 12, 23, 23-24, 35, 38, 46, 52, 81 from *Inventing Japan: 1853-1964* by Ian Buruma, copyright © 2003 by Ian Buruma. Used by permission of Random House, an imprint and division of Penguin Random House LLC. All rights reserved; Extracts on pages 9, 12, 14, 19, 21, 22, 23, 24, 26, 52 from *Japan, A Short History*, Oneworld Publications (Hane, M. 2015); Extracts on pages 12, 24, 30, 31, 49, 59, 63, 65, 75, 76, 77 from *Japan 1941: Countdown to Infamy* by Eri Hotta, copyright © 2013 by Eri Hotta. Used by permission of Alfred A. Knopf, an imprint of the Knopf Doubleday Publishing Group, a division of Penguin Random House LLC. All rights reserved; Extracts

on pages 18, 49, 58, 76 from *The Cambridge History of Japan, Volume 6: The Twentieth Century*, Cambridge University Press (Duus, P. (ed), 1995) p.282; Extract on page 23 from Jonathan N. Lipman, Imperial Japan: 1894–1945, 2008, http://aboutjapan.japansociety.org/content.cfm/imperial_japan_1894-1945_1, reproduced with permission from the author; Extracts on page 34, 38, 39 from *The Rise of Modern China* (Hsu, I. 1995), © 1995 by Oxford University Press, Inc. By permission of Oxford University Press, USA; Extracts on pages 50, 59, 59-60, 60, 66, 73, 81republished with permission of Blackwell Publishers from *The Causes of the Second World War*, Andrew J. Crozier, 1997, permission conveyed through Copyright Clearance Center, Inc; Extract on page 53 from *The Rape of Nanking* by Iris Chang copyright © 1997. Reprinted by permission of Basic Books, a member of The Perseus Books Group; Extract on page 82 from History Teaching and Historiography: the Textbook Controversy by Bandō, Hiroshi, *Historical Studies in Japan (VII) 1983-1987: Japan at the XVIIth International Congress of Historical Sciences in Madrid (VII, 198)*, pub Brill (ed. National Committee of Japanese Historians 1991), with permission from Koninklijke Brill; Extracts on pages 91, 106 from *Fascist Voices: An Intimate History of Mussolini's Italy*, Vintage Books (Dugan, C. 2012), with permission from Random House UK; Extract on page 94 from *The Fascist Experience in Italy*, 1st ed., Routledge (Pollard, J. 1998) p.93, copyright © 1998 Routledge, reproduced by permission of Taylor & Francis Books UK; Extract on page 101 from More Than Meets the Eye by Brian R. Sullivan, *The Origins of the Second World War Reconsidered: A.J.P. Taylor and the Historians*, 2nd ed., Routledge, p.197 (Gordon Martel, ed. 1999), copyright © 1999 Routledge, reproduced by permission of Taylor & Francis Books UK; Extract on page 105 from *The British Defence of Egypt, 1935-1940: Conflict and Crisis in the Eastern Mediterranean* 1st ed., Frank Cass (Morewood, S. 2005) p.80, copyright © 2005 Frank Cass, reproduced by permission of Taylor & Francis Books UK; Extract on page 105 from *1935 Sanctions Aganist Italy: Would Coal and Crude Oil Have Made a Difference?*, by Cristiano Andrea Ristuccia http://www.nuffield.ox.ac.uk/economics/history/paper14/14paper.pdf, reproduced with permission; Extract on page 109 from *The Second World War: Ambitions to Nemesis*, 1st ed., Routledge (Lightbody, B. 2004) p.21, copyright © 2004 Routledge, reproduced by permission of Taylor & Francis Books UK; Extract on page 109 from republished with permission of Cornell University Press from *Vital Crossroads: Mediterranean Origins of the Second World War, 1935–1940*, p.22 (Salerno, R.M. 2002), Copyright © 2002; permission conveyed through Copyright Clearance Center, Inc; Extract on page 111 from *Mussolini*, University of Chicago Press (Fermi, L. 1966) p.387 with permission from the University of Chicago Press; Extract on page 112 from *The Lights That Failed: European International History, 1919–1933*, Oxford University Press (Steiner, Z. 2005), by permission of Oxford University Press; Extracts on pages 116, 139 from *The Origins of World War II*, 3rd ed., Harlan Davidson (Eubank, K. 2004) p.12, Copyright © 1969, 1990, 2004 Harlan Davidson, Inc. All rights reserved. Reproduced with permission of John Wiley & Sons Inc; Extract on p.117 from *Republican and Fascist Germany: Themes and Variations in the History of Weimer and the Third Reich, 1918-45* by (Hiden, J. 1996), Copyright © 1996 Longman, p.117, reproduced by permission of Taylor & Francis Books UK; Extract on page 125 from An economy geared to war, *History Today*, Vol. 51, Issue 11, November, p.S27 (2001), with permission from History Today; Extract on page 127 from Interview of Adolf Hitler, *Daily Mail*, 19 October 1933; Extract on page 128 from Zalampas, Michael, *Adolf Hitler and the Third Reich in American Magazines, 1923-1939* © 1989 by the Board of Regents of the University of Wisconsin System. Reprinted by permission of The University of Wisconsin Press; Extract on page 132 from *Nazism 1919-1945 A History in Documents and Eyewitness Accounts, Volume II*, Exeter University Press (Noakes, J. and Pridham, G. 1988) p.675, Liverpool University Press; Extract on page 132 reprinted with the permission of Abner Stein and Simon & Schuster, Inc. from *The rise and Fall of the Third Reich*, by William L. Shirer, p.307 (1990), Copyright 1959, 1960 William L. Shirer, copyright renewed © 1987, 1988 William L. Shirer; Extract on page 146 from *Hitler and Mussolini: A comparative analysis of the Rome-Berlin Axis 1936-1940*, by Stephanie Hodgson 29 July 2011, with permission from Stephanie Hodgson; Extract on page 147 from *Poland, 1918-1945: An Interpretive and Documentary History of the Second Republic* by P. D. Stachura, Copyright © 2004 Routledge p.117, reproduced by permission of Taylor & Francis Books UK; Extract on page 150 from Winston S. Churchill's 'Arm yourselves and be ye men of valour' speech, 19 May 1940, Broadcast, London, reproduced with permission of Curtis Brown, London on behalf of The Estate of Winston S. Churchill; Extract on page 152 from *A World in Flames:A Short History of the Second World War in Europe and Asia, 1939-1945*, Routledge (Kitchen, M. 1990), copyright © 1990 Routledge, reproduced by permission of Taylor & Francis Books UK; Extract on page 157 from *The New Doublespeak: Why No One Knows What Anyone is Saying Anymore*, HarperCollins (Lutz, W. 1996), © 1996 by William Lutz. Used by permission of William Lutz in care of the Jean V. Naggar Literary Agency, Inc; Extracts on page 161 from Binational Pearl Harbor? Tora! Tora! Tora! and the Fate of (Trans)national Memory, *The Asia-Pacific Journal*, Vol. 8, Issue 52 No. 2, 27 December (Thorsten, M. and White, G.M. 2010), http://www.japanfocus.org/-Marie-Thorsten/3462/article.html#sthash.AtsvQ531.dpuf, with permission from the authors; Extract on page 161 from What historians think of historical novels, *Financial Times*, 15/02/2015 (Schama, S.), http://www.ft.com/cms/s/0/ec5583e2-b115-11e4-9331-00144feab7de.html, © The Financial Times Limited. All Rights Reserved.

Extract on p.97, Activity 5 from *Prelude to World War II*, Gollancz (Salvemini, G. 1953), p.67,originally published by Orion in 1953.

Text extracts relating to the IB syllabus and assessment have been reproduced from IBO documents. Our thanks go to the International Baccalaureate for permission to reproduce its intellectual copyright.

This material has been developed independently by the publisher and the content is in no way connected with or endorsed by the International Baccalaureate (IB). International Baccalaureate® is a registered trademark of the International Baccalaureate Organization.

Every effort has been made to trace the copyright holders and we apologise in advance for any unintentional omissions. We would be pleased to insert the appropriate acknowledgement in any subsequent edition of this publication.

There are links to relevant websites in this book. In order to ensure that the links are up to date and that the links work we have made the links available on our website at www.pearsonhotlinks.com. Search for this title or ISBN 978 1 292 10259 7.

Contents

Introduction

How will this book help you in your IB examination?

This book will help you prepare for Paper 1 in the International Baccalaureate History exam by equipping you with the knowledge and skills you need to demonstrate in your examination. It focuses on Prescribed Subject 3 (The Move to Global War), one of five prescribed subjects in Paper 1. Each prescribed subject includes two case studies. Below are the case studies covered in this book:

- Case Study 1: Japanese expansion in East Asia between 1931 and 1941
- Case Study 2: German and Italian expansion between 1933 and 1940.

This book includes three chapters on each of the two case studies, addressing the three areas of the material for detailed study as outlined in the IB History Guide. There is a chapter on how to approach Paper 1 exam questions, providing a useful explanation of the demands of the different question types, and offering advice on how to approach them. There is also a chapter on Theory of Knowledge (ToK). Together, these chapters enable you to gain an understanding of the aims of the IB History course, as well as the key concepts and skills that are reflected in the structure and assessment objectives of Paper 1.

The content of the book will also be useful for those taking the Higher Level Regional Option Paper 3, as the case studies are relevant to the history of their respective regions. It also covers a number of Paper 2 topics, such as Topic 10 (Authoritarian States – 20th Century) and Topic 11 (Causes and Effects of 20th-Century Wars). In addition, this book will assist you in choosing and researching suitable topics for the Internal Assessment (IA – Historical Investigation) or the History Extended Essays (EE).

How will this book help you prepare for Paper 1?

Prescribed Subject 3 (The Move to Global War) focuses on the interwar conflicts between 1931 and 1941 in order to examine how and why World War II became a worldwide conflict.

Case Study 1 focuses on Japanese expansionism in East Asia between 1931 and 1941, while Case Study 2 addresses German and Italian expansionism in Europe between 1933 and 1940. Your Paper 1 exam will be set on *one* of the case studies and will focus on one aspect of the material for detailed study as outlined in the IB History Guide. You will not know in advance which case study your exam is going to be set on. Therefore, it is important that you study both case studies and cover all material for detailed study in the History Guide.

Although exams are set on one case study, Japanese, German, and Italian expansions are no doubt interconnected. It is impossible to fully understand *how* World War II broke out without assessing these connections by, for instance, analysing the Japanese reactions to events in Europe. It is also difficult to understand *why* war broke out unless we consider the events that paved the way for Japanese, Italian, and German aggression before 1931, the starting date of this prescribed subject. For example, it is important to recognize the impact of the treaties signed at the end of World War I on Japan, Germany, and Italy in order to understand the nature and aims of these countries' aggressive foreign policies.

This book addresses each of the three main areas of the material for detailed study: causes of expansion, events, and responses. In doing so, it relates them to one another to help you gain an insight into how and why there was a move to global war between 1931 and 1941. Relating these areas will not only help you gain a better understanding of the prescribed subject itself but will also help you work with each of the six key concepts for DP History: continuity, change, causation, consequence, perspective, significance. Understanding these concepts is central to comprehending and interpreting sources.

What this book includes

Each case study includes:

- timelines of important events to help you put them into context
- specific focus on each of the six key concepts for DP History: continuity, change, causation, consequence, perspective, significance. Understanding and applying these concepts are central to evaluating and integrating sources in your answers
- analyses of the causes, events, and responses to the expansion
- primary and secondary sources, including reference to relevant historiographical approaches
- examples of students' responses to help you reflect on a variety of approaches used by students in tackling exam questions

- examiner's comments to explain the strengths and weaknesses of students' responses, and to make recommendations on how these could be improved
- review sections to help you reflect on your learning and revise key topics.

The book also has a chapter on how to approach Paper 1 questions and develop source analysis and evaluation skills and techniques, as well as a chapter on Theory of Knowledge (ToK) to help you think about the links between the study and writing of history and other areas of knowledge.

Important terms in each chapter are **emboldened** in the text; their definitions can be found in the glossary at the back of the book.

eBook

In the eBook you will find the following:

- additional worksheets containing student activities
- an interactive glossary
- practice examination quizzes
- revision quizzes

- biographies of key figures covered in the book
- links to relevant Internet sites
- enlargeable photos of useful resources, such as maps and source cartoons.

For more details about your eBook, see pages x–xi.

How this book works

In addition to the main text, there are a number of coloured boxes in every chapter, each with a distinctive icon. The boxes provide different information and stimulus:

Key facts and interesting facts

These boxes contain additional useful and interesting information that will add to your wider knowledge, but which does not fit within the main body of the text.

Names of emperors

The emperors of Japan may be referred to either by their title and personal name (for example, Emperor Mutsuhito) or by the title and the name given to their era (Emperor Meiji). Throughout this case study, where the full name of an emperor is mentioned, his personal name will appear in brackets, for example, Emperor Meiji (Mutsuhito).

'A splendid little war'

This phrase has been used many times in history to describe what belligerents had hoped would be a short and successful conflict. Vyacheslav Plehve, the minister of interior appointed by Tsar Nicholas II, is reported to have said that what Russia needed in 1904 was a 'little victorious war to stem a revolution'. Whether or not this is accurate is a matter of some speculation, but 'a splendid little war' (as a corruption of the above phrase) is commonly used to describe Russia's mistaken prediction of how the war against Japan would turn out.

International mindedness

These are activities that invite you to explore, for example, the similarities and differences between different states, or to reflect on how your knowledge contributes to a better understanding of the world we live in today.

With a classmate, consider the international context for the Brussels Conference. Carry out research on events taking place in Germany, Italy, and Spain in 1937, as well as on Stalin's purge of the military in 1937. How, and why, do you think, these events would have influenced Jiang's decision-making about going to war with Japan? Bear in mind Japan's relations with Germany and Italy at this time. Outline the case for and against war with Japan.

Challenge yourself

These boxes invite you to carry out additional research on an aspect discussed in the chapter.

CHALLENGE YOURSELF

Research, thinking communication, and self-management skills **ATL**

Write a short summary of how the international response to the Manchurian Incident could be seen as weakening the aims outlined in both the League of Nations and the Kellogg–Briand Pact.

Hints for success

These boxes can be found alongside questions, exercises, and worked examples. They provide insight into how to answer a question in order to achieve the highest marks in an examination. They also identify common pitfalls when answering such questions and suggest approaches that examiners like to see.

Look carefully at every part of the cartoon in Source C, including the caption. Try to identify the main characters; pay attention to the heaps of skulls in the background as well as the setting sun. All of these are symbolic and help you to understand what the cartoonist was trying to convey.

Weblinks

At the end of each chapter, you will find the URL for the Pearson hotlinks website in the weblinks box. To access websites relevant to a particular chapter, go to www.pearsonhotlinks.com, search for the book title or ISBN, and click on the relevant chapter number.

To access websites relevant to this chapter, go to www.pearsonhotlinks.com, search for the book title or ISBN, and click on 'Chapter 1'.

Relevant websites for each chapter can also be found in the Further Reading section at the end of the book. These websites contain video material and additional information to support the topic you are studying.

Theory of Knowledge

There are also Theory of Knowledge (ToK) boxes throughout the book – see page viii for more information about these.

IB History aims and assessment objectives

Whether you are studying history at Higher or Standard Level, you need to take a broad view of how past events have brought us to where we are today. The awareness of how events separated by both time and space are nevertheless linked together in cause and effect is one of the most important skills to be developed during the IB History course. For example, you need to understand what circumstances in Europe and Asia contributed to the aggressive foreign policies of Japan, Italy, and Germany, and to analyse the international response to them.

Although this book is essentially designed as a textbook to accompany Paper 1, Prescribed Subject 3 (The Move to Global War), as you work through it you will be learning and practising the skills that are necessary for different papers. This book also covers the assessment objectives relevant to Paper 1 – specifically, the assessment objectives on the following skills:

Assessment objective 1: Knowledge and understanding

You will learn how to demonstrate understanding of historical sources and their context.

Assessment objective 2: Application and analysis

You will learn to analyse and interpret a variety of sources, such as cartoons, tables, photographs, speeches, academic writings, and newspaper articles.

Assessment objective 3: Synthesis and evaluation

You will learn how to evaluate information from a variety of sources. You will also learn to evaluate historical sources and to recognize their value and limitations.

Assessment objective 4: Use and application of appropriate skills

You will develop the ability to synthesize sources by using evidence to support relevant, balanced, and focused historical arguments.

IB Learner Profile

When the IB set out a course curriculum, they have in mind certain qualities that they want a student to develop. These are not abstract ideas; everything you learn and do as part of the IB programme contributes to the development of these qualities. These objectives apply to the study of history.

Through the study of the prescribed subject in this book, you will become more knowledgeable about the world around you, and you will learn to evaluate

sources critically and to challenge them. History is not only about what happened in the past but also about how events have been interpreted at different times. Be prepared to change your mind; if you hold a particular opinion about an issue, find out about different points of view. It is useful to reflect on how the material you have learned and the skills you have acquired are relevant to areas other than history, and how they help you deal with your understanding, for example, of global issues.

Theory of Knowledge

History is a Group 3 subject in the IB Diploma. It is an 'area of knowledge' that considers individuals and societies. In the study of IB History, many different ways of obtaining knowledge are used. When working through this book you should reflect not only on the methods used by professional historians, but also those that you – as a student of history – use to gain knowledge. The methods used by historians are important to highlight, as it will be necessary to compare and contrast these with the other 'areas of knowledge', such as the Human Sciences and the Group 4 Sciences (Physics, Chemistry, and Biology). You should think about the role of individuals in history, the difference between bias and selection, and the role played by the historian. You will reflect in detail on these types of questions in the final section of your Internal Assessment.

Theory of Knowledge boxes

There are ToK boxes throughout the book. These boxes will enable you to consider ToK issues as they arise and in context. Often they will just contain a question to stimulate your thoughts and discussion.

In his account of the Abyssinian crisis, historian Piers Brendon notes how, in 1934, Haile Selassie asked Germany for supplies of conventional and chemical weapons, and how Hitler sent him rifles and machine guns. How does knowing that Haile Selassie tried to obtain chemical weapons from Hitler influence the way you evaluate this event? To what extent does the rightness of an action depend on the context? What does this reveal about the role of emotions in the study of history?

We have also included a chapter on Theory of Knowledge, which has been updated for the latest ToK curriculum with the help of ToK expert Malcolm Price. In it, you will be encouraged to reflect on the methods that historians use, by thinking about questions such as:

- What is the role of the historian?
- What methods do historians use to gain knowledge?

- Who decides which events are historically significant?

These types of questions require you to reflect on and engage with how historians work, and will help you with the reflection section of the Internal Assessment.

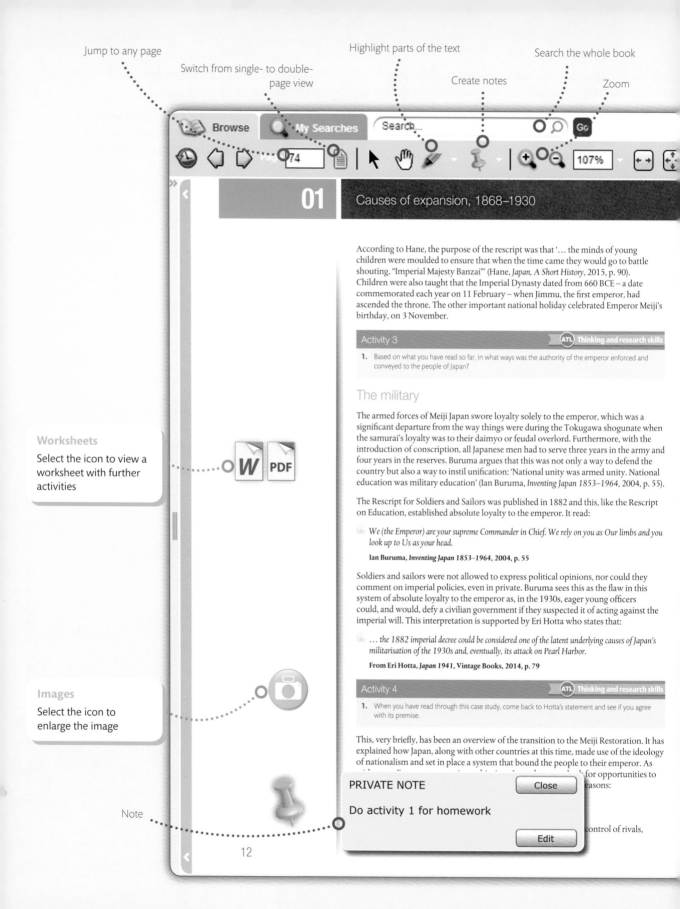

Jump to any page

Switch from single- to double-page view

Highlight parts of the text

Create notes

Search the whole book

Zoom

Browse   My Searches   Search...   Go

Page 74   107%

Worksheets

Select the icon to view a worksheet with further activities

Images

Select the icon to enlarge the image

Note

01   Causes of expansion, 1868–1930

According to Hane, the purpose of the rescript was that '… the minds of young children were moulded to ensure that when the time came they would go to battle shouting, "Imperial Majesty Banzai"' (Hane, *Japan, A Short History*, 2015, p. 90). Children were also taught that the Imperial Dynasty dated from 660 BCE – a date commemorated each year on 11 February – when Jimmu, the first emperor, had ascended the throne. The other important national holiday celebrated Emperor Meiji's birthday, on 3 November.

Activity 3   (ATL) **Thinking and research skills**

1. Based on what you have read so far, in what ways was the authority of the emperor enforced and conveyed to the people of Japan?

The military

The armed forces of Meiji Japan swore loyalty solely to the emperor, which was a significant departure from the way things were during the Tokugawa shogunate when the samurai's loyalty was to their daimyo or feudal overlord. Furthermore, with the introduction of conscription, all Japanese men had to serve three years in the army and four years in the reserves. Buruma argues that this was not only a way to defend the country but also a way to instil unification: 'National unity was armed unity. National education was military education' (Ian Buruma, *Inventing Japan 1853–1964*, 2004, p. 55).

The Rescript for Soldiers and Sailors was published in 1882 and this, like the Rescript on Education, established absolute loyalty to the emperor. It read:

> We (the Emperor) are your supreme Commander in Chief. We rely on you as Our limbs and you look up to Us as your head.

Ian Buruma, Inventing Japan 1853–1964, 2004, p. 55

Soldiers and sailors were not allowed to express political opinions, nor could they comment on imperial policies, even in private. Buruma sees this as the flaw in this system of absolute loyalty to the emperor as, in the 1930s, eager young officers could, and would, defy a civilian government if they suspected it of acting against the imperial will. This interpretation is supported by Eri Hotta who states that:

> … the 1882 imperial decree could be considered one of the latent underlying causes of Japan's militarisation of the 1930s and, eventually, its attack on Pearl Harbor.

From Eri Hotta, Japan 1941, Vintage Books, 2014, p. 79

Activity 4   (ATL) **Thinking and research skills**

1. When you have read through this case study, come back to Hotta's statement and see if you agree with its premise.

This, very briefly, has been an overview of the transition to the Meiji Restoration. It has explained how Japan, along with other countries at this time, made use of the ideology of nationalism and set in place a system that bound the people to their emperor. As for opportunities to ...asons:

PRIVATE NOTE   Close

Do activity 1 for homework

...control of rivals,   Edit

12

See the definitions of key terms in the glossary

ate a bookmark   Switch to whiteboard view

1.1

First stages of imperialism

Activity 5   **ATL** Thinking and research skills

Study the map below and answer the question that follows.

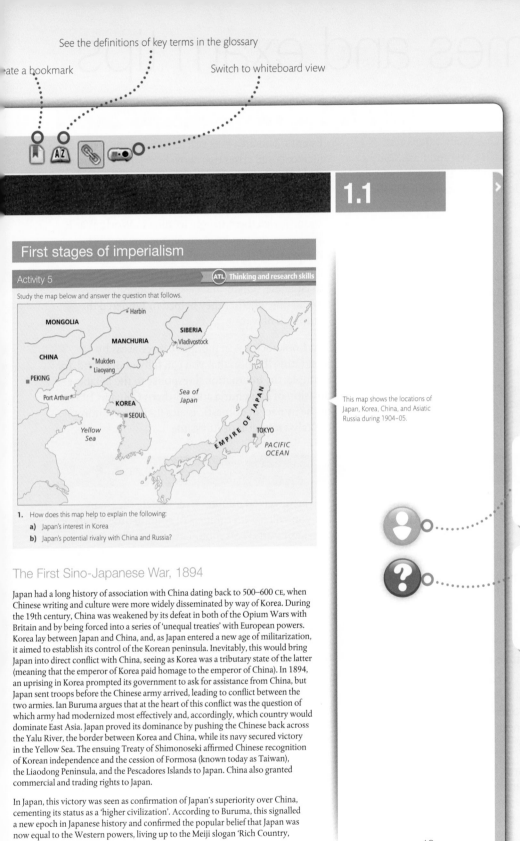

This map shows the locations of Japan, Korea, China, and Asiatic Russia during 1904–05.

1. How does this map help to explain the following:
   a) Japan's interest in Korea
   b) Japan's potential rivalry with China and Russia?

Biographies

Select the icon to open biographies of key figures mentioned in the text

Quiz

Select the icon to take an interactive quiz to test your knowledge or practise answering exam essay questions

The First Sino-Japanese War, 1894

Japan had a long history of association with China dating back to 500–600 CE, when Chinese writing and culture were more widely disseminated by way of Korea. During the 19th century, China was weakened by its defeat in both of the Opium Wars with Britain and by being forced into a series of 'unequal treaties' with European powers. Korea lay between Japan and China, and, as Japan entered a new age of militarization, it aimed to establish its control of the Korean peninsula. Inevitably, this would bring Japan into direct conflict with China, seeing as Korea was a tributary state of the latter (meaning that the emperor of Korea paid homage to the emperor of China). In 1894, an uprising in Korea prompted its government to ask for assistance from China, but Japan sent troops before the Chinese army arrived, leading to conflict between the two armies. Ian Buruma argues that at the heart of this conflict was the question of which army had modernized most effectively and, accordingly, which country would dominate East Asia. Japan proved its dominance by pushing the Chinese back across the Yalu River, the border between Korea and China, while its navy secured victory in the Yellow Sea. The ensuing Treaty of Shimonoseki affirmed Chinese recognition of Korean independence and the cession of Formosa (known today as Taiwan), the Liaodong Peninsula, and the Pescadores Islands to Japan. China also granted commercial and trading rights to Japan.

In Japan, this victory was seen as confirmation of Japan's superiority over China, cementing its status as a 'higher civilization'. According to Buruma, this signalled a new epoch in Japanese history and confirmed the popular belief that Japan was now equal to the Western powers, living up to the Meiji slogan 'Rich Country,

13

Themes and exam tips

What should you study?

You should study both Case Study 1 (Japanese expansion in East Asia, 1931–41) and Case Study 2 (German and Italian expansion, 1933–40), focusing on the material for detailed study specified in the IB History Guide for Prescribed Subject 3.

The material for detailed study is divided into three areas:

- **Causes of expansionism:** This area asks you to consider what circumstances contributed to the aggressive nature of the foreign policies of Japan, Italy, and Germany. Some of these circumstances preceded the rise of the expansionist governments, such as Japan's desire to extend its control over Korea and then Manchuria; while others, such as the role of Nazi ideology, became significant with their rise. Looking at long- and short-term causes of expansionism will help you understand which circumstances played a part in the move to global war.

- **Events:** This area asks you to consider different incidents and crises that show how Japan, Germany, and Italy tried to achieve territorial expansion by either threatening to use or by using force. You will examine how the foreign policies of these three countries led them to fight as allies in World War II and assess the results of the alliance up to 1941.

- **Responses:** This area asks you to consider the international, diplomatic, and military responses to Japanese, Italian, and German aggression by evaluating whether they helped or hindered the outbreak of war.

This book focuses on the above three areas by integrating them so that you can fully understand, for example, the international response to the Japanese invasion of Manchuria and northern China in 1931, or the impact of domestic issues (like the economy) on Italy's invasion of Abyssinia.

What does Paper 1 look like?

Whether you are taking History as a Higher or Standard Level, you will be sitting Paper 1.

Paper 1 will clearly indicate which case study is being tested but you will need to use your learning to decipher which part of the case study to focus on from the sources and questions given. Below is what you will see at the top of your section of the paper:

Section C: The move to global war

Read sources A to D carefully and answer the questions that follow. The sources and questions relate to the following aspect of the syllabus: Japanese expansion in East Asia (1931–41): Events.

Sources in this paper have been edited: word additions or explanations are shown in square brackets [ ]; substantive deletions of text are indicated by ellipses... ; minor changes are not indicated.

You are given 60 minutes to complete the exam, but you will have 5 minutes of reading time before the exam starts. You should use the reading time effectively to familiarize yourself with the sources and questions.

The paper will include four sources, which will be a combination of primary and secondary sources (one will always be a visual source, for example, a cartoon, photograph, or map); sometimes you may find a table-based source. Sources are approximately 750 words long and include source attributions. Attributions are very important as they tell you where and when each source was produced, and they can offer useful information about the author of each source.

> Throughout this chapter, you will see how the information in the attributions can help you answer some of the questions.

Paper 1 will have four questions that you are required to answer. These questions will follow a specific format and order. You will find many examples of these questions and possible answers throughout this book. They will help you familiarize yourself with the specific demands of each question type.

There are a maximum of 24 marks to be gained in this paper. The marks awarded for each question are indicated in the exam paper. Like the format and order of the questions, the marks do not change from session to session.

The following chart provides an overview of the structure of Paper 1.

Question	Aim of the question	Marks awarded
First question, Part A	This question will test understanding of one of the sources.	3 marks
First question, Part B	This question will test understanding of one of the sources.	2 marks
Second question	This question will ask students to analyse the value and limitations of one of the sources. In their analysis of value and limitations, students should refer to the origin, purpose, and content of the specified source.	4 marks
Third question	This question asks students to compare and contrast two of the sources in terms of what they reveal to a historian studying a particular aspect of the prescribed subject.	6 marks
Fourth question	This will be an evaluative question that asks students to draw both on the sources and their own knowledge in their evaluation.	9 marks

(Table taken from the IB History Guide ® IBO, 2016)

Paper 1 question formats

First question, part A (3 marks)

What, according to the source, was…?

- Make three distinct points to obtain one mark per relevant idea.
- Express each point separately. For example:
  - *One of the aims/reasons given by the source is…*
  - *The second aim/reason is…*
  - *Finally,…*
  (Using separate paragraphs for each point is another way of highlighting this.)
- Provide supporting evidence from the source by quoting a few words from it, or paraphrase.
- Work only with the source. Outside knowledge can help you put the source in its historical context and understand it better but including it in the written response will not count towards the marks.

First question, part B (2 marks)

What is the message conveyed by the source?

- This question usually relates to the visual or graphic source (for example, a cartoon, a table, or a map).

- If a source features historical characters, its attribution and caption will usually provide you with the information about who they are. For example, on page 16, you will find a cartoon from 1906 of US president Theodore Roosevelt with his hands on the shoulders of the tsar of Russia and the emperor of Japan. The cartoon – taken from a postcard – was drawn at the time of the Treaty of Portsmouth that ended the Russo-Japanese War. The caption reads: 'Assez, Enough, Genug'. To interpret the message of the source fully you need to use your knowledge of its context.
- Some cartoons use symbols to put their message across; while most symbols will probably be explained in the attribution, there are some very well-known ones you should be able to identify yourself.
- This question is asking you what messages the source is putting across. Therefore, do not just describe what you see in the source. Use what you see to *support* the messages you have identified. You may begin your paragraph like this:
  - *One of the messages of the source is that… This can be clearly seen in the cartoon in…*

- You can also express your points separately as different paragraphs by using phrases like these to introduce each point:

- ○ *The first message…*
- ○ *Another message…*
- ○ *A further message…*

Activity 1

 Social and communication skills

1. In pairs, identify the following symbols and what they represent.

Second question (4 marks)

With reference to its origin, purpose, and content, analyse the value and limitations of the source…

- This question asks that you examine how valuable a source is to a historian studying a specific topic (mentioned in the question), by focusing on the source's origin, purpose, and content.
  - ○ Examining the **origin** means looking at *who* produced the source, and *where* and *when* it was written. The attribution will include the author as well as the time and place where the source was produced. Look at the source below and state its origins.
  - ○ Examining the **purpose** means asking *why* this source was produced. Ask yourself what type of source it is; this will help you understand for *whom* the source was produced (that is, its intended audience). Look carefully again at the attribution. If the source is from an academic book, its title can tell you whether the book is an in-depth study of the topic or something concerning a broader subject.
  - ○ Examining the **content** means asking yourself: *what is the source saying?* (But also consider if there is something important you think the source is not saying.) What is its tone?

Activity 2

 Social, communication , and thinking skills

This is an extract taken from a speech by Mussolini to the workers of Milan, 1934.

> ❝ *This is not a crisis in the traditional sense of the term. It is the passage from one phase of civilization to another. It is no longer an economy aiming at individual profit, but an economy concerned with collective interests […] The future cannot be planned like an itinerary or a timetable. One must not take out a mortgage too long into the future. Indeed, as we have said before, we are absolutely convinced that fascism is bound to become the standard type of civilization of our century for Italy and for Europe.*

1. Look at the attribution. What do you think is the purpose of this source?

2. With reference to its origin, purpose, and content, analyse the value and limitations of this source for a historian studying the impact of the Great Depression on Mussolini's foreign policy.

3. In pairs, think of other points you could include in your evaluation of this source, in addition to the points covered in the table.

You may find the table below useful in helping you plan your answer to the above question. It lists some of the arguments you could use to evaluate Mussolini's speech in relation to its origin, purpose, and content.

	Value	Limitations
Origin	It is contemporary to the Great Depression.	The Great Depression may still be having an impact.
Purpose	It shows the methods used by Mussolini to motivate workers at the time of the Great Depression.	As a speech to workers, it has an element of propaganda.
Content	Mussolini recognizes the existence of a crisis and the need for change.	His ideas on what changes the Great Depression is bringing about are rather vague.

Avoid saying that because a source has been translated it has limitations. Also, do not say that because it is only an extract of the original source it is of limited value. Primary sources are not necessarily valuable because they are primary.

Third question (6 marks)

Compare and contrast what Sources A and B reveal about…

- This question requires that you discuss the ways in which two sources are similar and how they are different. The similarities and differences usually relate to a point of view. A typical question may be: **Compare and contrast what Source A and Source B reveal about Mussolini's foreign policy in the 1930s.**
- Because the question is asking about the views expressed in the sources, do not compare and contrast the origins and purpose of the sources. Focus instead on the *content*: that is, what the sources *say*.
- Offer both comparisons and contrasts. Ideally, you should find three of each, but some sources may have more points of contrast than comparisons (or the other way around). In any case, try to offer six different arguments.
- Write each comparison or contrast as a separate paragraph and clearly indicate whether you are comparing or contrasting. Use the following words and phrases to shape your arguments:
  - Comparisons: *Also… / Both sources reveal… / Similarly…*
  - Contrasts: *However… / On the other hand… /… as opposed to Source B…*

- Indicate what you are comparing and contrasting by making explicit references to the sources, either by paraphrasing the sources or including brief quotations.
- Write full answers; do not include bullet points or charts.
- If you merely state in a paragraph that something is mentioned in one source and not in the other (*'Source A discusses such-and-such while Source B does not.'*), it will not be counted as a valid contrast and you will not gain any marks for it.

Markbands used to mark the third question

Marks	Level descriptor
0	• The response does not reach a standard described by the descriptors above.
1–2	• There is superficial discussion of one or both sources. • The response consists of description of the content of the source(s), and/or general comments about the source(s), rather than valid points of comparison or of contrast.
3–4	• There is some discussion of both sources, although the two sources may be discussed separately. • The response includes some valid points of comparison and/or of contrast, although these points may lack clarity.
5–6	• There is discussion of both sources. Explicit links are made between the two sources. • The response includes clear and valid points of comparison and of contrast.

(Table taken from the IB Online Curriculum Centre ® IBO, 2016)

CHALLENGE YOURSELF

Read the above markbands for the third question in the paper. In groups, discuss what the differences between each level descriptor are. How can you make sure an answer fits the highest markband?

Fourth question (9 marks)

Using the sources and your own knowledge, evaluate…

- Take some time to plan your answer as this question carries the most number of marks. Decide how you would like to use each source and what relevant knowledge you would like to recall for this question.
- Make sure your answer focuses on the specific question. Do not limit it to a summary of what the sources say or what you know about the question topic in general.
- It is important that you use both the sources from the paper and your own knowledge to answer the question. Your own knowledge can be used to further support or refute a source.
- Make sure every argument you offer is supported either by the sources, your own knowledge, or both. Use the following sentences to open an argument:
  - *This idea is supported by Source A as it states that…*
  - *The fact that… suggests that…*
- If the question asks you to discuss the extent to which you agree with a statement, you should provide arguments both for and against it. With reference to the sources, start by deciding which side of the argument each source supports – though a source can sometimes be used to support both sides! You need to show clearly how each source contributes to your arguments.
- When using a source, make specific reference to it by either naming it ('*Source C claims…*') or by quoting from it. Keep your quotations short, however, as you will not have much time to write your answer.
- When referring to your own knowledge, provide as much information as possible. Include specific names, dates, and any other relevant detail to demonstrate your understanding of the topic you are discussing.
- After you have finished writing your main arguments, refer back to the question and offer a brief conclusion.

Markbands used to answer the fourth question

Marks	Level descriptor
0	• The response does not reach a standard described by the descriptors above.
1–3	• The response lacks focus on the question. • References to the sources are made, but at this level these references are likely to consist of descriptions of the content of the sources rather than the sources being used as evidence to support the analysis. • No own knowledge is demonstrated or, where it is demonstrated, it is inaccurate or irrelevant.
4–6	• The response is generally focused on the question. • References are made to the sources, and these references are used as evidence to support the analysis. • Where own knowledge is demonstrated, this lacks relevance or accuracy. There is little or no attempt to synthesize own knowledge and source material.
7–9	• The response is focused on the question. • Clear references are made to the sources, and these references are used effectively as evidence to support the analysis. • Accurate and relevant own knowledge is demonstrated. There is effective synthesis of own knowledge and source material.

(Table taken from the IB History Guide ® IBO, 2016)

CHALLENGE YOURSELF

Read the markbands for the fourth question in the paper. In groups, discuss the differences between each level descriptor. How can you make sure your answer fits the highest markband?

Preparation tips

- Even though you will not know in advance whether the exam will be set on Case Study 1 or Case Study 2, you do know what the questions will be like. Familiarize yourself with these question types by practising how to answer them.
- Use the reading time to go over the questions and the sources. Start by looking at the heading of the exam paper as it will tell you which case study the exam is based on. Then read the questions. When you read the sources, keep the fourth question in mind and make some mental notes on how to answer it. Remember, you will not be allowed to make notes during your reading time.
- You have 60 minutes to answer the questions in Paper 1. There is no set time distribution, but it is wise to leave at least 20 minutes to answer the fourth question.
- Follow the order in which questions are set on the paper. They enable you to work through the sources in such a way that, by the time you get to the fourth question, you have a deep understanding of each source. This will help you address the question more confidently than if you had answered it first. Remember, the fourth question is worth 9 out of 24 marks.
- If you are stuck on a question, move on to the next one but leave some space in case you have time to return to it later.

CASE STUDY

1

JAPANESE EXPANSION IN EAST ASIA, 1931–41

JAPANESE EXPANSION IN EAST ASIA, 1931–41

Note on Japanese and Chinese names

In accordance with usual practice, all Japanese and Chinese names in this book have been written with the family name first. Pinyin Romanization has been used for Chinese names and place names: for example, Jiang Jieshi (not Chiang kai-shek), Nanjing (not Nanking), Guandong Army (not Kwantung Army). However, depending on when they were written, you will find that some of the sources or names mentioned in the chapter use Wade–Giles spellings.

On 7 December 1941, Japan launched an attack on the United States naval base at Pearl Harbor in Hawaii, leading to the outbreak of war in the Pacific. Japan's ally Germany then declared war on the United States, resulting in a global conflict that lasted until 2 September 1945 when the Japanese Instrument of Surrender was signed aboard the USS *Missouri* in Tokyo Bay.

As with all wars, there were long- and short-term causes of this global conflict. However, the events leading up to December 1941 can be linked back to the early 1930s – in particular, the Japanese incursion into Manchuria. Focusing on Japan, this case study examines the nature of its imperialism and its expansionist policies to understand the role Japan played in the run-up to World War II.

The case study is divided into three chapters, each dealing with a different aspect of Japan's role in events in the Far East and on the world stage up to the attack on Pearl Harbor.

- Chapter 1 addresses the changes that transformed Japan from a feudalistic country controlled by the shogunate to a modernized, democratic nation-state of international significance that was dominated, nonetheless, by the cult of the emperor.
- Chapter 2 focuses on the domestic and international repercussions of Japan's invasion of Manchuria in 1931 and of China in 1937.
- Chapter 3 examines events that led to Japan's military alliance with Nazi Germany and Fascist Italy, its conquest of Southeast Asia, and the attack on Pearl Harbor.

Key concepts:

The case study analyses all these decisive actions within the rapidly evolving context of international events during the period 1938–41. As you read through the three chapters, consider the following key concepts we use when studying history and how they apply to this case study:

- **Change:** Japan underwent immense change after the Meiji Restoration. Consider therefore the impact that social, cultural, and economic change has upon the ordinary citizen. Think about how it may have changed the self-awareness of the Japanese as subjects of the emperor, as well as the international opinion of Japan.

- **Continuity:** Despite the changes brought in after the end of the *bakufu* period, how far were the soldiers of the modern Japanese army similar in ideology to the samurai?

- **Consequence:** How far was the Manchurian Incident of 1931 a consequence of the Great Depression?

- **Causation:** What were the causes the Second Sino-Japanese War in 1937? Can we determine these without knowing the aims of the military authorities who sanctioned it?

- **Perspective:** How does the passage of time influence our perspective of events? For example, how is the Japanese invasion of China talked about today? How and why has this changed over the past 80 years?

- **Significance:** The Yasukuni Shrine in Tokyo was built in the 1870s. Why is it so significant today? Consider how and why places and events change in significance over time.

1853

- Commodore Perry sails into Nagasaki harbour to open trade negotiations with the Japanese emperor.

1868

- January: Restoration of Meiji rule is declared.

1870

- Commoners are allowed to adopt surnames, a privilege previously reserved for samurai.

1871

- Samurai are allowed to cut their topknots, to lay down their swords, and to intermarry with commoners.

1872

- Compulsory elementary education is introduced.

1873

- Mass conscription is introduced.

1874

- *Meirokusha* (Meiji Six Society) is formed to promote what is called 'civilization and enlightenment'.

1889

- 11 February: The emperor presents the Constitution of the Empire of Japan. On the same day, the House of Representatives Election Law is passed giving the vote to men over 25 who pay at least ¥15 in national taxes (which is just over 1 per cent of the population).

1890

- 30 October: The Imperial Rescript on Education is issued. This document is distributed to all schools. It emphasizes civic responsibility and imperial loyalty as the moral basis for education. It will be displayed together with a portrait of the emperor and read on ceremonial occasions until its repudiation in 1948.

1894–95

- The Sino-Japanese War breaks out on 1 August 1894 and ends with the Treaty of Shimonoseki on 17 April 1895.

1902

- The Anglo-Japanese Alliance is signed.

1904–05

- The Russo-Japanese War breaks out in 1904. It ends in 1905 with the Treaty of Portsmouth being signed in 1905.

1912

- The Taishō era begins, following the death of Emperor Meiji (Mutsuhito).

1914

- Japan enters World War I on the side of the Entente powers.

1915

- Japan presents the Twenty-One Demands to China.

1918

- Takashi Hara is appointed the first 'commoner' prime minister.

1919

- Paris Peace Conference takes place.
- Japan lays claim to Shandong province in China.

1921–22

- The Washington Naval Conference takes place leading to the Washington Naval Treaty and the Nine-Power Treaty.

1925

- The Peace Preservation Law is passed.
- Universal male suffrage is introduced.

1926

- Emperor Taishō (Yoshihito) dies. The Shōwa era begins with the coronation of Crown Prince Hirohito.

1927

- Start of the banking crisis and onset of the Great Depression/Wall Street Crash.

1928

- The Assassination of China's warlord, 'Old Marshal' Zhang Zuolin.

1930

- The London Naval Conference takes place.
- Prime Minister Hamaguchi Osachi is shot and critically wounded.

1931

- A bomb explodes in Manchuria, leading to its takeover by the Guandong Army. This is known as the Manchurian Incident.

1932

- Manchuria is renamed Manchukuo.
- The League of Nations sends the Lytton Commission to investigate the incident.
- 15 May: Prime Minister Inukai Tsuyoshi is assassinated during an attempted coup by young naval officers. It becomes known as the May 15th Incident.

1933

- Japan withdraws from the League of Nations.
- The Tanggu Truce is signed with China.

1936

- Ultra-nationalist officers carry out an attempted coup in Tokyo.
- Japan signs the Anti-Comintern Pact with Germany.
- The first of three Neutrality Laws is passed by the US Congress.
- The Second United Front is established between China's GMD and CPC.

1937

- Prince Konoe Fumimaro is appointed prime minister.
- Italy joins the Anti-Comintern Pact.
- The Marco Polo Bridge Incident leads to the Japanese invasion of China.
- Japanese forces attack Nanjing.
- President Roosevelt of the United States delivers his Quarantine Speech.

1938

- The National Mobilization Law is passed.

1939

- Border conflicts take place on the Soviet border of Manchuria.
- The Tianjin (Tientsin) Incident takes place.
- The United States announces the abrogation of the 1911 Treaty of Commerce and Navigation with Japan.
- Konoe resigns as prime minister.

1940

- Konoe returns as prime minister.
- Japan signs the Tripartite Pact with Italy and Germany.
- The United States limits trade with Japan on materials such as cotton, scrap metal, and certain types of oil.
- Japan occupies northern Indochina.

1941

- April: The Soviet-Japanese Neutrality Pact is signed.
- June: Operation Barbarossa begins when Germany invades the Soviet Union.
- August: The Atlantic Conference takes place.
- November: General Tojo Hideki is appointed prime minister; the Hull Note is delivered.
- December: Pearl Harbor is attacked.

01

Causes of expansion, 1868–1930

This chapter examines the background to the rise of Japan as a modern military power in the period leading up to the invasion of Manchuria in 1931. Key events to be discussed include:

- the dramatic changes undertaken during the period of the Meiji Restoration and the attendant emergence of the notion of national unity
- the emergence of Japan as a significant influence on international relations, both in the Far East and on the world stage
- the impact of World War I on the Japanese economy, politics, and its imperial ambitions.

1.1 The impact of Japanese nationalism and militarism on foreign policy

During the 1930s, Japan expanded its territory into Manchuria; it withdrew from the **League of Nations**; it invaded China; it signed a military alliance with Italy and Germany; in 1941, it launched an attack on the United States. To some extent, such aggressive policy-making was prompted by changes that Japan underwent after the late 1800s when it opened its doors to Western influences, abandoned its traditional military government, and elevated the emperor to a position of authority imbued with god-like status.

These changes were meant to transform Japan into a strong and modern nation able not only to defend itself against the encroachment of Western imperialism, but also to compete with and establish itself as a first-class power equal to the United States and the European Great Powers such as Britain, France, Germany, and Russia. To accomplish this, Japan needed a prosperous economy to fund and equip a strong military. It also needed to educate its population and instil a strong sense of nationalism. Between 1868 and 1930, many of these aims were achieved as Japan fought and won the Sino-Japanese War of 1894 and the Russo-Japanese War of 1904–05, signed a treaty of alliance with Britain in 1902, and entered World War I in August 1914.

This period of momentous change can be traced back to the arrival of Commodore Perry and what contemporary observers referred to as the 'four black ships of evil' in 1853 (Buruma, *Inventing Japan 1853–1964*, 2004, p. 11), an event that led to a crisis of seismic proportions as different political and military factions within Japan called either for the country's continued isolation or, alternatively, for the rapid absorption of all knowledge that could be gleaned from the Western powers.

Before 1868, Japan was in theory ruled by an emperor but, in practice, power was wielded by a military government known as the **shogunate** or *bakufu*. Since 1603, the Tokugawa had been the dominant clan of military leaders. Its head was called the shogun, a title that translates as 'chief barbarian-quelling generalissimo' (Livingston et al, *Imperial Japan 1800–1945*, 1973, p. 13). Below the shogun in rank were the daimyo, the feudal overlords with territory that they ruled. The daimyo, together with samurai warriors who were loyal to them, lived by a strict code of honour known as **Bushido**.

As with many European countries in the 19th century, Japan also experienced economic changes that impacted the organization of its society and politics. The feudalistic system with its very strict hierarchy had started to break down because:

During the shogunate, Kyoto – where the imperial court was located – was the capital of Japan. However, the real seat of power was Edo, where the shogun lived. With the Meiji Restoration in 1868, Edo was renamed Tokyo (meaning 'eastern capital') and became the capital; the imperial court was moved there the following year.

CHALLENGE YOURSELF

ATL **Thinking, research, communication, and social skills**

Working with a classmate, find out about Francis Xavier and the Jesuits who went to Japan in 1543. How did the Japanese respond to the arrival of Christian missionaries on their shore? Why was there such a hostile reaction to Christianity in later years? Share your research with the class.

This Japanese print from around 1930 shows Commodore Perry's marines 'testing the girth' of a sumo wrestler.

- population growth created an increased demand for food and goods
- the merchant class, considered inferior to the samurai, grew in wealth and importance
- the various obligations of the samurai to attend the imperial court at Edo (later named Tokyo) led them into debt
- the emergence of the Satsuma and Chōshū clans, ambitious rivals to the Tokugawa clan, who saw opportunities to seize power.

Commodore Perry and the 'black ships'

Commodore Matthew Calbraith Perry of the United States Navy sailed into Edo (Tokyo) harbour on 8 July 1853; under his command was a fleet referred to as the 'four black ships of evil' by the Japanese. Perry came to demand open trade with a country that, despite some early contact with Christian missionaries during the 17th century, had retreated into isolation from the West.

According to Ian Buruma,

> *Japanese rulers, fearful of foreign aggression and worried that Christianity, promoted by European missionaries, would make their subjects unruly, had outlawed the Christian religion, expelled most foreigners and all priests, and forbidden Japanese to go abroad.*

From Ian Buruma, *Inventing Japan 1853–1964*, Modern Library, New York, 2004, page 11

Activity 1 **ATL** **Thinking and research skills**

The source below is a contemporary Japanese print. Study the source and answer the question that follows.

1. What does this source convey about how the Americans were perceived at this time in Japan?

Perry brought the emperor a letter from US President Millard Fillmore demanding that American ships be allowed to trade with Japan. However, it was the shogun and not the emperor who would rule on such matters; this is just one example of how little Japan was understood by the West at this time. Perry's meetings were not very successful as few Japanese could speak English, although some did speak Dutch, as the Netherlands was the only nation whose merchants were allowed to trade directly with Japan.

Perry returned to Japan once more in 1854, more heavily armed this time. He ordered his fleet to fire cannons to impress upon the Japanese that resistance was useless, as the United States had far greater force at its disposal. Concessions were made and, in 1858, a treaty giving further trading and residency rights to the United States was signed by a representative of the *bakufu*. The signatory, however, would later be assassinated by a samurai critical of the submission of Japan to a foreign power.

By the 1860s, it seemed that if Japan were to become not a colony but an equal of the Western powers, it would need to industrialize and modernize. To do so, it needed to cast off the centuries-old rule of the *bakufu*, and to replace the deeply traditional samurai warriors with a well-equipped and well-trained army that would fight not with swords but with guns. Not unexpectedly, factions emerged with some supporting and others resisting this proposed shift in Japanese culture and values. Eager to seize the opportunity to remove the Tokugawa shogunate, the Satsuma and Chōshū clans joined forces; with a modernized army, they challenged the *bakufu*. This was made easier by the death of Emperor Kōmei (Osahito) in 1866, given that his successor, Emperor Meiji (Mutsuhito), was a young man of fifteen who could be influenced by opponents of the *bakufu*.

In 1867, the Tokugawa shogunate ceded political power, although what followed was a short and bloody civil war, from 1868 to 1869, between the *bakufu* and the imperial army. This ended with the defeat of the samurai and the 'restoration' of the emperor whose place of residence was moved from Kyoto to Edo, now referred to as Tokyo. This two-year period was known as *bakumatsu* (which means 'the end of the *bakufu*'). As Mikiso Hane argues, the population needed to be convinced that this was not a new system of government but the restoration of imperial rule. As stated in a public declaration, it was the restoration of the indissoluble link between the emperor and the common people:

> *Our country is known as the land of the gods, and of all the nations in the world, none is superior to our nation in morals and customs… All things in this land belong to the Emperor…*

From Mikiso Hane, *Japan: A Short History*, Oneworld Publications, 2015, pp. 68–69

The Meiji era signalled the introduction of an elaborate personality cult of the emperor as the divine leader of the nation of Japan. He was to be revered as the descendent of the sun goddess and thereby treated as a 'living god'. **Shintoism** briefly became the official religion of Japan; although this ceased in 1872, Shinto shrines remained under state control and the Shinto belief that the imperial family was descended from the sun goddess remained of great importance. In this way, religion, emperor worship, and nationalism were intertwined, and '… anyone who questioned the mythological origin of the imperial dynasty got into trouble' (Hane, *Japan: A Short History*, 2015, p. 88). Among the new shrines erected was the Yasukuni shrine in Tokyo where the souls of those who had died for the emperor were worshipped.

CHALLENGE YOURSELF

Thinking and research skills (ATL)

In Chapter 2 of this case study, you can read about the response of militant young soldiers to the signing of the London Naval Treaty of 1930 (see page 34). See what comparisons you can draw with the response of the samurai to the concessions made to the United States in 1858.

Names of emperors

The emperors of Japan may be referred to either by their title and personal name (for example, Emperor Mutsuhito) or by the title and the name given to their era (Emperor Meiji). Throughout this case study, where the full name of an emperor is mentioned, his personal name will appear in brackets, for example, Emperor Meiji (Mutsuhito).

TOK

What ways of knowing did the Japanese population use to reconcile the process of modernization and the **deification** of the emperor?

CHALLENGE YOURSELF

(ATL) **Thinking, self-management, social, and research skills**

Today, the Yasukuni shrine remains controversial among the Japanese; it appears in the news almost every year. See what you can find out about it. Share your research with the class.

The Meiji Restoration – a period of social and political change

As the Tokugawa shogunate lost power, the authority of the emperor was enhanced. A new constitution was promised and, when complete, was referred to as *Bunmai Kaika* (meaning 'Civilization and Enlightenment'). According to Ian Buruma, an elaborate ceremony had preceded the presentation of the constitution to the people: Emperor Meiji entered the Shinto shrine at the royal palace and explained the new constitution to his divine ancestors, assuring them that it meant not the end but rather a restoration of imperial authority. A small percentage (just over 1.14 per cent) of the population, composed of men over 25 years of age who paid above a certain amount of tax, was now given the right to vote for members of the National Diet, a bicameral system made up of the House of Peers and the House of Representatives. The House of Peers was made up of nobility, senior civil servants, and high-ranking military officers, while the House of Representatives was made up of elected members. The purpose of the Diet was to assist the emperor in his decision-making; he could both veto legislation and enact his own imperial edicts when the Diet was not in session. In reality, the emperor was expected to accept the advice offered by the *Genrōin*, a group of advisors whose role was not outlined in the constitution but who were, nevertheless, very influential and 'acted as a link between the emperor and the government' (Hunter, *Concise Dictionary of Modern Japanese History*, 1984, p. 48). One very important aspect of the new constitution was that the military was responsible directly to the emperor. Supreme authority lay with the emperor, but as he was meant to be 'above' politics, decisions would be made in his name. This meant that although all his subjects owed him their loyalty, and although he held ultimate power, the emperor was not expected to make political decisions.

Activity 2 Thinking and research skills

Study the sources below and answer the questions that follow.

Source A

An image of Emperor Meiji of Japan, from 1910.

Source B

A print of the Imperial Diet, from 1890.

Thinking and research skills **ATL**

After reading about the new constitution, how democratic, do you think, was Japan at this time? Begin by listing the characteristics of a democratic state and check these against what you have learned about Meiji Japan. Compare this with a contemporary democratic state from a different region.

1. When created, the cartoon in Source A would have been aimed at a European audience. What kind of image of the Japanese emperor do you think it was trying to convey?

2. Source B is a print of the Imperial Diet in 1890. What impression does this convey of the kind of body that governed Japan at this time?

The inspiration for the new Japanese constitution had actually come from Germany. Officials, including Itō Hirobumi, president of the Privy Council (advisors of the emperor), were sent abroad to 'shop around' for a political system. They looked at several examples but decided that the US constitution was too democratic and 'smacked of disorder', and that the British system was unsuitable. So they opted for the rather more autocratic German style of government. An admirer of Bismarck, Itō not only imitated the way he held his cigar but also agreed with the German chancellor's opinion that 'popular sovereignty would be a very dangerous thing'. Ian Buruma describes the resultant constitution as 'a mixture of German and traditional Japanese authoritarianism' (Buruma, *Inventing Japan 1853–1964*, 2004, p. 38).

Social changes – education

Like Russia in the second half of the 19th century, reform was needed so that the military could be trained and equipped to rival the armies and navies of Western powers. Japan had to move quickly from centralized **feudalism** – with a privileged caste of samurai warriors – to a state in which ordinary citizens would be conscripted into its army. Soldiers would be recruited in large numbers and taught to obey only the emperor and their nation. A basic level of universal literacy was necessary as recruits needed to read basic orders and operate new technology. To aid this, a new system of elementary schooling was introduced in 1872. It was not free and, at first, attendance was relatively low. According to Mikiso Hane, by 1876, 46 per cent of boys, (though only 16 per cent of girls) attended school (Hane, *Japan, A Short History*, 2015, p. 85). Education would also be the means by which nationalism was instilled into the population. In 1890, the Imperial Rescript on Education was introduced; the rescript had to be memorized and recited each morning by teachers and pupils – an edict that remained in place until World War II.

The rescript began with the assertion 'Know ye, our subjects' and outlined the various obligations of Japanese subjects of the emperor including the following:

> *… should any emergency arise, offer yourselves courageously to the state; and thus guard and maintain the prosperity of our Imperial throne, coeval with heaven and earth. So not shall ye be good and faithful subjects but render illustrious the best traditions of your forefathers.*

From Livingston et al, *Imperial Japan 1800–1945*, Pantheon, 1973, pp. 153–54

According to Hane, the purpose of the rescript was that '… the minds of young children were moulded to ensure that when the time came they would go to battle shouting, "Imperial Majesty Banzai"' (Hane, *Japan, A Short History*, 2015, p. 90). Children were also taught that the Imperial Dynasty dated from 660 BCE – a date commemorated each year on 11 February – when Jimmu, the first emperor, had ascended the throne. The other important national holiday celebrated Emperor Meiji's birthday, on 3 November.

Activity 3

1. Based on what you have read so far, in what ways was the authority of the emperor enforced and conveyed to the people of Japan?

The military

The armed forces of Meiji Japan swore loyalty solely to the emperor, which was a significant departure from the way things were during the Tokugawa shogunate when the samurai's loyalty was to their daimyo or feudal overlord. Furthermore, with the introduction of conscription, all Japanese men had to serve three years in the army and four years in the reserves. Buruma argues that this was not only a way to defend the country but also a way to instil unification: 'National unity was armed unity. National education was military education' (Ian Buruma, *Inventing Japan 1853–1964*, 2004, p. 55).

The Rescript for Soldiers and Sailors was published in 1882 and this, like the Rescript on Education, established absolute loyalty to the emperor. It read:

> *We (the Emperor) are your supreme Commander in Chief. We rely on you as Our limbs and you look up to Us as your head.*

> **Ian Buruma, *Inventing Japan 1853–1964*, 2004, p. 55**

Soldiers and sailors were not allowed to express political opinions, nor could they comment on imperial policies, even in private. Buruma sees this as the flaw in this system of absolute loyalty to the emperor as, in the 1930s, eager young officers could, and would, defy a civilian government if they suspected it of acting against the imperial will. This interpretation is supported by Eri Hotta who states that:

> *… the 1882 imperial decree could be considered one of the latent underlying causes of Japan's militarisation of the 1930s and, eventually, its attack on Pearl Harbor.*

> **From Eri Hotta, *Japan 1941*, Vintage Books, 2014, p. 79**

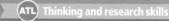

Activity 4

1. When you have read through this case study, come back to Hotta's statement and see if you agree with its premise.

This, very briefly, has been an overview of the transition to the Meiji Restoration. It has explained how Japan, along with other countries at this time, made use of the ideology of nationalism and set in place a system that bound the people to their emperor. As with many European countries at this time, Japan began to look for opportunities to expand the territory under its control. It did so for a number of reasons:

• to elevate its status as an imperial power
• to access resources for a growing population
• to secure territory that might, otherwise, have fallen under the control of rivals, especially Russia, Britain, France, or the United States.

First stages of imperialism

Study the map below and answer the question that follows.

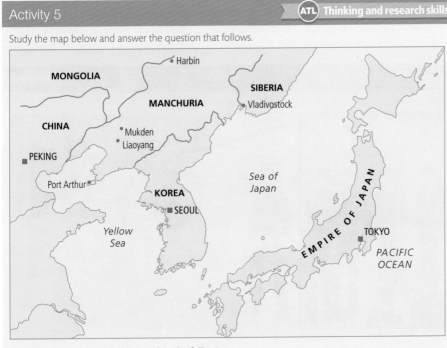

This map shows the locations of Japan, Korea, China, and Asiatic Russia during 1904–05.

1. How does this map help to explain the following:

    a) Japan's interest in Korea

    b) Japan's potential rivalry with China and Russia?

The First Sino-Japanese War, 1894

Japan had a long history of association with China dating back to 500–600 CE, when Chinese writing and culture were more widely disseminated by way of Korea. During the 19th century, China was weakened by its defeat in both of the Opium Wars with Britain and by being forced into a series of 'unequal treaties' with European powers. Korea lay between Japan and China, and, as Japan entered a new age of militarization, it aimed to establish its control of the Korean peninsula. Inevitably, this would bring Japan into direct conflict with China, seeing as Korea was a tributary state of the latter (meaning that the emperor of Korea paid homage to the emperor of China). In 1894, an uprising in Korea prompted its government to ask for assistance from China, but Japan sent troops before the Chinese army arrived, leading to conflict between the two armies. Ian Buruma argues that at the heart of this conflict was the question of which army had modernized most effectively and, accordingly, which country would dominate East Asia. Japan proved its dominance by pushing the Chinese back across the Yalu River, the border between Korea and China, while its navy secured victory in the Yellow Sea. The ensuing Treaty of Shimonoseki affirmed Chinese recognition of Korean independence and the cession of Formosa (known today as Taiwan), the Liaodong Peninsula, and the Pescadores Islands to Japan. China also granted commercial and trading rights to Japan.

In Japan, this victory was seen as confirmation of Japan's superiority over China, cementing its status as a 'higher civilization'. According to Buruma, this signalled a new epoch in Japanese history and confirmed the popular belief that Japan was now equal to the Western powers, living up to the Meiji slogan 'Rich Country,

Strong Army' (Buruma, *Inventing Japan 1853–1964*, 2004, pp. 50–51). Victory led to new tensions, however, as Russia also wanted control over Korea and the Liaodong Peninsula. Under pressure from Britain, France, and the United States, Japan was persuaded to relinquish the Liaodong Peninsula – an act that, to many Japanese nationalists, proved Japan was still regarded as inferior to the Western powers, despite its military prowess.

> **Activity 6** | **ATL** Thinking skills
>
> Study the source below and answer the question that follows.
>
>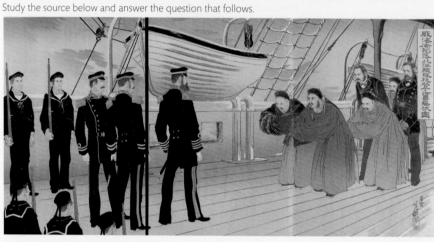
>
> Source: Art Object Photograph © 2016 Museum of Fine Arts, Boston.
>
> **1.** What is the message of this source? Look carefully at the dress of the Japanese soldiers receiving the surrender of the Chinese. What impression does this give about the differences between the two groups?

This print shows the Chinese surrendering to the Japanese.

The Russo-Japanese War (1904–05) and the Anglo-Japanese Alliance (1902)

The outcome of the First Sino-Japanese War displeased Russia as it wanted to secure its own interests in Manchuria and Korea. In 1898, Russia had secured permission from China to extend the Trans-Siberian Railway to Vladivostok as well as to build the South Manchurian Railway. Furthermore, it secured a 20-year lease on the Liaodong Peninsula and Port Arthur, all of which led to worsening relations with Japan. It seemed increasingly likely that conflict would break out; in anticipation of this, Japan signed the Anglo-Japanese Alliance in 1902. This stated that both Britain and Japan would 'maintain the status quo in the Far East' and one party would remain neutral in a conflict unless the other was attacked by more than one power (Hane, *Japan, A Short History*, 2015, p. 109).

Efforts to negotiate an agreement with Russia (whereby Russia would recognize Japanese interests in Korea, and Japan the interests of Russia in Manchuria) failed, and the Japanese navy attacked the Russian Pacific Fleet on 8 February 1904, declaring war on 10 February. The war was fought both on land and sea, with the sinking of the Russian Baltic Fleet in the Tsushima Straits probably being one of the most memorable events in this nine-month conflict that ended in October 1905. Famously, this turned out not to be the 'splendid little war' anticipated by Tsar Nicholas II and his advisors, and it made Japan a 'major player in the Far East' (Hane, *Japan, A Short History*, 2015, p. 110). Under the terms of the Treaty of Portsmouth, negotiated by US President

Theodore Roosevelt, Japan acquired South Sakhalin, the leasehold over the Liaodong Peninsula and Port Arthur, as well as control over the South Manchurian Railway. Russia also recognized Japanese interests in Korea, which became a protectorate of Japan in 1906 and its colony in 1910.

As with the European powers at this time, nationalism was boosted by imperialism. Japan's foreign policy was extremely successful in expanding its interests in Korea and Manchuria but, inevitably, this aroused a mixed response on the international scene.

'A splendid little war'

This phrase has been used many times in history to describe what belligerents had hoped would be a short and successful conflict. Vyacheslav Plehve, the minister of interior appointed by Tsar Nicholas II, is reported to have said that what Russia needed in 1904 was a 'little victorious war to stem a revolution'. Whether or not this is accurate is a matter of some speculation, but 'a splendid little war' (as a corruption of the above phrase) is commonly used to describe Russia's mistaken prediction of how the war against Japan would turn out.

Activity 7 — Thinking, research, and self-management skills

Study the sources below and answer the questions that follow.

Source A

G.B   *Le péril jaune – Cauchemar Européen*

This French cartoon is entitled 'Le peril jaune' ('Yellow Peril').

Source B

Here is an extract from 'Why the Russians lost in the recent war', from the *New York Sun*. (Transcribed version reprinted in *The Army and Navy Register*, 11 August 1906.)

> *Our conclusion is that in the military operations of which Manchuria was the theatre the Russians were not signally outgeneraled by the Japanese, otherwise their losses must have been much greater than were actually experienced. As for the supposed superiority of the Japanese in naval strategy, Mr. Jane, for his part, concedes that Rojestvensky's [the Commander of the Russian fleet] formation in Tsushima Straits, in view that he expected only a torpedo attack, was not a bad formation at all, and that it is hard to conceive that Togo, with Rojestvensky's general orders and with the special problems to be solved by the latter, would have done anything materially different up to the hour of battle. Nevertheless, we cannot conceive of Togo as losing the ensuing fight, because every individual officer and every individual seaman would have died rather than forfeit victory. This brings us to the capital reason for the success of the Japanese. The Russians were not so much outgeneraled as they were outfought, and they were outfought because they were lukewarm and not wrought to desperation as they had been in the Crimea and in resistance to Napoleon's invasion; whereas every Japanese soldier and sailor believed, as was indeed the truth, that his country's fate was at stake and that his personal conduct might decide the issue.*

Source C

ROOSEVELT : Assez ! — Enough ! — Genug ! (Collection T. Bianco)

The text in the cartoon reads 'Roosevelt: Assez! Enough! Genug!' (All three words mean the same in French, English and German.)

Look carefully at every part of the cartoon in Source C, including the caption. Try to identify the main characters; pay attention to the heaps of skulls in the background as well as the setting sun. All of these are symbolic and help you to understand what the cartoonist was trying to convey.

Kanno Sugako

A socialist and feminist, Kanno Sugako opposed the Russo-Japanese War; she wrote many articles that criticized the status of women in Japan, who she felt 'were in a state of slavery'. Kanno also stated that, '(in) accordance with long-standing customs, we have been seen as a form of material property ... Japan has become an advanced, civilised nation but we women are still denied our freedom by an invisible iron fence'. In 1910, Kanno was involved in a plot to assassinate the emperor. Along with 11 others, she was put on trial and sentenced to death. She was executed in 1911 (Hane, *Japan, A Short History*, 2015, p. 114).

1. Source A is a French cartoon of the 'Yellow Peril', a term that was used to describe the perceived threat of the Japanese as they grew in strength. What is the message of this cartoon? (See if you can identify the figures in the beds.)
2. According to Source B, why did the Russians lose the Battle of Tsushima Straits?
3. What is the message of the cartoon in Source C?

Yamamoto Isoroku was a Japanese naval cadet who was seriously wounded at the Battle of Tsushima. He went on to become one of the people responsible for planning the attack on Pearl Harbor in 1941 (Hotta, *Japan 1941*, 2014, p. 97).

The Taishō era: World War I and its immediate aftermath

The Meiji era came to an end with the death of the emperor in 1911. Emperor Meiji was succeeded by his son Prince Yoshihito, who became Emperor Taishō, and the Meiji era gave way to the Taishō era, meaning 'the era of great righteousness' (Hotta, *Japan 1941*, 2014, p. 86). Japan had, seemingly, become a successful modern empire with a modern army, a constitution, and a democracy of sorts. There were indications, however, that the changes were superficial: underneath this veneer of modernization Japan remained deeply traditional, with political power entrenched in the emperor and his circle of advisors. Freedom of expression was severely limited and political ideas such as **socialism** and demands for greater equality for women were swiftly suppressed.

In August 1914, almost immediately after the outbreak of World War I in Europe, Japan, in keeping with the spirit of the 1902 alliance it had signed with Britain (though not strictly necessary, as the latter had not been attacked by two powers) declared war on Germany. This was not entirely altruistic as the war offered opportunities for Japan to stand in for Britain in the Far East and, in particular, to take over German-leased territory in the Shandong province in China. The Japanese army moved quickly to surround the German port of Tsingtao and, after a two-month siege, received its surrender. Similarly, German colonies in the Pacific surrendered without many casualties. When the Allied Powers asked for Japanese troops to be sent to Europe however, this request was denied, although some destroyers were sent to act as convoy escorts in the Mediterranean.

In 1915, Japan imposed what became known as the **Twenty-One Demands** on China, insisting on the following concessions:

• that German interests in China be transferred to Japan
• that Japanese interests in Manchuria be recognized
• that Japan be given an increased role in the administration and policing of China.

These demands reflected not only Japanese ambition but also Chinese weakness during this period of **warlordism** and weak central government. American and British support helped China to resist some of the more aggressive demands to share its governance, but the territorial demands were conceded. To some extent, this backfired on Japan as it aroused Chinese nationalism as well as American suspicions that Japan would seize any opportunity to impose its influence over China. Indeed, when civil war broke out in Russia in 1918 in the wake of the **Bolshevik** Revolution, Japan sent soldiers to Siberia to halt the progress of the Bolshevik Red Army. The United States also sent soldiers with the intention of 'maintaining a limited Eastern front against Germany and limiting Japanese gains' (Stone and Kuznik, *The Untold History of the United States*, 2013, p. 29).

The Paris Peace Conference

An armistice ended World War I in November 1918. It was followed by the Paris Peace Conference, during which the Japanese delegation sought occupation of the following German colonies in the North Pacific: the Mariana, Marshall, and Caroline islands. Of even greater importance to its foreign policy was Japan's request to take over German interests in Shandong province, as had been outlined in the Twenty-One Demands. In China, the **May Fourth Movement** of 1919 protested vehemently against such a violation of the principle of **self-determination**.

For US President Woodrow Wilson, whether to accede to Japan's demands or (preferably for him) champion those of the Chinese was among the most difficult of the dilemmas he faced at the conference. Japan did get Shandong but this decision was influenced by another event linked to the establishment of the League of Nations. A number of people, including Prince Konoe Fumimaro, a member of the Japanese delegation, were critical of the concept of the League, an organization that was believed to preserve the economic and political supremacy of the Western powers. The prince also railed against the racism inherent in the attitudes of the British and the Americans, who seemed to consider Japan, despite its military prowess, to be a second-class power. In particular, Japan was deeply offended by the treatment of Japanese immigrants to the United States and now demanded that the League should support racial equality. A proposal was made that the Covenant of the League of Nations, which already mentioned the equality of all religions, should also make reference to the equality of all races. In 1919, this was considered incendiary as it would have immediate repercussions in European colonies in Africa and Asia, as well as threatening the Australian whites-only immigration policy. Japan lost the debate and the racial equality clause was shelved. President Wilson also feared that denying Japan its claim on Shandong might result in Japan leaving the conference and refusing to sign the Treaty of Versailles; it was a risk he was not prepared to take. So Japan gained Shandong but, as Margaret Macmillan notes, it was not an easy decision for Wilson, who complained to his doctor: 'Last night, I could not sleep, my mind was so full of the Japanese–Chinese controversy' (Macmillan, *Paris 1919*, 2003, p. 338).

May Fourth Movement, 1919

A student-led movement that sprang up in May 1919, in response to the treatment of China at the Paris Peace Conference and its acceptance of Japan's demands.

Whites-only policy

Australia had a whites-only immigration policy from 1902 onwards. This was finally ended in 1973 when it was stated that race could not be considered as a factor influencing immigration into Australia.

For question 3, don't forget that the best way to approach this type of question is to use a comparative structure. For instance, don't be tempted just to describe the content of Source A and then that of Source B. It is better to have one paragraph stating the similarities in the views and another stating the differences. It is also quite helpful to use certain phrases, for example:

- 'Both sources agree that...'
- 'Similarities between the sources include...'
- 'Whereas Source A says..., Source B says that...'
- 'The sources differ on...'

Beginning your answer with phrases like those above will help make it very clear to the examiner what you are comparing or contrasting.

CHALLENGE YOURSELF

 Thinking, research, communication, and social skills

Disarmament was one of the most important aims of the world leaders who gathered in Paris in 1919. Work in groups to research the following topics and share your research with the class:

1. Why was disarmament considered to be so vital during the inter-war period?

2. What were the disarmament terms set out in the **Treaty of Versailles** and the **Treaty of St Germain**?

3. Japan was a victor, not a loser, in World War I. Why were Britain and the United States so eager to limit the growth of the Japanese navy?

Activity 8

Study the sources and answer the questions that follow.

Source A

Here is an extract from *The Deluge* (2014, p. 325), a book by British historian Adam Tooze.

> *The idea that Japan might be speaking on behalf of Africans would no doubt have caused indignation in Tokyo. What was at stake were European–Asian relations and specifically the right of Asians to join Europeans in the settlement of the remaining open territories of the world.*

Source B

Here is an extract from an article entitled 'Illusions of the White Race' (1921) by Okuma Shigenobu (1838–1922), a leading Japanese politician who served as prime minister in 1898 and again from 1914 to 1916.

> *It is, of course, true that there are still peoples in this world who are so backward in civilisation that they cannot at once be admitted into the international family on an equal footing… What is needed by them is proper guidance and direction… Although most Asiatic nations are fully peers of European nations, yet they are discriminated against because of the colour of their skin. The root of it lies in the perverted feeling of racial superiority entertained by the whites.*

1. In Source A, what is meant by 'the remaining open territories of the world'?

2. With reference to its origin, purpose, and content, analyse the value and limitations of Source B for a historian studying the impact of the Paris Peace Conference upon Japanese public opinion.

3. Compare and contrast the views expressed in both sources on Japanese views on racial equality.

The Paris Conference and the Treaty of Versailles were followed by the Washington Conference of 1921–22, giving rise to the term the 'Versailles–Washington System' to describe the new international order that 'had been organised to protect the interests of the two major victorious powers, Great Britain and the United States' (Duus, *The Cambridge History of Japan, Volume 6: The Twentieth Century*, 1995, p. 282). The outcome of the conference resulted in a sense of increasing disillusionment in Japan and a deepening of its inferiority complex for the following reasons:

- It confirmed the end of the Anglo-Japanese Alliance and with it, the loss of Japanese control over Shandong.
- It required the withdrawal of Japanese troops from Siberia.
- It imposed a 5:5:3 ratio in battleships (Britain: United States: Japan), thus limiting the size of the Japanese fleet in relation to that of the other two Western powers.

This was not all. In 1922, the Nine-Power Treaty 'liquidated all existing treaties between the powers and China and replaced them with the Open Door principles so long espoused by the United States' (Duus, *The Cambridge History of Japan, Volume 6: The Twentieth Century*, 1995, p. 283). Further limits on the Japanese navy would be imposed at the 1930 London Conference, when a 10:10:6 ratio (Britain: United States: Japan) was agreed for heavy cruisers and a 10:10:7 ratio for destroyers, although parity between the United States and Japan was allowed for submarines. Mikiso Hane notes that during the inter-war period, disarmament became a source of discontent among the ultra-nationalists, and the signatories of the London Treaty were all targeted for assassination by right-wing militants.

1.2 Japanese domestic issues and their impact on foreign relations

Between 1918 and 1932, Japanese politics went through a period known as Taishō democracy. In 1918, Hara Takashi formed the first party government as leader of the *Rikken Seiyūkai* (the Constitutional Society of Political Friends), later known only as the *Seiyūkai*, which had been established since 1900. The party's support had come mostly from rural areas and its aim, generally, was to improve the economy and Japanese standards of living. It was the majority party in the Diet until 1914, when it became the minority briefly; the party regained the majority in 1918, which was when it entered a golden age. Its leader at the time, Hara Takashi, was the first 'commoner' prime minister, so-called because he led the majority political party and sat in the House of Representatives.

Hara was assassinated in 1921: allegations of corruption as well as his suppression of left-wing groups were probably the main reasons for this, but his assassin claimed it was both 'to gain fame and to bring about revolutionary change' (Hane, *Japan, A Short History*, 2015, p. 120). Hara's assassination, however, paled in comparison with the catastrophe of 1923, when a severe earthquake led to the devastation of Tokyo and the deaths of 100,000 of its inhabitants. Around 700,000 of Tokyo's mainly wooden houses were rapidly destroyed in the fire that raged. Rumours quickly spread that the fire had been started deliberately by Tokyo's Korean population, with an estimated 2,613 people being killed in the ensuing riots. In this mayhem of fear and hysteria, labour leaders were also arrested and executed. Overall, this tragedy and its racist aftermath led to the enforcing of right-wing ideologies and demands for greater security.

Even so, the appointment of the leader of the majority party as prime minister had been established; this practice continued up until 1932. In 1924, the *Kenseikai* (Constitutional Government Party), a party that had long since called for universal suffrage and civil rights, came to power and in the following year a legislation was passed to grant universal suffrage to men over the age of 25. It also passed the Peace Preservation Law, however, which was intended to 'curb dangerous thought' and was directed against communists and anarchists. In 1927, a new party, the *Minseitō* (Liberal Party), was formed. It supported more liberal policies and depended on urban rather than rural support. It was closely allied with business interests, a conciliatory foreign policy, and the enforcement of the London Naval Treaty.

Political developments – from Taishō democracy to militarism

Although in the period following World War I political parties did multiply, the bureaucracy was so entrenched and the constitution so limited that they never established a strong presence in Japan's political landscape. Furthermore, they were weakened by a 'lack of popular support, rife factionalism, corruption, lack of any clear political ideology and failure to cooperate with each other to oppose antiparty elements' (Hunter, *Concise Dictionary of Modern Japanese History*, 1984, p. 169).

As we shall see, as economic conditions worsened and relations with China over Manchuria reached a critical point, Japanese democracy also faltered; prevented by constitutional limitations, or perhaps a lack of will, the country found itself failing to challenge effectively the growing right-wing ultra-nationalism.

Thinking, social, self-management, and research skills (ATL)

World War I marked a transition point in many different countries. For victors and losers, the cost of the war, both in economic terms and in human suffering, led to much reflection on whether or not the war was 'worth it'. Compare the social and economic post-war conditions of either Italy or Germany to those of Japan. Share your findings with your class.

Left-wing movements

An interesting question to ask when looking at the political landscape in Japan after World War I is: where was the Left? Despite military incursions into Siberia during the Russian civil war, the Bolshevik Revolution did have an impact on Japanese politics: the Japanese Communist Party (JCP) was secretly established in 1922 but was closed down in 1924 after the arrest of its leaders. An attempt was made in 1926 to re-form the party, but the movement was harshly suppressed: its members, if uncovered, were arrested and often tortured. The JCP remained banned until after World War II. A socialist party had been established in 1906 but was banned in 1907. In 1920, the Japanese Socialist League was formed: it was split into different factions and finally emerged as the Social Mass Party in 1932. Although the expansion of suffrage in 1925 did make possible increased support for various labour-farmer parties, according to Christopher Gerteis ('Political Protest in Interwar Japan, Part 1', *Asia Pacific Journal*, 2014), it came at a time when political power was slipping away to the entrenched 'constitutionally independent state bureaucracy'. Also, the Peace Preservation Law of 1925 limited freedom of speech and was intended to limit the impact of universal male suffrage upon the status quo. The general election of 1928 did not see any significant increase in the number of left-wing representatives in the House of Representatives either. One reason for this was the financial backing of the **zaibatsu** for traditional parties; trade union activity was allowed, although the right to strike was blocked by the powerful business interests that were closely entwined with the major political parties. In 1940, trade unions were banned altogether.

An election poster from 1928 for the Japan Labour-Farmer Party (a radical left-wing party).

Activity 9   **ATL** Thinking skills

日本勞農黨

1. What is the message conveyed in the poster above?

Social and cultural change in the 1920s

During the 1920s, urban society was being particularly influenced by Western culture and customs. Not unexpectedly, this led to a deepening rift between life in the countryside and that in the city. Sophisticated city dwellers expressed contempt for rural inhabitants, as the latter were considered to be ignorant people leading desperate, poverty-ridden lives. Equally, for many rural farmers, the cities were dens of iniquity mired in corruption, their inhabitants dismissive of Japanese culture and tradition. Mikiso Hane notes that although literacy was improving across both groups as a result of compulsory elementary education, those who lived in towns and cities inevitably had better access to secondary and higher education. In the 1930s, ultra-nationalists found support in the countryside whose conservative and highly traditional inhabitants rejected Western cultural and political influences.

Economic challenges – industry and agriculture

World War I had a strong impact on the expansion of the Japanese economy, as the war offered immense opportunities to develop the country's arms and export industries. The preoccupation of the West's producers with the war effort also meant that there was less competition for Japanese producers. As a result, the consumption of Japanese goods increased not only at home, but also in nearby Asian countries, as well as across Europe and the United States.

Even though the production of industrial goods grew significantly in the 1920s, Hane notes that over 50 per cent of workers were still involved in the primary industries of farming, fishing, and mining (Hane, *Japan, A Short History*, 2015, p. 134). According to a government survey conducted in 1927, family income among farming communities was just 70 per cent of that of city office-workers, while urban workers' incomes were only slightly ahead of their rural counterparts. Even though urban and rural working families together comprised 84 per cent of the population, they accounted for less than 50 per cent of household income. What these statistics show is an unequal distribution of wealth, with much of it being the preserve of the top echelons of the business community, in particular the zaibatsu. At the top of this group were Mitsui, Mitsubishi, Sumitomo, and Yasuda. The heads of these economic powerhouses, with interests in everything from shipbuilding to mining, banking, and textiles, had close ties with the government and the major political parties. According to Hane,

> [government] leaders did nothing to curb the monopolistic thrust of the zaibatsu. In fact, they were integral to the goal of building 'a rich nation and a powerful military', and military and political expansion abroad went hand in hand with zaibatsu control of markets and resources

Hane, *Japan, A Short History*, 2015, p. 136

Indeed, the 1927 Banking Crisis demonstrated that the Japanese economy was becoming more monopolistic. Many small banks went out of business, while control of much of the country's finances went to a few large and powerful banks, with the zaibatsu growing in size and authority. Then came the Wall Street Crash of 1929, a calamity that impacted not just the economy of the United States but that of all its trading partners.

The Great Depression and its aftermath

As with all other countries that depended upon the export markets for their livelihood, Japan suffered from the collapse in world trade associated with the Great Depression. The response of the government was an austerity programme, with a focus on deflationary measures. Niall Ferguson argues that Japan's decision to pursue austerity and return to the gold standard in 1929, just before the Wall Street Crash, was ill-timed and only worsened the situation. Exports fell by 6 per cent between 1929 and 1931; unemployment rose to 1 million; and agricultural incomes slumped.

In the face of the overvalued Yen and increasing protectionism by the British Empire and American markets, the Japanese government took the wise decision to come off the gold standard in 1931. The Yen was allowed to float, meaning there would be no fixed rate of exchange. At the same time, the government abandoned its austerity programmes and started to spend money on military equipment. There was a shortage of raw materials that continued through the 1930s, squeezing the small to medium-sized producers, but benefiting the zaibatsu, whose political clout and economic power enabled them to direct scarce resources their way. Hugely dependent on the British Empire for imports of raw materials (such as jute, lead, tin, zinc, iron ore, and cotton) and on the Americans (for cotton, scrap metal, and oil), Japan needed good access to resources. As Ferguson notes, Japan's exports needed a strong world economy, but when protectionist measures led to a drawing in of world markets, Japan had to reassess its political and military position.

The weak demand in a protectionist world economy adversely affected Japan. In addition, Japan had a rapidly growing population that needed living space and more access to food. All this added weight to a call for what Hane refers to as the acquisition of its own 'imperial market' (Hane, *Japan, A History*, 2015, p. 153). According to Ferguson, imperial expansion led to the emigration of around 315,000 Japanese citizens between 1935 and 1940. However, Ferguson notes that the problem with imperial expansion was that '… it required increased imports of petroleum, copper, coal, machinery and iron ore to feed the nascent Japanese military–industrial complex' (Ferguson, *The War of the World*, 2006, p. 297). In other words, the more imperialistic Japan became, the greater its dependence on imported raw materials. At some stage, presumably, its empire would both provide the resources and absorb the goods it needed, but that time was yet to come.

The growth of ultra-nationalism and its threat to democracy

After becoming the leader of the *Seiyūkai* in 1925, General Tanaka Giichi was appointed prime minister in 1927. His policies were both repressive of left-wing movements and aggressive abroad. An important event was the assassination in 1928 of Zhang Zuolin, a warlord of Manchuria (for more, see page 30). Emperor Shōwa (Hirohito) had been angered by Japanese complicity in this event, and even though Tanaka had not been part of the planning of this event, his failure to provide an explanation for the emperor reflected the weakness of the government and made him feel compelled to resign. Tanaka was succeeded by Hamaguchi Yūkō, leader of the *Minseitō* whose government was responsible for signing the London Naval Treaty. According to Hane, the military officers who objected most vehemently to the treaty's restrictions on Japan's naval capability now accused the government of overstepping its authority, claiming it did not have the right 'to override the naval general staff in matters of defence' (Hane, *Japan, A Short History*, 2015, p. 139). Hamaguchi was shot in an assassination attempt; although he survived, he resigned as prime minister and died not long afterwards. Hamaguchi's successor, Wakatsuki Reijirō, was caught up in the Manchurian Incident (see Chapter 2, page 30) and resigned soon after; he was replaced by Inukai Tsuyoshi, leader of the *Seiyūkai*. Although he criticized the London Treaty, Inukai was also assassinated by ultra-nationalists in May 1932.

According to Hane, 'Inukai's assassination was the turning point in Japan's move towards militaristic extremism' (Hane, *Japan, A Short History*, 2015, p. 145). Buruma, similarly, equates this time with the end of party democracy and even compares it to contemporaneous events in Germany where the Weimar Republic was being buffeted by the combination of harsh economic circumstances and the rise of **fascism**. As Buruma points out, although Japan had neither a Nazi party nor a führer, it had an emperor whose political opinions are still, to this day, shrouded in mystery, while its rival power-grasping factions 'in the court, the military, the bureaucracy and the Diet… fought each other with almost as much zeal as they displayed towards external enemies' (Buruma, *Inventing Japan, 1853–1964*, 2004, p. 91). The period of Taishō democracy was drawing to a close.

Activity 10

Study the sources below and answer the questions that follow.

Source A

The following is taken from historian Mikiso Hane's book *Japan, A Short History* (Oneworld Publications, 2015, pp.141–42).

One of the officers arrested and put on trial for Inukai's assassination reflected the anguish felt by many soldiers who saw an enormous gap between the seemingly extravagant lifestyle in the cities and impoverished lives of the peasants in rural villages. He said,

> In utter disregard of the poverty-stricken farmers, the enormously rich zaibatsu pursue their private profit. Meanwhile, the young children of the impoverished farmers of the north eastern provinces attend school without breakfast, and their families subsist on rotten potatoes.

Source B

Jonathan N Lipman is a professor of history. The following is taken from his essay 'Imperial Japan: 1894–1945' (2008).

> Young men, both military officers and their colleagues in civilian organizations such as the Kokuryukai (Amur River Society), expressed their nationalist passions through assassinations of politicians, industrialists, intellectuals, and others who did not conform to their rigid standards of 'pure Japanese' behaviour and beliefs. Prime Minister Hamaguchi was murdered at Tokyo Station in 1930, and Prime Minister Inukai was killed in 1932. Both assassinations were perpetrated by ultranationalists impatient with the corruption of party politics and eager for Japan to be driven by their own heroic values, which were expressed most obviously in the military and the drive to dominate Japan's neighbours, especially China.

1. With reference to the origin, purpose, and content, analyse the value and limitations of Source A to historians studying post-World War I politics in Japan.

2. To what extent does Source A support the reasons given in Source B for the assassination of political leaders?

The Shōwa era

On the death of this father Emperor Taishō in 1926, and having served as regent for the previous four years, Crown Prince Hirohito ascended to the Imperial throne and became Emperor Shōwa. The new emperor was a young man who had rarely left Japan, with one exception being in 1921 when, warned beforehand about the 'poison of European liberal thought', he had been sent on a tour of Europe. According to Buruma, educated to believe absolutely in 'the myths of Japanese racial purity and the divine provenance of his own blood lines as though they were historical facts', the young Crown Prince Hirohito was apparently impressed by the 'informality of British aristocratic manners, even at Buckingham Palace' that contrasted with the elaborate and strictly enforced code of behaviour at the imperial palace in Tokyo (Buruma, *Inventing Japan, 1853–1964*, 2004, pp. 82–83).

If Hirohito had wanted to introduce some informality, however, he would have been rapidly disabused of any such idea in a culture that had been built upon the veneration of the emperor. In accordance with Shinto rituals, the coronation on 14 November 1926 took place after Hirohito spent the night at Ise, the holiest of Shinto temples, communing with his ancestor, the sun goddess. The following morning, 'reborn' as a living god, Hirohito could assume his role as emperor and take Japan from the Taishō era to the Shōwa era, meaning 'a time of illustrious peace' (see Buruma, *Inventing Japan, 1853–1964*, 2004, pp. 83–84).

One of the side trips made by Hirohito during his European tour was to the site of the Battle of Ypres, which was said to have contributed to his 'aversion of war'. According to Eri Hotta, the young prince was taken on a tour of the battlefield (remember that this was only three years after the end of World War I) by a Belgian officer who had lost a son in the war. Upon hearing about the plight of the officer, Hirohito's eyes 'welled up with tears' (Hotta, *Japan 1941*, 2014, p. 87).

A photo taken in 1925 of Emperor Shōwa (Hirohito) in his coronation robe.

Having read through this section, you can see how Japan emerged out of World War I as a modern and ambitious country, growing in prosperity and moving towards a more democratic system of government as it entered the Shōwa Era. Even so, there was a lingering disaffection with the outcome of the Treaty of Versailles, as well as the Naval Treaties. Many of its citizens felt that Japan was being denied its rightful place as an equal of the Western powers. Within the Japanese military, which owed allegiance only to the emperor, there were groups of militant nationalists wanting to purify Japan. One such organization was the *Sakurakai* (Cherry Blossom Society), established in 1930. Opposed to political corruption and disarmament policies, its intention was to set up a military government and to rid Japan of its corrupt politicians. According to a society pamphlet produced by the *Sakurakai*,

> ... the poisonous sword of the thoroughly degenerate politicians is being pointed at the military. This was clearly demonstrated in the London treaties. It is obvious that the party politicians' sword that was used against the navy, will soon be used to reduce the size of the army. Hence... we must arouse ourselves and wash out the bowels of the completely decadent politicians.

Extract from a Cherry Blossom Society pamphlet, in Hane, *Japan, A Short History*, Oneworld Publications, 2015, p. 142

CHALLENGE YOURSELF

Thinking, research, communication, and self-management skills

See what you can find out about the *Ketsumeidan* (Blood Brotherhood Society), a Japanese ultra-nationalist society similar to the *Sakurakai*. Compare the ideologies of these Japanese societies with those of the NSDAP (Nazi Party) in Germany. Share your research with the class.

1.3 Political instability in China

The demise of the **Qing dynasty**, the last of China's empires, began on 10 October 1911 in what became known as the Double Tenth Rebellion. This was followed by a long period of weak government known as warlordism, when regional leaders (largely self-appointed) with their own private militias controlled whole provinces with scant regard for the nominal government in Beijing. As mentioned earlier, Japan entered World War I mainly to take over German interests in China, an aim it achieved and attempted to build on with the Twenty-One Demands it presented to the Chinese central government. Had it not been for the protection of the United States, motivated by both a long-established link to China as well as concern over Japanese expansion, it is likely that all 21 of the demands would have had to be conceded.

China and Japan, 1911–22

Sino-Japanese rivalry over Korea has already been discussed in the first section of this chapter; relations between the countries did not improve as World War I came to an end. Negotiations over the Shandong province and whether it should remain with Japan or be returned to China (which had also entered the war on the side of the **Allies** in 1917) led to heated debates in Paris. Presenting the case for China was Wellington Koo, the Chinese ambassador to Washington. American-educated with degrees from Columbia University, Koo was immensely engaging and erudite.

Wellington Koo and his wife in a photograph taken in 1920.

Activity 11   (ATL) Thinking skills

Taken from the book *Paris 1919* (Random House, 2003) by Margaret Macmillan, below is a description of Wellington Koo by Georges Clemenceau, the French prime minister:

> ❝ *[He is] a young Chinese cat, Parisian of speech and dress, absorbed in the pleasure of patting and pawing the mouse, even if it was reserved for the Japanese.*

1. According to the quotation above, what is the 'mouse' meant to symbolize? What impression does this source give of Wellington Koo?

Despite his eloquence, Koo's arguments could not overcome the fact that it was pragmatic – at least in the short term – to give Shandong to Japan. This greatly incensed public opinion in China and the supporters of the May Fourth Movement (the latter mainly comprising students from Peking University), who condemned the Western leaders for deserting China during what they claimed was a 'life and death struggle' (Macmillan, *Paris 1919*, 2003, p. 340). Despairing over the lack of support from the West, many Chinese turned to an alternative system adopted by the Soviet Union; indeed, the Communist Party of China, set up in 1921, grew out of the May Fourth Movement.

Very soon it was clear that the resolution of the Shandong question was seen as a mixed blessing for Japan: it had aroused the hostility of many of its wartime allies, underlining that this was a prize given grudgingly. According to Macmillan, in China, resentment affected Japanese business, while Britain began to seriously rethink the Anglo-Japanese Alliance. Unsurprisingly, this concerned Japan greatly; discussions were initiated by the Japanese in 1920 to return Shandong to China, though China did not respond. The matter was eventually resolved during the Washington Conference in 1921–22, when it was agreed that Shandong should be given back China, albeit with economic concessions to the Japanese. (For more on the Washington Conference, see page 18).

According to Hane,

> At the Washington Conference, a settlement between Japan and China was reached. Japan agreed to return the German holdings in Shandong Peninsula to China but it got China to agree to allow Japan to retain the railroad on the peninsula for fifteen years. Sino-Japanese relations grew increasingly strained however, as Japanese authorities intervened in Chinese political affairs during the 1920s when a power struggle between the different warlord factions was taking place.

From Mikiso Hane, *Japan, A Short History*, Oneworld Publications, 2015, p. 119

Activity 12 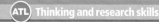 **Thinking and research skills**

The countries that attended and signed the Washington Treaty also agreed on the Nine-Power Treaty signed in February 1922, which guaranteed the sovereignty of China and an open-door trading policy.

Below is the first article of the treaty.

ARTICLE I

> The Contracting Powers, other than China, agree:
> (1) To respect the sovereignty, the independence, and the territorial and administrative integrity of China;
> (2) To provide the fullest and most unembarrassed opportunity to China to develop and maintain for herself an effective and stable government;
> (3) To use their influence for the purpose of effectually establishing and maintaining the principle of equal opportunity for the commerce and industry of all nations throughout the territory of China;
> (4) To refrain from taking advantage of conditions in China in order to seek special rights or privileges which would abridge the rights of subjects or citizens of friendly States, and from countenancing action inimical to the security of such States.
>
> Addendum: [Elihu Root, a US statesman]… drafted the Nine Power Treaty. In the course of that Hughes [prime minister of Australia] produced the secret promise made by Japan as part of the Lansing–Ishii arrangement that she would not interfere with other nations in China and without saying anything to anybody this secret agreement was put into the Root draft… It became verbatim the corresponding obligation in the Nine Power Treaty. (File no. 500. A4d/240 1/2.)

1. With reference to its origin, purpose and content, analyse the value and limitation of this source to historians studying the postwar settlements.

The Guomindang and the Northern Expedition

Despite some attempts at unity, China in the 1920s was riven with discord. Back in 1923, following the advice of the **Comintern**, members of the **Communist Party of China (CPC)** had joined the **Guomindang** (Chinese Nationalist Party, or GMD for short) to form the United Front, aimed at ridding China of warlords. The year 1925 saw the death of Sun Yixian, founder and head of the GMD; he was succeeded by Jiang Jieshi, the vehemently anti-communist head of the National Revolutionary Army (NRA). In 1926, Jiang launched the Northern Expedition to end the rule of the warlords, beginning in Guangdong province and heading north towards Shanghai, Beijing, and Manchuria. One of Jiang's best-known sayings was to be 'the Japanese are a disease of the skin but the Communists are a disease of the heart': in 1927, he demonstrated the depth of his hatred of the CPC by launching a campaign known as the White Terror to purge the GMD of Communists.

The GMD advanced northwards. By 1928, they were moving towards the territory controlled by Zhang Zuolin (see page 22), who according to Jonathan Fenby was 'China's biggest warlord' (Fenby, *The Penguin History of Modern China; The Fall and Rise*

Study closely the content of this source, in particular the addendum at the end that refers to a 'secret' agreement which Japan had accepted. This is an official document, but how reliable is this source for understanding what actually happened during the signing of the treaty or what was agreed by the nations?

While primary sources such as this may be useful in your studies, do not assume they are always more reliable or valuable than secondary sources!

of a Great Power, 2009, p. 183). Known also as the Old Marshal, Zhang had actively cooperated with the Japanese who had controlled the South Manchurian Railway. For the Japanese army in Manchuria, known as the Guandong Army (Guandong is pinyin for Kwantung), the Northern Expedition posed a threat to Japanese interests in Manchuria. Increasingly, the Japanese doubted the loyalty of Zhang Zuolin, preferring to deal with his son Zhang Xueliang, known (unsurprisingly) as the Young Marshal. A plot was hatched to dispose of the Old Marshal by first killing him and then waiting for the his army to take to the streets to seek revenge; the Guandong Army would then intervene to restore peace and, in doing so, establish control over Manchuria. The first part of the plot worked: a bomb was dropped on the Old Marshal's train carriage as he returned to Mukden in 1928. The critically injured warlord was taken to hospital where he died. Unexpectedly, however, Zhang's army did not respond, thus presenting no opportunity for the Guandong Army to 'defend' Japanese interests. To make matters worse for the plotters, the Young Marshal came to an agreement with Jiang Jieshi and, in return, was given autonomy over Manchuria. Fenby notes that, unlike his father, Zhang Xueliang refused to cooperate with the Guandong Army and showed every intention of seeking 'further integration' with China by building a railway to compete with the Japanese-run South Manchurian Railway. The Guandong Army did not try again to gain control until 1931 (Fenby, *The Penguin History of Modern China*, 2009, p. 232).

 A review of Chapter 1

This chapter has focused on Japan's rise as a modern nation state from the late 19th century through to the 1920s. In particular, it has examined how the Meiji restoration established an economic and military basis for Japanese expansion and its aspiration to be regarded as a world power. It has also looked at the relationship between Japan and its neighbours, including its response to the decline of the Chinese Manchu Empire and growing rivalry with the Romanov Empire of Russia. The impact of World War I upon Japan – and the opportunities it offered – has been outlined, as has Japan's role in the Paris peace-making of 1919. The chapter has ended with an overview of the political and social changes that Japan underwent during the 1920s, as well as an analysis of its growing tension with Nationalist China over the future status of Manchuria.

'Young Marshal' Zhang Xueliang (on the right) posing in 1929 with General Connell, an American officer, after he had joined forces with Jiang Jieshi against further Japanese and Soviet incursions in Manchuria. The United States had offered aid to help combat Soviet and Japanese raids in Manchuria.

 Activity 13    **(ATL) Thinking and research skills**

Now that you have read through this chapter, answer the following question. This is very similar to the kind of mini essay that you would get asked to write in the fourth question of the Prescribed Subject exam paper.

Using the sources and the text in this chapter, examine the factors that influenced Japanese foreign policy between 1919 and 1931.

 To access websites relevant to this chapter, go to www.pearsonhotlinks.com, search for the book title or ISBN, and click on 'Chapter 1'.

 It isn't a good idea to try and start your exam by answering the fourth question first (even though it carries the highest marks). Always answer the questions in the order they are written in the exam: in other words, start with the first question and work your way through to the last. By doing so, you become familiar with the sources and you are better prepared to tackle this mini-essay question. Don't forget that the question asks you to include references to the material in the sources as well as your own knowledge. To write a good answer, you need to include references to all the sources (there are always four sources included in the exam paper), and use your own knowledge as well as the sources to support your argument. Allow yourself around 20 minutes of the exam time to answer the fourth question – don't forget to plan your answer before you start writing.

For this particular question on Japanese foreign policy, you could list the following factors:

• the Treaty of Versailles and the treatment of Japan at the Peace Conference
• the Naval Treaties
• the Japanese economy that both prospered and faced crises in the 1920s.

Think of other factors you could add to this list. Once you have done this, go through the sources in the last section of this chapter and see if you could use some of them in your answer. Don't forget to include an introduction and a conclusion.

Japanese expansion and foreign
policy, 1931–38

This chapter examines Japan's foreign policy from 1931 to 1938. In particular, it focuses on the ways in which it was perceived by the following world powers:

- the United States and the Soviet Union: both considered Japan to be an ambitious neighbour with interests that might potentially clash with their own
- Britain and France: both had imperial possessions in the Far East that made them wary of Japanese expansion
- Germany and Italy: both would form closer relations with Japan during this period.

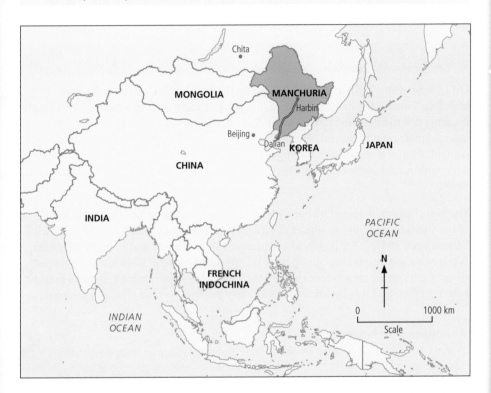

Map of East Asia (with location of South Manchurian Railway), 1931

The chapter begins with the invasion of Manchuria in 1931 and ends with the Battle of Nanjing in December 1937, giving an overview of events that contributed to growing tension as the world moved closer to war.

2.1 The Japanese occupation of Manchuria and northern China, 1931

As you will recall from the previous chapter, in 1928 a faction within the Guandong Army attempted to manufacture a *casus belli* in Manchuria by assassinating its warlord, 'Old Marshal' Zhang Zuolin. This act of terrorism had been motivated in part by the northward movement of the Guomindang (GMD) under the leadership of Jiang Jieshi, who wanted to unite all of China under a centralized government; if successful, it would have compromised Japanese control over the South Manchurian Railway as well as its trading interests throughout the region. Japan was also concerned about the growing support offered to Jiang Jieshi by the Western powers and how this might strengthen China. Furthermore, the Soviet Union was rapidly industrializing and, in time, might prove a troublesome neighbour. Finally, perhaps most importantly, China was in disarray and unlikely to have the military capacity to prevent a takeover of Manchuria.

Zhang's assassination had been an attempt to provoke a hostile response from the warlord's army, providing a pretext for the Guandong Army to intervene and secure its control over Manchuria. Although this act of murder roused anti-Japanese feeling in Manchuria, there was no military response and the Guandong Army's plan failed. Shocked by the murder of Zhang Zuolin and suspecting a plot, Emperor Shōwa (Hirohito) demanded an explanation; Prime Minister Tanaka Giiji, though having played no part in events, felt compelled to resign.

Manchuria, however, remained of great economic and historical importance and, in 1931, the Guandong Army, acting once again on its own initiative, made another attempt to consolidate its control over this region of China.

The Manchurian Incident

On 18 September 1931, a bomb exploded on the South Manchurian Railway near Mukden. 'Young Marshal' Zhang Xueliang, son of Zhang Zuolin, issued instructions to his army not to intervene, but the Guandong Army immediately blamed the Chinese, asserted their right to defend Japanese interests against the Chinese bandits, and took control of cities along the whole length of the South Manchurian Railway. This was done without the authority of the emperor, the Japanese Diet, or the military chiefs in Tokyo.

The Manchurian Incident had been planned by Lieutenant Colonel Ishiwara Kanji of the Guandong Army, an officer described by Eri Hotta as 'magnetic and eccentric' (Hotta, *Japan 1941*, 2014, p. 44), who was motivated by a fear that Jiang Jieshi, under Western influence, was becoming increasingly anti-Japanese. Ishiwara also worried about the looming presence of the Soviet Union, which had embarked on its first Five-Year Plan and was building up its military presence on the Manchurian border.

An invasion or an incident?

In Japan, the occupation of Manchuria was referred to as the Manchurian *Incident*, which made it sound like a brief event that had been quickly dealt with. In history textbooks, however, it is commonly referred to as the Manchurian *Invasion*. The use of the term is debated: on the one hand it could be argued that this was not an *invasion* as such, as the Guandong Army was already present in Manchuria and had the right to protect Japanese interests. On the other hand, the army did invade Chinese territory, bringing it under Japanese control.

Activity 1	**ATL** Thinking and communication skills

Source A

Eri Hotta is a Japanese historian who was educated in Japan, the United States, and the United Kingdom. The following extract is taken from her book *Japan 1941*

> ❝ To many in Japan, the Western support garnered [gathered] by Jiang […] represented a betrayal […] By the end of the 1920s, Japan was equally obsessed with the rise of Bolshevism […] All these factors compelled Ishiwara and his followers to go far beyond the call of duty and invade Manchuria. Their reckless initiative came as a surprise to most leaders in Tokyo, though the plotters may well have had supporters in the higher ranks of the Army General Staff. At the beginning of the campaign, [Japanese] Prime Minister Wakatsuki Reijiro […] wanted to contain hostilities. Japanese public opinion, however, fuelled by a jingoistic [nationalistic] media, keenly supported Ishiwara's adventures.

Eri Hotta, *Japan 1941*, Vintage Books, USA, 2014, p. 45

Source B

Jonathan Fenby is a British writer, journalist, and analyst. Here is an extract from his book *The Penguin History of Modern China: The Fall and Rise of a Great Power.*

> A leading politician, Prince Konoe [he later became prime minister] thought it 'only natural for China to sacrifice itself for the sake of Japan's social and industrial needs'. Rising unemployment under the impact of the Great Depression, growing hardships at home and food problems made expansion across the sea all the more attractive. For those who had envisaged an anti-communist crusade, the north-east was an ideal springboard for an attack on the Soviet Union.

Jonathan Fenby, *The Penguin History of Modern China: The Fall and Rise of a Great Power*, Penguin, UK, 2009, p. 231

1. Compare and contrast the views expressed in Sources A and B on the reasons for the Manchurian Incident of 1931.

Student answer – Sara

Both sources talk about the Soviet Union and how Japan reacted to it. Source B mentions Prince Konoe but Source A doesn't. Source B also talks about unemployment in Japan but Source A doesn't. Both sources talk about invading Manchuria.

Student answer – Ben

Both Source A and Source B refer to the importance of the Soviet Union as a reason for the Japanese invasion of Manchuria. Source A mentions how Japan was 'obsessed with the rise of Bolshevism' and Source B states that Manchuria (the northeast) 'was an ideal springboard for an attack on the Soviet Union'. Both Sources A and B also comment on how the politicians – in Source A, Prime Minister Wakatsuki and in Source B, Prince Konoe – were both swayed by public opinion to support the invasion. Source B places more emphasis on unemployment and other economic motives, however, while Source A refers to the importance of nationalism (**jingoism**). Both Sources A and B refer to Japan's attitude towards China but in different ways: Source B states that China had to 'sacrifice itself' for Japan's needs, while Source A refers to the frustration felt in Japan by the support given to China by the West.

Examiner's comments

Ben has written a much fuller answer than Sara. His answer is also more clearly structured, as he refers firstly to comparisons and then to contrasts, whereas Sara's structure is less coherent. Ben has also included short phrases, which are always helpful in enabling an examiner to see why certain points have been made. Notice also that Sara has implied some contrasts but only by stating that Source B mentions Prince Konoe and Source A doesn't. Do try to avoid this kind of response as it is a bit like giving half an answer. Ben handles this better by saying that Source B discusses unemployment while Source A focuses on nationalism. It would be even better if Ben linked this to the question by emphasizing nationalism as a reason for the Manchurian Incident.

The creation of Manchukuo

Once it had taken control of the region around the South Manchurian Railway, the Guandong Army continued to march forward and, by March 1932, occupied the three Manchurian provinces of Liaoning, Heilongjiang, and Jilin. The Guandong Army claimed that the people of Manchuria had been liberated and had spontaneously declared their independence; supported by Japan, Manchuria was renamed as the state of Manchukuo.

The independence of Manchukuo was proclaimed on 1 March 1931, although it was commonly referred to as a 'puppet state'; it was also termed as a 'client regime' (Hotta, *Japan 1941*, 2014, p. 40) as, in reality, it was administered by Japan. To rule over the Manchu people, Japan nominated 28-year-old Puyi, the last of the Manchu (Qing) emperors of China deposed in 1912, as regent in the new capital city of Changchun. In 1934, when the conquest of Manchuria was complete, Puyi was officially enthroned as emperor. As was customary with Japanese emperors, Puyi was given a name that also referred to the era of his reign: his was Kangde, meaning 'prosperity and virtue'.

Regardless of his position and title, Kangde was head of state in name only as he took his orders from the Japanese military.

Yoshioka Yasunori, an officer in the Guandong Army, was appointed as a 'minder' for Emperor Kangde: in other words, the former told the latter what to do. According to Jonathan Fenby, when news came of Japanese victories, Kangde was instructed to bow in the direction of the battlefield. Japanese police were also posted in the Imperial Palace to keep a watch on what went on there (*The Penguin History of Modern China: The Fall and Rise of a Great Power*, 2009, p. 249).

Activity 2

Source A

Taken in 1934, this is a photo of Empress Wanrong of Manchukuo. She became addicted to opium and died in 1945.

Source B

Emperor Kangde (Puyi) with Emperor Shōwa (Hirohito) on a state visit to Japan in April 1935.

1. Looking at the photos in Sources A and B, what impression do they give of the status of the emperor and empress of Manchukuo?

Some reasons behind the Manchurian Incident

Manchukuo, 1932.

- Jiang Jieshi was moving northwards with the GMD to bring all of China (including Manchuria) under centralized control and this would have limited Japanese control over its interests in the region.
- Chinese nationalism and anti-Japanese feelings were increasing in Manchuria and other regions of China, which were important trading partners for Japan.
- There were growing concerns about the Soviet Union and the potential expansion of communism into Manchuria.
- The Great Depression badly affected the Japanese economy; it needed cheap, plentiful resources as well as a market for its goods.
- Officers in the Guandong Army believed that it was Japan's destiny to expand its empire to Manchuria and beyond.

 TOK **Thinking, research, and communication skills** **ATL**

The events of 1931 are referred to as either the Manchurian *Invasion* or the Manchurian *Incident*; the Japanese government at the time preferred the latter. When you go on to read about the Second Sino-Japanese War of 1937, you will see that it too was referred to in Japan as the *Chinese Incident*. Do the names we give to such events really make a difference to how we think of them and respond to them? Can you think of other conflicts that were/are given different names to arouse support or opposition?

2.2 The response in Japan and China to the Manchurian Incident

It is fairly clear that the Guandong Army was controlling events in Manchukuo in 1931, but who had control of the events in Tokyo? Overall, it is quite difficult to determine which factions (and there were many) within the military, the parliament, and the imperial court supported or condemned the actions of the Guandong Army.

Japan – a political response

Hamaguchi Yūkō was appointed prime minister in June 1931. The year before, he had been responsible for signing the naval agreement at the London Naval Treaty (see Chapter 1, page 22) that further limited the growth of the Japanese navy, an action that was deeply unpopular among the ultra-nationalists in Japan. Hamaguchi was targeted by an assassin in November 1930 and was severely wounded; he was, however, reappointed as prime minister in 1931, shortly before his death later that same year. He was succeeded by Wakatsuki Reijirō (who resigned in December 1931). Wakatsuki's response to the actions of the Guandong Army was lukewarm, at best; a 'credibility gap' was developing in Japanese politics as the government reiterated its policy of non-expansionism while the military in Manchuria continued to advance (Hsu, *The Rise of Modern China*, Oxford, 1995 p. 549). Wakatsuki was succeeded by Inukai Tsuyoshi, who also expressed misgivings about the creation of Manchukuo, stating that it should not be recognized as an independent state from China. In 1932, Inukai agreed to a ceasefire when fighting broke out in Shanghai: for this, he was assassinated by right-wing nationalists. His assassination has been seen as marking the end of the Taishō democracy and the start of a new era in which a government by 'national unity cabinets' was ushered in, made up mainly of senior bureaucrats with only some representation from the political parties. This was meant to restore stability. Ian Buruma compares this to contemporary events in Germany, where Weimar democracy came to an end in 1933 (Buruma, *Inventing Japan 1853–1964*, 2004, p. 91).

 Research, communication, social, and self-management skills

With a classmate, carry out research on why democracy came to an end in Germany in 1933. Draw up a list of comparisons and contrasts between what was happening in Germany and events in Japan during this period, focusing on the economy, the ideology of the ruling party, and the parliamentary system. See what other factors strike you as similar. Share your research with the class.

Japan – a popular response

The legacy of the Russo-Japanese War (which in 1904 had cost the lives of approximately 100,000 Japanese soldiers) had been an important reason for public support for the takeover of Manchuria (Gong, *Memory and History in East and South East Asia*, 2001, p. 52). Propaganda emphasized how much Japanese blood had already been spilled over Manchuria, claiming that the Guandong Army was not seizing but merely defending hard-won territory.

Activity 3  **ATL** Thinking and communication skills

A photo taken in 1933 of a young girl holding dolls. These were made both to commemorate the first anniversary of the establishment of Manchukuo and to foster good relations with Japan.

1. What impression, do you think, were these dolls meant to convey to the people of Manchukuo?

According to Ian Buruma, those who supported the takeover of Manchuria maintained that the region was rich in resources (such as coal and iron ore) that were vital for Japan's continued industrialization: without them, Japan would surely collapse. For some, Manchuria was seen as an impoverished region, needing only economic investment and good (Japanese) governance so it could be turned into a paradise; it was believed that, under the benevolent rule of Japan, the different ethnic groups living in Manchuria would coexist in peace (Buruma, *Inventing Japan 1853–1964*, 2004, pp. 93–96). It is significant that by propagating this vision of harmony and justice, many left-wing Japanese were enticed to go to Manchuria to be part of this social experiment. Conveniently, this rid Japan of some of its more troublesome left-wingers.

In the early 20th century, the five main ethnic groups living in Manchuria were Russian, Chinese, Korean, Japanese, and the Manchu. The Manchu people formed only a small percentage of the region's population.

Activity 4 **ATL** Thinking skills

Ian Buruma is an Anglo-Dutch writer and academic. The following extract is taken from his book *Inventing Japan 1853–1964*.

> *Japanese novelists and essayists flocked to Manchukuo to write about its remarkable modernity, the speed of its trains, the fine parks of Dalian and the cosmopolitan nightlife of Harbin. Some of the best filmmakers worked for the Manchu film studios, where they were given the most advanced facilities to make films about brave Japanese pioneers helping their Asian brethren [brothers]. Many of the artists and writers were in fact Marxists, whose sentiments were anti-capitalist and thus anti-Western anyway. Pan-Asianism appealed to their sense of idealism. All they had to do was switch from socialism to a brand of national-socialism.*

Ian Buruma, *Inventing Japan 1853–1964*, Modern Library, New York. 2004, pp 96–97

1. According to the source above, for what reasons did filmmakers, writers, and artists go to Manchukuo?

Now read the following sample answers.

Student answer – Michelle

Filmmakers went to Manchukuo because of the up-to-date facilities they were given at the Manchu film studios. Artists and writers often went there because they were anti-capitalist and its Pan-Asian ethos appealed to their idealism. Also, Manchukuo was modern and living standards were good, with fast trains and nice surroundings.

Student answer – Mike

The reasons why writers and artists went to Manchukuo was that the trains were fast and the nightlife was lively. Also, writers were **Marxist** and anti-capitalist.

Examiner's comments

Mike has mentioned two points but both could be a little more fully developed. Michelle has given a much fuller and nicely structured answer: she has made three clear points, using her own words.

Don't forget that part A of the first question in the Paper 1 exam is worth 3 marks – this means an examiner will be looking for three clear points in order to award the full marks.

As World War II in Asia came to an end in August 1945 – when the Soviet Union declared war on Japan and the Red Army crossed the border into Manchuria – the Japanese settlers were abandoned to their fate and an estimated 120,000 were killed. Professor Takemaro Mori states that many settlers ended up in Siberian gulags (prison camps) and would not return to Japan until after 1972, when diplomatic relations between Japan and the Soviet Union were resumed.

Remember, reading a historical document in translation is not, necessarily, a limitation to its value unless you have a particular reason for saying so. If that is the case, you need to mention it.

Manchuria was also seen as an area with plenty of 'living space' for Japan's growing population, offering opportunities to relieve the poverty that blighted the lives of farmers in the Japanese countryside. This policy was given official support in 1932 when the so-called Rural-Rescue Diet funded an investigation into how best to promote and support the emigration of farmers to Manchuria. The aim was to send a million households to Manchuria; however, by 1945, only 320,000 Japanese emigrants had settled there.

Takemaro Mori, a professor of economic research, notes that emigration to Manchuria was favoured not only for economic reasons but also to support militaristic aims, as farmers were encouraged to settle along the route of the South Manchurian Railway and on the border with the Soviet Union ('Colonies and Countryside in Wartime Japan: Emigration of Manchuria' in *The Asia-Pacific Journal: Japan Focus*, originally published in 2003).

Activity 5

This source is an extract from a conversation held in March 1936, between Katō Kanji (an agronomist – a scientist who studies plants) and Tanaka Nagashige, a senior civil servant in the Ministry of Agriculture and Forestry.

> *KATŌ: On the question of land, there's plenty available [in Manchuria] now at one or two yen per tan. Worrying about what we'd do if the price rises, the way some people do, makes no sense at all. In my opinion, we should just get on with it as quickly as possible. The Chinese and the Koreans don't bother trying to find out who owns the land they want. They just move in and take it over. If we waste time trying to track down owners and agree prices, we'll get left behind. The first group of armed emigrants didn't buy land before they left Japan, they bought it after they arrived. In Manchuria, no one knows who owns which parcels of land. If we Japanese don't get cracking, the Koreans and the Chinese will grab all the land there is.*
>
> *TANAKA (laughing): It sounds like theft to me.*
>
> *KATŌ: The conditions over there are not like those here at home. If you call what I'm talking about 'theft' then you'd have to be against war, too, because war also involves theft as well as killing.*

1. According to the origin, purpose, and content, analyse the value and limitations of the source above for a historian studying how the Manchurian Incident was viewed in Japan.

Activity 6

Source A

The cover of a tourist brochure for Manchukuo, January 1937.

Source B

A propaganda poster encouraging Japanese farmers to move to Manchukuo.

1. What is the message conveyed in Source A?
2. What is the message conveyed in Source B?
3. What does each source tell us about the intended audience? Who were they meant to persuade and how?

China's response to the Manchurian Incident

By 1931, Jiang Jieshi had established an alliance with 'Young Marshal' Zhang Xueliang. In the aftermath of the Manchurian Incident, Jiang had urged Zhang not to react to provocation by the Guandong Army. According to Jonathan Fenby, Jiang had not wanted to fight the Japanese; he had hoped that the seizure of territory would be limited and that Western powers would step in to 'reverse the situation' (Fenby, *The Penguin History of Modern China: The Fall and Rise of a Great Power*, 2009, p. 230).

Activity 7 (ATL) Thinking and research skills

1. Why, do you think, was Jiang Jieshi so confident about the involvement of foreign powers 'to reverse the situation'? How had the Western powers responded to Japanese expansion in the past?

The Guandong Army had proceeded to take over the whole of Manchuria, however, meeting any resistance with force and carrying out bombing raids on cities. Additional Japanese troops were sent from Korea, without permission being sought from Tokyo, to assist in what Fenby calls 'the biggest land grab in history' (Fenby, *The Penguin History of Modern China: The Fall and Rise of a Great Power*, 2009, p. 234). Jiang also prevaricated over whether or not to challenge Japanese expansion as he was also fighting the Chinese Communists in Jiangxi province in southeast China.

Despite Jiang's reluctance, there was popular opposition to the Japanese: demonstrators in Shanghai called for a boycott of Japanese shops and the purchase of Japanese goods; in Nanjing, men demanded to be sent north to fight and women volunteered to accompany them as nurses. With demonstrators shouting slogans such as 'Death before Surrender' and 'Supreme Sacrifice', Japanese banks were boycotted, workers in Japanese-owned factories went on strike, and imports from Japan fell by 30 per cent by the end of 1931 and 90 per cent in 1932 (Fenby, *The Penguin History of Modern China: The Fall and Rise of a Great Power*, 2009, p.235). Despite this outpouring of public anger, Jiang did nothing. According to Fenby, this was 'widely seen as the first episode of appeasement of the revisionist **Axis powers** that would stretch up to 1939' (Fenby, *The Penguin History of Modern China: The Fall and Rise of a Great Power*, 2009, p. 235). Furthermore, Japanese reports stated that Jiang had been heard to say, 'If Japan will be satisfied with Manchuria,

The description of Japanese soldiers as 'human bullets' was not new; it was first coined during the Russo-Japanese War. In 1932, this term would have resonated with the Japanese public and reminded them (as intended) of the successful war of 1904–05. A lieutenant in the Japanese army called Tadayoshi Sakurai also included the term in the title of his memoirs *Human Bullets: A Soldier's Story of the Russo-Japanese War.*

well, we aren't happy about it, but we can pretend they aren't there' (Fenby, *The Penguin History of Modern China: The Fall and Rise of a Great Power*, 2009 p. 23).

Jiang's decision not to confront the Japanese was based on a number of reasons, including the following:

- The GMD army was no match for the well-trained Guandong Army and resistance would probably have ended in defeat.
- Sending his best soldiers to Manchuria would have weakened Jiang's precarious hold on the rest of China, which still needed to be brought under centralized control.
- Defeating the Communists whom he referred to as 'the disease of the heart' remained his priority.
- Many senior GMD officials and officers were from southern China, so Manchuria was a region unfamiliar to them and of limited importance.

According to Immanuel Hsu, Jiang's reaction was 'a combination of non-resistance, non-compromise and non-negotiation'. Hsu also suggests that some organized resistance might have boosted the moderates in Tokyo, who could have used it to call for an end to the conflict (Hsu, *The Rise of Modern China*, Oxford, 1995, p. 550). Instead, Jiang chose to approach the League of Nations, hoping that it would step in to solve the problem.

The Shanghai Incident

Since the mid-19th century, Shanghai, a densely populated and prosperous city on the estuary of the Yangtze River, had been a centre for international trade. Around 50,000 foreigners lived there, in the French Concession, the Japanese Concession, and the International Settlement that combined the British and American Concessions.

In January 1932, a series of anti-Japanese riots and disturbances broke out in Hongkou, an area of Shanghai known as Little Tokyo. Japanese marines were sent to restore order; they were, however, supported by a Japanese cruiser and 12 destroyers that proceeded to bombard the Chinese section of Hongkou. Extensive aerial bombing also destroyed houses and factories. A local warlord fought back against the Japanese with the assistance of the Green Gang, a triad gang that ran the drugs trade in Shanghai. Jonathan Fenby asserts that Jiang Jieshi also sent in GMD troops, but only after he realized there would be no support from the Western powers that had allowed the Japanese to use the International Settlement as a base. A ceasefire was agreed on 3 March 1932, making Shanghai (outside of the International Settlement) into a demilitarized zone.

Inukai Tsuyoshi, the Japanese prime minister who agreed to this truce was assassinated. According to Ian Buruma, however, propaganda back home in Japan glorified the bravery of its soldiers who were described in the media as 'human bullets' (Buruma, *Inventing Japan 1853–1964*, 2004, p. 93).

International Settlements

The British government had been given access to a number of treaty ports in China in accordance with the Treaty of Nanking (Nanjing), signed after the First Opium War in 1842. In Shanghai, this led to the establishment of the British Concession, an area of the city that came under British control. Later, having been combined with the American Concession, the area became known as the International Settlement. It was run by an Anglo-American municipal council and was independently administered with its own soldiers and police. There existed also a French Concession, administered from French Indochina, and a Japanese Concession. Outside of these areas lay what was known as the Chinese Municipality. In 1937 the entire Chinese Municipality came under Japanese control. In December 1941, after attacking Pearl Harbor, the Japanese forces attacked and took over the International Settlement.

A propaganda poster from 1933, illustrating how anti-Japanese Manchurians would go to hell, while pro-Japanese Manchurians would go to heaven.

2.3 The international response to the Manchurian Incident

Despite Jiang's hopes that the Western powers would condemn the actions of the Guandong Army in Manchuria, the response from the international community was quite muted. According to Immanuel Hsu,

> The London Times stated that, 'Japan had a strong case but had put herself regrettably and unnecessarily in the wrong'. The United States took the easy position that Tokyo could not be held responsible for the violation of the Paris Pact since the Kwantung Army had acted without its authorisation. The Soviet Union also took no action as long as its Siberian border remained unviolated. Thus China was left to face the enemy alone.

Immanuel Hsu, *The Rise of Modern China*, 1995, p. 529

The League of Nations and the Lytton Commission

Even so, Jiang asked for assistance from the League of Nations and also from the United States, as it had signed the Nine-Power Pact defending Chinese sovereignty and was a signatory of the Kellogg–Briand Treaty of 1928.

The League of Nations

This was an organization set up in Geneva in 1920 to provide collective security for its member states. It was meant to make alliances unnecessary and to provide guarantees against aggressive actions, such as the invasion of Manchuria, because League members would present a united front against aggressors. Both China and Japan were members of the League. The United States, however, was not a member.

Article 11 of the Covenant of the League

Any war or threat of war, whether immediately affecting any of the Members of the League or not, is hereby declared a matter of concern to the whole League, and the League shall take any action that may be deemed wise and effectual to safeguard the peace of nations. In case any such emergency should arise the Secretary General shall on the request of any Member of the League forthwith summon a meeting of the Council.

http://avalon.law.yale.edu/20th_century/leagcov.asp

The Kellogg–Briand Treaty, 1928
Named after Frank B Kellogg (US secretary of state) and Aristide Briand (French foreign minister), this was an agreement made between the United States and France to renounce the use of war to solve disputes between countries. By 1929, there were over 62 signatories, including China and Japan.

Events leading up to the Lytton Commission proceeded in the following order:

1. On 22 September 1931, the Council of the League of Nations debated the Manchurian Incident, only days after the bomb blast in Mukden. The Japanese delegate was described as 'conciliatory'. It was proposed that an enquiry be held into the events in Manchuria and for both Japan and China to stop fighting.

2. The League hoped for American support (the United States was not a member of the League) but Henry Stimson, the US secretary of state, sent a note advising against an enquiry, given that Japan did not agree with the proposal. The non-involvement of the United States at this stage may have influenced the Japanese army's decision to move further into Manchuria.

3. In mid-October, the League gave Japan a deadline of 16 November to withdraw from all occupied territory, which was ignored.

4. Japan now changed its mind and requested a commission of enquiry, a proposal that the League accepted while suspending any 'coercive measures against Japan'. A commission was then formed chaired by Lord Lytton, the acting viceroy of India.

5. At the start of January 1932, China asked the League to impose economic sanctions on Japan but the worldwide economic depression made it difficult for member states to accept a reduction in trade and this was not done.

6. On 7 January 1932, Henry Stimson published a note that came to be known as the Stimson Doctrine. It stated that the United States would not recognize 'any treaty or agreement between Japan and China that violated US rights or treaties to which the US subscribed'. This meant the United States would not accept any changes to the open-door policy that guaranteed free trade and would also refuse to recognize the state of Manchukuo. Furthermore, as Japan had violated the Nine-Power Pact, the US no longer considered itself bound by the naval limitations that had been agreed to. Historian AJP Taylor pointed out that the United States did not, however, intend to 'curtail its trade with Japan' (Taylor, *The Origins of the Second World War*, 1962, p. 63).

7. For now, Britain rejected the Stimson Doctrine, stating that Japan had given assurances that there would be an 'open door' for trade in Manchuria and so did not intend to violate the Nine-Power Pact. Furthermore, when the question of recognizing the state of Manchukuo was debated in the British parliament, the government stated that Japan had not requested this and that any such decision would be made after the Lytton Commission had presented its report.

8. In October 1932, the Lytton Report was published and, although sympathetic to Japan's grievances over Manchuria, it condemned Japanese aggression, indicating that Manchukuo was no more than a puppet state where 'the territory was de facto under Japanese occupation' (Turns, 'The Stimson Doctrine of Non-Recognition', *Chinese Journal of International Law*, 2003, 2 (1): p. 126).

9. In February 1933, the report was accepted by the League, prompting Japan to withdraw its membership from the League. At the same time, Japan began occupation of Jehol province (known as Rehe today), beyond the borders of Manchuria.

10. In May 1933, Japan and China signed the Tanggu Truce: it attached Jehol province to Manchukuo; it handed over the control of the Shanhaiguan Pass between Manchuria and China to the Guandong Army; and it declared the region to the north of Beijing a demilitarized zone. According to Jonathan Fenby, on reading the terms of the truce, the Chinese response was to say it was purely military and without political significance but 'they were told "to shut up and sign", which they did' (Fenby, *The Penguin History of Modern China: The Fall and Rise of a Great Power*, 2009 p. 247 – also based on Mowat, *Britain Between the Wars*, p. 420, 1976; Hane p. 147, 2015).

The League of Nations had been slow to react to the Japanese takeover of Manchuria, but Japan was admonished for its bad behaviour and instructed to withdraw from the territory it had occupied. The government in Tokyo did not appear to have authority over the Guandong Army, however, and Japanese popular opinion was unlikely to support any submission to the demands of the League.

In defence of the League, AJP Taylor points out that it had acted as it had been designed to do, in that it 'limited the conflict and… brought it to an end'. Furthermore, although the League's response was limited to 'moral sanction', it was the Manchurian Crisis that prompted the creation of a process to impose economic sanctions and these were applied against Italy in 1935 (Taylor, *The Origins of the Second World War*, 1962, p. 64).

Jiang Jieshi proceeded to coexist with the Japanese presence in Manchukuo until an upsurge of popular opposition compelled him to oppose them and to agree to a United Front with the Communist Party of China (CPC) in 1936.

 The Hoover–Stimson Doctrine (Herbert Hoover was the US president between 1929–33, Stimson his secretary of state) is also known in international law as the doctrine of 'non-recognition' as it established the precedent of one state refusing to recognize the legality of another. Previously, states either recognized each other or not without making a specific declaration of 'non-recognition'. After the League of Nations' acceptance of the Lytton Report, no state recognized Manchukuo other than Japan.

 According to AJP Taylor, the League did not condemn Japanese 'aggression' but, rather, criticized it for 'resorting to force before all peaceful means of redress were exhausted' (Taylor, *The Origins of the Second World War*, 1962, p. 64).

CHALLENGE YOURSELF

Research, thinking communication, and self-management skills ATL

Write a short summary of how the international response to the Manchurian Incident could be seen as weakening the aims outlined in both the League of Nations and the Kellogg–Briand Pact.

Henry Stimson, secretary of state in the Hoover administration and author of the Stimson Doctrine.

Source A

Here is a cartoon on the Lytton Report, published in *Punch*.

THE ULTIMATUM.

JAPAN. "IF YOU GO ON SAYING I'M NAUGHTY, I SHALL LEAVE THE CLASS."

1. What is the message conveyed in the source above?

Soviet Union's response to events in the East

The Soviet Union shared a border with Manchuria; Japan's possible encroachment on Soviet territory was Stalin's 'greatest fear' (Taylor, *The Origins of the Second World War*, 1962, p. 78). Meanwhile, the GMD's continual attacks on the CPC's Red Army at a time when Jiang was unwilling to fight Japanese troops in Manchuria provided excellent propaganda for the Chinese Communists. Acting on an initiative formulated by Mao Zedong, the Chinese Soviet government declared war on Japan on 15 April 1932 (Pantsov and Levine, *Deng Xiaoping: A Revolutionary Life*, 2015, p. 103). The CPC was further supported in its opposition to Japan when, on 1 August 1935, the Comintern instructed all Communist parties to cooperate with all anti-fascist parties to form united fronts against the fascists in the West and against Japan in the East. In 1936, as we shall see, this led to the creation of the Second United Front, formed by the CPC and the GMD against Japan; despite Stalin's initial concerns, following 'the formation of a united Chinese Communist–Nationalist front in 1936 and the Soviet fortifications of the Manchurian–Soviet border, both China and the Soviet Union began to stand their ground' (Chickering and Forster (eds), *The Shadows of Total War*, 2007, p. 330).

A move to global war?

Although the response of the Japanese government in Tokyo to events in Manchuria was muted, Japan's moral standing in international affairs was damaged by the behaviour of the Guandong Army. Rather than being seen as a cooperative and peaceable member of the League of Nations, Japan was criticized as expansionist and unwilling, or maybe unable (due to governmental weakness), to abide by treaties it had signed in the 1920s. With hindsight, it is possible to view the Manchurian Incident as a step towards the isolation of Japan, a country that was determined to take its place among the elite of world powers.

Meanwhile, Italy and Germany were observing events in the Far East and the weak response of the League towards Japan. In January 1933, Hitler was appointed chancellor of Germany and moved quickly to end democracy and to establish a single-party state. He withdrew Germany from the League of Nations in October 1933, citing the unfairness of demands made of Germany in the Geneva Disarmament Conference. In violation of the Treaty of Versailles, he proceeded to rearm Germany

The League of Nations was replaced by the United Nations (shown here) in 1945, after the League failed to prevent the outbreak of the Second World War.

and to remilitarize the Rhineland in March 1936. In Fascist Italy, Mussolini challenged collective security by invading Ethiopia in October 1935; by 1937, Italy had also withdrawn from the League. (You can read more about these events in Chapters 5 and 6 of Case Study 2 in this book.)

All these actions were to further divide global powers into two sides: those that continued to hope for collective security, and those intent upon challenging it, including, it seemed, Japan.

Activity 9   **(ATL) Thinking skills**

This cartoon is from the 25 February 1933 edition of the *New York World-Telegram.* Its caption reads 'Moral Isolation'.

1. What is the message conveyed in the source above?

The Second United Front

Despite the emergence of the 'fascistic Blue Shirt movement' within the GMD (Ferguson, *The War of the World*, 2006, p.305), Jiang Jieshi declared in 1934 that China was not yet ready for war with Japan, predicting (accurately) that a much wider global conflict was brewing. In order to improve the training of his soldiers, Jiang had enlisted the services of General von Seeckt, a German veteran of World War I, who helped train 80,000 GMD soldiers, mainly to combat the Communists. The Guandong Army, however, continued to make incursions into China's northern provinces and to tighten its grip on Manchuria. Matters came to a head when Jiang was persuaded to halt his campaigns against the 'Red Bandits' (the Communists) and to focus instead on the 'Dwarf Bandits' (the Japanese) by agreeing to a Second United Front.

The First United Front was established in 1923, when the CPC was instructed by the Comintern to join forces with the GMD (see Chapter 1, page 26). This union came to a bitter end during the White Terror when the GMD turned on the Communists and attempted to eradicate them. Conflict between the Communists and the GMD continued up until 1936 when, for different reasons, both the CPC and the GMD once again agreed to work together, this time to defeat the Japanese.

The Blue Shirts Society

You may have come across the terms '**Brownshirts**' (Hitler's militia) and '**Blackshirts**' (Mussolini's militia). These were private armies identifiable by their uniforms and insignia. In China, a secret organization called the **Blue Shirts** Society emerged from within the GMD. Its members were committed to anti-communism and a determination to fight the Japanese; they held the belief that only a strong dictator could unite and rule China. Historians differ on whether the society had elements of fascism. It was disbanded in 1938.

Why was the Second United Front established?

Most of the Communist Red Army was driven out of Jiangxi province in 1934 when it began the Long March to Yan'an, where it would be safe from attack by the GMD and better situated to wage guerrilla war against the Japanese in Manchuria. In 1935 instructions came from the Comintern that, once again, the CPC were to ally with the GMD. This had been a public declaration and Jiang was willing to consider better relations with the Soviet Union, even if it meant ending his campaign against the CPC, because he believed that if global war were to break out, he would need Soviet support to fight Japan. In public, Jiang maintained that no such union was needed as the GMD had more or less succeeded in suppressing the CPC; but secret negotiations took place, resulting in a verbal agreement that the Red Army would be renamed the Eighth Route Army and brought under the control of the GMD (Mitter, *China's War with Japan 1937–1945*, 2014, p. 67).

The Xi'an Incident

A twist to this story came when 'Young Marshal' Zhang Xueliang – unaware of the secret talks, afraid that he was about to be removed as commander of the northeast army, and frustrated by Jiang's lack of action against the Japanese – plotted the kidnapping of Jiang Jieshi. Zhang was joined in this exploit by another former warlord, General Yang Hucheng, who was also fearful of losing his command. In December 1936, on a routine inspection in Xi'an, Jiang was taken prisoner by his two generals and held hostage. Jiang was only released when the Second United Front was publicly announced, stating that the Communists and the GMD would join forces to defend China against Japan.

A short time after the Xi'an Incident, Jiang arrested Zhang Xueliang and put him under house arrest. In 1949, when the GMD was defeated in the Chinese civil war, Zhang was transferred to Taiwan where he remained as a prisoner of the regime until 1990. He remains a hero to many Chinese who believe he was responsible for making Jiang agree to the Second United Front.

According to Rana Mitter, Stalin was anxious that Jiang Jieshi was not killed during the kidnapping. (Mao Zedong later made much of how he could have had Jiang killed but, in the interests of Chinese unity, chose not to.) Stalin's concern was that if Jiang were removed as leader of the GMD he could be replaced by someone more inclined to join the Anti-Comintern League, and the Soviet Union would therefore be surrounded by its signatories, namely, Germany, Japan, and China (Mitter, *China's War with Japan 1937-1945*, 2014, p. 67).

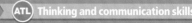
This is an extract from *China's War with Japan 1937–1945* by Rana Mitter, published in 2014. A historian who has written extensively on Chinese history, Mitter is a professor of history at St Cross College, Oxford, in the UK.

> *Zhang Xueliang is today seen in China as a patriot who was shocked by the Generalissimo's unwillingness to face the 'real' threat of Japan, and his insistence on fighting his fellow Chinese, the CCP. In this version of events, Zhang kidnapped Chiang [Jiang] in order to force a change of direction. In fact, Zhang's motive may have been more straightforward: Jiang was likely to deprive him of his military command.*

1. According to its origin, purpose and content, analyse the value and limitations of this source for historians researching the Second United Front.

Political tensions within Japan

In February 1936, political tension increased in Japan when a group of young military officers attempted a coup to remove what they perceived as obstacles preventing a closer union between the emperor and his people.

Known as the February Coup, this event emphasized the division of the military into two factions:

- The Imperial Way Faction (*Kōdōha*) wanted a revolution to remove the zaibatsu, overthrow **capitalism**, assist the poverty-stricken countryside, and establish a military dictatorship loyal only to the emperor.
- The Control Faction (*Tōseiha*) envisioned a future war against the West. Pragmatically, this would require cooperation with the bureaucracy that, to a large extent, governed Japan, as well as the zaibatsu in order to ensure a build-up of armaments to make Japan a formidable military and naval power.

In 1935, a military officer, given the task of demoting some of the Imperial Way officers, was attacked and 'slashed to death by a young officer wielding a samurai sword' (Buruma, *Inventing Japan 1853–1964*, 2004, p. 99). This was a disturbing event and although the Control Faction was able to retain its authority within the army, the Imperial Way remained popular. On 26 February that year, over a thousand of Imperial Way's supporters attempted to take over central Tokyo. Three senior government ministers were assassinated. The prime minister was saved only because, in a case of mistaken identity, his brother-in-law was killed instead. Emperor Shōwa (Hirohito), anxious to stem this tide of unrest, condemned the attempted coup but disturbances continued until 29 February, when the navy was called in to restore order and the rebels surrendered.

The Control Faction within the army was now fully in control and, to assert its authority, demanded that the army and navy ministers would have the right to approve all civilian appointments to the cabinet. This was an important step towards the increase of military authority in Japan. Prime Minister Kōki Hirota proceeded to increase the military budget to finance rearmament. He also signed the **Anti-Comintern Pact** with Germany (Italy joined in 1937).

The Anti-Comintern Pact, 1936

According to Mitter, the Anti-Comintern Pact was not intended as a precursor to a military alliance, or even a fascist alliance: Japan signed the pact because it was increasingly concerned about the threat of the Soviet Union to its interests in Manchuria and northern China. Furthermore, Japan tried, unsuccessfully, to get both Britain and Poland to join the pact. Nevertheless, a secret clause stipulated that if one of the co-signatories went to war with the Soviet Union, the other(s) would not aid the Soviet Union (Mitter, *China's War with Japan 1937–1945*, 2014, p. 67). Whatever the intention, to all outward appearances, it looked as though Japan was aligning itself with the fascist powers of Europe.

One of the ironies of the Anti-Comintern Pact and, later, the Tripartite Pact was that Aryan Germans now had a link to non-Aryans. To overcome any difficulties that might arise, the title 'Honorary Aryans' was bestowed upon the Japanese. Meanwhile, the Italians had already been 'Aryanized' by Mussolini, who had declared that they were the Mediterranean branch of the Aryan race.

Activity 11
ATL Thinking skills

An American cartoon published in November 1938 at the time of the Anti-Comintern Pact. Its caption reads 'Up "Nordics" and at 'em'.

1. What is the message conveyed in this source?

2.4 The Sino-Japanese War, 1937–41

Also referred to as the Second Sino-Japanese War (the First Sino-Japanese War took place in 1894, see Chapter 1, page 13), this conflict was known in Japan as the 'China Incident' as there was never an official declaration of war. It was clear to Japan that control over China was of great importance, especially if, as was feared, it were to move closer to the Soviet Union.

The Marco Polo Bridge Incident, 1937

The Marco Polo Bridge (*Lugouqiao* in Chinese) is lined with 500 carved statues of guardian lions.

The Marco Polo Bridge in the town of Wanping, 15 kilometres to the southwest of Beijing, was so named because the Venetian explorer Marco Polo had once described it as 'one of the finest bridges in the world'.

Some historians have compared the Marco Polo Bridge Incident to the shooting of the Archduke Franz Ferdinand in Sarajevo on 28 June 1914, claiming that the former marked the true outbreak of World War II. Certainly, for China, this was a momentous step towards full-scale war with Japan. The incident took place in 1937 on the Marco Polo Bridge, which was located in an area where, according to an agreement made at the turn of the century, Japanese soldiers could be stationed. On the evening of 7 July, the Japanese commanding officer discovered one of his soldiers had gone missing (most sources state that the soldier had gone to relieve himself and then wandered away into the demilitarized zone) and immediately called for a search, implying that the man had either been kidnapped or killed by Chinese forces. There was an exchange of fire with Chinese troops and a two-day standoff ended with a truce being signed on 9 July. When informed of the incident, Jiang Jieshi had to decide whether this was yet another skirmish with Japanese troops or whether it signalled an attack on Beijing and the heartland of China. This was the point at which he had to decide whether to concede northern China to the Japanese or to fight back. In his diary, Jiang wrote: 'This is the turning point for existence or obliteration' (Mitter, *China's War with Japan 1937–1945*, 2014, p. 76).

In June 1937 Prince Konoe Fumimaro, an aristocrat and close confidante of the emperor, was appointed prime minister of Japan. He was a very popular choice and his response to the incident proved very significant. Despite the truce of 9 July, Konoe used the media to stir up nationalism and showed strong support for the military by sending additional troops to northern China. It is uncertain how much control he actually had over the rapidly worsening situation as, later, he tried to shift the blame elsewhere.

Activity 12
ATL Thinking skills

Rana Mitter is a British historian who specializes in the history of Republican China. This source is taken from his book *China's War with Japan 1937–1945*, Penguin (2014).

> 'Japan is destined sooner or later to clash with the Soviet Union', said Itagaki Seishirō (then chief of staff of the Kwantung Army) to foreign minister Arita Hachirō, 'and the attitude of China at the time will gravely influence operations'.

1. According to its origin, purpose, and content, analyse the value and limitations of this source for historians studying the Marco Polo Bridge Incident.

Activity 13
ATL Thinking and communication skills

Source A
This source is taken from *Japan 1941* (Vintage Books, 2014, p.31) by Eri Hotta. Hotta is a Japanese historian educated in Japan, the United States, and the United Kingdom.

> The truce had become a dead letter by July 20th with Chiang (Jiang) taking his time to give it his official approval. As the war spread and intensified, Japan bombed Nanjing, Shanghai, Hangzhou and other major cities – Konoe blamed it on others, especially, the army's bellicose [warlike] elements who were conveniently nameless and faceless.

Source B
Below is an extract from *The Cambridge History of Japan, Volume 6: The Twentieth Century* (Cambridge UP, 1995, p. 305), edited by Peter Duus, an American historian who specializes in the history of Japan.

> It was a reflection of the split in army circles that decisions to mobilise were made and cancelled four times before a decision was made to send three divisions to northern China on July 27th. Neither Prime Minister Konoe nor Foreign Minister Hirota had clear views about what to do. In the final analysis, they simply followed the lead of the expansionist faction within the Japanese army.

1. According to Source A what reasons were there for the escalation of hostilities in China?
2. Compare and contrast the views expressed in Sources A and B on how decisions were made to mobilize Japanese troops for China.

The Battle for Shanghai, August–October 1937

On 26 July 1937, the Chinese forces were issued an ultimatum by the Japanese demanding that they withdraw from Wanping within 24 hours, although attacks had already begun before the ultimatum had expired. The Chinese government in Nanjing officially declared war on Japan on 7 August, stating a week later that this was a war of self-defence; meanwhile, according to Jonathan Fenby, the emperor in Tokyo called for a 'war-ending' battle (Fenby, *The Penguin History of Modern China: The Fall and Rise of a Great Power*, 2009, p. 275).

Business as usual at the Chartered Bank (a British overseas bank) in 1937, despite the spread of the conflict to Shanghai.

Although there was no intention to compromise the neutrality of the International Settlement, on Saturday 14 August Chinese planes aiming for Japanese destroyers anchored on the Yangtze River accidentally dropped bombs on the crowded Bund (riverfront), killing over 1,000 people. Despite this tragic error, the Chinese forces fought desperately to prevent the fall of Shanghai and, by showing that he no longer tolerated Japanese aggression, 'Jiang forced the world to take notice' (Mitter, *China's War with Japan 1937–1945*, 2014, p. 94). The world did take notice but action was limited, and the League did little, other than condemn the bombing of civilians.

The Brussels Conference

Seeking support for its struggle against Japan, China appealed to the signatories of the Nine-Power Pact who agreed to hold a conference in Brussels in October 1937. Britain was especially concerned, as British investment in Shanghai at the time 'exceeded that of any comparable area outside the United Kingdom' (Crozier, *The Causes of the Second World War*, 1997, p. 135). However, it was reluctant to risk conflict with Japan given that tension was already building within Europe. Economic sanctions against Japan were considered, but Britain would not risk those unless the United States also participated. Given that the latter seemed unwilling to depart from its policy of isolationism, no action was taken in the end. Other countries offered little support: the foreign minister of Spain sent a note to China that read 'Spain sends the great Chinese people the warmest expression of their solidarity' (Mitter, *China's War with Japan 1937–1945*, 2014, p. 97).

Activity 14	 **Thinking and research skills**

1. Why did the Spanish foreign minister express 'solidarity'?

The *Panay* Incident

An incident took place in December 1937 that could have sparked a global war: the bombing of the American patrol boat USS *Panay* by Japanese forces. A British gunboat, HMS *Ladybird*, also came under fire while anchored in the Yangtze River. The British government was willing to 'make a display of force' and send up to nine **capital ships** on the condition that the United States would do the same. However, the British Ambassador in Washington was told that the United States would 'only participate in the most modest gestures… [if] Japan did something really outrageous to provoke American opinion' (Crozier, *The Causes of the Second World War*, 1997, p. 136).

By now, the British government was increasingly aware that it could expect little direct assistance from an isolationist United States (for more on American foreign policy, see Chapter 3, page 68). Furthermore, there had been minimal support coming from Britain's dominions, such as South Africa, Canada, Australia, and New Zealand: at the Imperial Conference held in London in May–June 1937, representatives from each of these dominions expressed reservations about entering into another war. Given the apparent lack of support from the dominions, Crozier believes it is unsurprising that Neville Chamberlain, who became prime minister of Britain in 1937, was of the opinion that 'further attempts at conciliation with Germany and Italy were better advised than confrontation' (Crozier, *The Causes of the Second World War*, 1997, p. 137).

One country that did offer more than words of comfort to Jiang Jieshi in 1937 was the Soviet Union. On 1 August, a non-aggression pact was signed between the Nationalist government of China and the Soviet Union; by mid-1938, significant aid was delivered to China in the form of 300 military aircraft, ammunition, and US$250 million.

CHALLENGE YOURSELF

 **Thinking, research, communication, and self-management skills**

For British dominions such as South Africa, whether or not to support British views on matters of war became a political issue during the late 1930s. See what you can find out about the foreign policies of some of the British dominions between 1937 and 1939. Share your research with the class.

Activity 15

This is an extract from *The Origins of the Second World War* by AJP Taylor, a British historian who first published this book in 1960. Taylor was a professor at Oxford University but also wrote on current events for newspapers as well as presenting televised lectures on history. He was well known for having argued, controversially, that Hitler did not plan World War II but that it arose out of the confused polices of the European powers, especially those of Britain.

> *As before [during the Manchurian Crisis] the Americans would do nothing. They wanted the moral satisfaction of non-recognition and also the material satisfaction of their profitable trade with Japan. Non-recognition was an American device, unconscious no doubt, for pushing others, particularly the British, forward against the Japanese. The Americans would express the indignation; the British would provide the opposition. This was not an attractive offer. The Brussels Conference did nothing to help China […]*

AJP Taylor, *The Origins of the Second World War*, Hamish Hamilton, London, 1962, p. 127

1. With reference to its origin, purpose, and content, analyse the value and limitations of the source above for historians researching the international response to the Sino-Japanese War.

2. Compare and contrast the American response as viewed by AJP Taylor in the source above with that of the Stimson Doctrine of 1932.

Activity 16

The photo below shows refugees fleeing across the bridge to the relative security of the International Settlement, Shanghai, in November 1937.

1. What is the message conveyed in this source?

By the end of November, the Nationalist forces retreated from Shanghai and Jiang announced that his capital would be transferred from Nanjing to Chongqing (Mitter, *China's War with Japan 1937–1945*, 2014, p. 100).

Social, thinking, communication, and research skills (ATL)

With a classmate, consider the international context for the Brussels Conference. Carry out research on events taking place in Germany, Italy, and Spain in 1937, as well as on Stalin's purge of the military in 1937. How, and why, do you think, these events would have influenced Jiang's decision-making about going to war with Japan? Bear in mind Japan's relations with Germany and Italy at this time. Outline the case for and against war with Japan.

Amid tensions between Britain, China, and Japan during this period, celebrations were held in London over a new Japanese world record. On 6 April 1937, a Mitsubishi aircraft named Kamikaze (Divine Wind) set off from Tokyo and reached London after a flight of 51 hours, 93 minutes, and 53 seconds. According to *The Times*, the two pilots were greeted by a crowd of 4,000 'shouting *Banzai* (meaning "live forever") and decked with garlands of flowers'.

Refugees try to get into the French concession in Shanghai to escape the bombing.

The fall of Nanjing, December 1937

Nanjing was the capital of Nationalist China and this became Japan's next target. Known also as the Rape of Nanjing, this was probably the most horrendous battle of the Sino-Japanese War. After capturing the city in mid-December 1937, the Japanese forces rounded up and killed males of military age, raped and killed women and girls; the soldiers behaved with extreme brutality towards the Chinese population.

For decades, there has been much speculation as to why Japanese soldiers carried out acts of such appalling cruelty towards a civilian population. Rana Mitter suggests that the length of time it had taken to end Chinese resistance in Shanghai had led to frustration among the Japanese officers and soldiers, which made them 'deeply angry' (*China's War with Japan 1937–1945*, 2014, p. 138). Other historians offer different explanations. Racism was certainly a factor in the brutality demonstrated in Nanjing. Jonathan Fenby notes that one Japanese soldier wrote of the Chinese as being equivalent to 'ants crawling on the ground' (Fenby, *The Penguin History of Modern China: The Fall and Rise of a Great Power*, 2009, p. 282).

Activity 17

Source A

In his book *Inventing Japan 1853–1964*, Ian Buruma argues that prevailing racist views in Japan towards the Chinese caused the victims to be stripped of their humanity.

 For years, the Japanese had been told that the Chinese were inferior and the Japanese a divine race. Contempt for the Chinese goes back to the Meiji prints in which the Japanese are tall, white and vigorous and the Chinese are cowering yellow cretins; Government propaganda, parroted by the jingoistic Japanese press, told soldiers they were fighting a holy war.

Anything they did in the name of the emperor, no matter how savage, was sanctioned by the holiness of their cause. An American chaplain in Tokyo's Sugamo prison, where Japanese prisoners were held after the war, concluded [...] that they 'had the belief that any enemy of the emperor could not be right, so the more brutally they treated their prisoners, the more loyal to the emperor they were being.'

Ian Buruma, *Inventing Japan 1853–1964*, Modern Library, New York, 2004, p. 105

Source B

Mikiso Hane (1922–2003) was renowned scholar of Japanese history. Below is an extract from his book, *Japan, A Short History*, which was published in 2015.

The inculcation [teaching by repeating endlessly] of the samurai spirit in which brutal behaviour was idealised was an integral part of military training. Absolute submission to authority and harsh treatment of those lower in rank governed military life. The tight discipline enforced in the military keeps the soldier in line but what happens when the bonds of discipline are loosened? [...] In society in general respect for the strong and contempt for the weak prevailed. People identified themselves narrowly with members of their own circle and village. Thus concern and compassion towards others were not likely to be fostered. A sense of individuality and individual responsibility were not values stressed. Thus when mob violence breaks out, people may become part of the mob.

Mikiso Hane, *Japan, A Short History*, Oneworld Publications, UK, 2015, p. 156

1. According, to Source A, why did Japanese troops behave with such violence in Nanjing?
2. To what extent does Source B agree with Source A about the behaviour of the soldiers?

Iris Chung recounted a number of survivor tales in her famous book, *The Rape of Nanking*, first published in 1997. According to Chung, the purpose of the book was to bring to light a largely forgotten massacre that was rarely mentioned in school textbooks. In the Introduction, she asserted that, unlike Auschwitz and Hiroshima, in Nanjing 'the victims remained largely silent'. Chung wondered why this was so, suggesting that '[it] soon became clear to me that the custodian of the curtain of silence was politics', and attributing the silence to the Cold War and the shifting alliances that transformed Japan from an enemy into an ally and post-war Communist China from an ally into an enemy. She also quoted George Santayana's warning: 'Those who cannot remember the past are condemned to repeat it.' Perhaps this could also be written as 'those who do not learn about the past are condemned to repeat it'?

How important is it, do you think, that present-day students in Japan are taught about the Rape of Nanjing?

By the time the Japanese soldiers entered Nanjing, Jiang Jieshi had already left and was setting up a new capital in Chongqing, in the interior of China.

Popular response to Nanjing

In February 1938, a conference of the International Peace Campaign was held in London. Protesting against a Japanese invasion of China, the conference called for a boycott of Japanese goods. Although it was accepted that governments were unlikely to support such a boycott, it was argued that 'private boycotts' could be effective. In the British city of Southampton, dock workers refused to unload cotton bales from Japan. In Le Havre, French workers refused to load munitions destined for Japan (*The Adelaide Advertiser*, 14 February, 1938). In the United States, the Washington Commonwealth Federation spearheaded a campaign to boycott Japanese goods coming into Seattle and, in October 1937, women were urged to wear stockings made of cotton rather than imported Japanese silk.

To coincide with the London conference of the International Peace Campaign in February 1938, marchers in London call for a boycott of Japanese goods.

Japanese reaction to the 'China Incident'

Japanese schoolgirls wave flags in front of the Imperial Palace in Tokyo to celebrate the victory in Nanjing, December 1937.

Although celebrations were held across Japan to mark the fall of Nanjing, the Japanese government was still frustrated by the failure to secure the surrender of the Chinese government, despite having taken control of the capital city. The fighting had dragged on; even though Japan had occupied the most densely populated coastal region, it had failed to end what was still referred to as the 'China Incident'.

In the next chapter, you will look at the diplomatic response to the Sino-Japanese War and how the period between 1938 and 1941 forms the backdrop to the outbreak of war between the United States and Japan.

World War II and the Olympic Games

In 1936, Tokyo won the right to host the 1940 Olympic Games. When the Sino-Japanese War broke out in 1937, there were hints of a boycott by countries that were deeply concerned by what was perceived as Japanese aggression. In 1938, however, a demand for resources for arms production meant that the government strictly controlled the use of timber and cement, for example, and Tokyo had to forfeit its offer to host the Games. Although the International Olympic Committee then awarded the Games to Helsinki, the outbreak of World War II meant that in 1940 and 1944 they had to be cancelled. The summer Olympics, held in London, were resumed in 1948.

A review of Chapter 2

Outlining events from 1931 to 1938, this chapter set the scene for the descent into global war. You saw how, prompted in part by the apparent disarray of the Chinese government, Japan extended its control over Manchuria in 1931. You also looked at the repercussions of the invasion both at home and abroad, as the military steadily gained strength in Tokyo, and Japan became increasingly isolated on the international stage. By 1938, Japan had left the League of Nations, joined Italy and Germany in the Anti-Comintern Pact, and abandoned the limitations imposed on it by the Washington and London naval treaties. However, despite extending its control in China along the coastal provinces, Japan had yet to secure a decisive victory. Events in Europe would soon have a dramatic impact upon the Far East and Japan's foreign policy.

Activity 18 ATL Thinking skills

Now that you have read through this chapter, answer the following question.

Using the sources and the text in this chapter, discuss the reasons why Japan decided to expand its control over China between 1931 and 1938.

This question is typical of the fourth question you will get in the Paper 1 exam. It is worth returning to the final hint for success at end of Chapter 1 for tips on how best to approach this type of question. Think of this particular question as a short essay where you need to combine the content of some of the sources (but not all of them – just the ones you decide are relevant) with what you have read here about Japan's motives for increasing its control over Manchuria and then China. Don't forget that events happening both in China and in Japan are significant. Also, you may consider the extent to which the Guandong Army was *a law unto itself*, and whether the government in Tokyo was therefore responding to, rather than controlling, events.

 To access websites relevant to this chapter, go to www.pearsonhotlinks. com, search for the book title or ISBN, and click on 'Chapter 2'.

03

The road to war, 1937–41

The final chapter of this case study focuses on events leading to the outbreak of war between Japan and the United States, with analysis of how and why Tokyo and Washington finally made the decision to go to war.

Topics to be investigated in this chapter include:

- the impact of the China Incident/Sino-Japanese War of 1937–39; the New Order in East Asia
- Japan's relations with Europe between 1938 and 1939, in particular the outbreak of war in Europe and its impact on Japan
- Japan's relations with the United States and Britain
- the signing of the Tripartite Pact
- an overview of US foreign policy after 1936
- the move to global war – the final stages
- a **historiography** focusing on various interpretations of the outbreak of war.

In Chapter 1, we saw the emergence of Japan as a nation ambitious to take its place as a world power, establishing its interests in Manchuria as well as in China by 1929.

In Chapter 2, we learned how Japan extended its control over Manchuria and northern China and, by 1937, over much of coastal China. By 1938, where Chapter 2 ended, we saw the ways in which Japanese foreign policy was being influenced by the following factors:

- The Sino-Japanese War was continuing with no decisive victory in sight.
- The Soviet Union was ready to confront Japanese expansion along the Manchurian border.
- Both Britain and the United States were wary of Japanese aggression because, at this stage, neither wanted to end up at war with Japan (although Japan could not be sure of this).
- Nazi Germany officially recognized Manchukuo in 1938, heralding a weakening of support for China and closer relations with Japan.
- Fascist Italy had joined Japan and Germany in the Anti-Comintern Pact and was also looking for better relations with Japan.

Japan was being courted by Germany and Italy, while becoming increasingly isolated from Britain and the United States. Meanwhile, inside Japan itself there were many different factions at work within the government, the court, and the military: one wanted to wage war against the Soviet Union, another wanted to wage war against the United States, and then there were those who wanted peace.

3.1 The impact of the Sino-Japanese War

That the events of 1937 and the invasion of China did not end in a quick, decisive victory for Japan caused some consternation in Tokyo; there was also concern as to how far Japan could go in extending its occupation of China before provoking a response from Britain and the United States.

As was so often the case during the 1930s, the Japanese government was not making policy so much as responding to events. The military continued to grow in power and influence, while Prime Minister Konoe Fumimaro made every effort to build up public support for the war in China. It could be said that, with the passing of the National Mobilization Act of 1938, Japan now entered a period of total war: labour unions were dissolved and the government was given total control over the economy and the distribution of resources; workers were urged to work hard for the war effort; school children were given textbooks that instilled nationalism; and censorship of the media was enforced to ensure that news from the war front was always positive.

Prime Minister Konoe announced Japan's war aims, stating its intention to struggle against what he called 'the old order of Western imperialism and its principle Chinese agent, Chiang Kai-shek (Jiang Jieshi)' and to establish a 'New Order in East Asia led by Japan' (Duus (ed), *The Cambridge History of Japan, Volume 6: The Twentieth Century*, 1995, p. 134).

Activity 1	Thinking and communication skills

Source A

This photo, taken in January 1939, shows a group of schoolchildren who had been mobilized to work in the factories.

Source B

This photo shows a Japanese soldier looking at a wall of anti-Japanese cartoons in the captured city of Wuhan, 1938.

Source C

This photo, published in a German newspaper in July 1939, shows young Chinese peasants bringing a gift of a young pig to Japanese soldiers as a gesture of peace.

1. What is the message conveyed in Source A?
2. What is the message conveyed in Source B?
3. What is the message conveyed in Source C?

A New Order in East Asia

This new stage in Japanese policy was decided at a meeting of the Imperial Conference. A number of moderates, even within the Japanese army, had hoped for a negotiated end to the China Incident, but they were unable to influence events, and the establishment of the New Order demonstrated a significant shift of power towards the Imperial Way faction that wanted a 'subjugation of China' (Crozier, *The Causes of the Second World War*, 1997, p 211). In essence, the New Order envisaged that Japan would cease to recognize Jiang Jieshi's Chinese government unless the latter accepted an ultimatum that demanded:

- the formal recognition of Manchukuo
- the establishment of neutral zones in northern China and Inner Mongolia
- the payment of reparations to Japan
- Sino-Japanese cooperation in the areas of central China occupied by Japan at the time.

Rapidly, Japan was being drawn into a war that was to drain its resources and its economy.

The New Order for East Asia was announced officially in November 1938. Jiang Jieshi had refused the ultimatum and continued to resist, so a substitute government for the GMD was set up – a puppet regime (officially recognized by Japan in 1940) based in Nanjing and led by Wang Jingwei, one-time rival of Jiang Jieshi. The New Order also stated that Japan would become China's main trading partner (although Britain, France, and the United States could continue to trade with it); this was a departure from the Washington System of 1922 that had guaranteed the sovereignty of China and the open-door trading policy. Prime Minister Konoe had hoped that 'China and

The Imperial Conference

This term was used to describe official meetings with the emperor. Policies would be discussed and, according to Eri Hotta, 'the imperial approval was a mere formality with no constitutionally binding power. Yet it bore the stamp of uncontested authority, and there was no historical precedence of it having been overturned. By acquiring imperial sanction, policy decisions would become divine, suddenly apolitical, and political leaders would be collectively relieved of any personal responsibility for the newly approved policy' (Hotta, *Japan 1941*, 2014, p. 131).

Manchukuo would cooperate, politically, economically and culturally' to defeat communism and to establish a new economic union in the region (Crozier, *The Causes of the Second World War*, 1997, p. 213). In reality, in spite of the establishment of the New Order, Sino-Japanese relations remained intractable; Konoe, unable to bring the China Incident (Sino-Japanese War) to a satisfactory conclusion, resigned in 1939.

Activity 2

(ATL) Thinking and communication skills

The following is an extract from a statement about the New Order by General Tojo Hideki, made after the war was over when he was in prison for war crimes. Tojo had been vice-army minister in 1938 and prime minister from 1941 onwards.

> *The basic intention was that the raw materials which China possessed in abundance would be contributed by China and the technique, capital and skilled personnel [would be] contributed by Japan for the mutual benefit of both countries. Manchuria would come into the picture similarly [...] The idea of profit or loss did not enter in. The idea of mutual benefit was the main one. It had a moral basis.*

From Andrew Crozier, *The Causes of the Second World War*, Blackwell, 1997, p. 213

1. According to the source, what were the reasons for the application of a New Order in China?

Student answer – Jenny

The source states that China had 'raw materials' and that there was 'mutual benefit'.

Student answer – Kyla

The source mentions that whereas China could contribute a lot of resources such as raw materials, Japan would provide the skills and the expertise that would then allow both countries to benefit. The source also emphasizes that this would not be carried out in order to make a 'profit' but that it was based on a moral purpose such as helping each other.

Examiner's comments

As you can see, Jenny's response is a little too brief and it also quotes rather than paraphrases the source. The points she makes are quite accurate, but she doesn't really show that she understands the source. Kyla, however, tries to put the main points into her own words and so an examiner would see that she has not only understood the question, but that she also understands the source. She states two points very clearly.

Activity 3

(ATL) Thinking skills

This is a Japanese propaganda poster meant to show how life would improve under the Japanese. It was published in January 1939. You can just about read the comments where the Chinese script has been translated. These include:

- 'This is what China will be like if you let us take over.'
- 'If you keep on fighting, all the Chinese will die.'
- 'It's all colony (sic) propaganda.'

1. What is the message conveyed by this source?

An arch is being built to commemorate the first anniversary of the Japanese-supported collaborationist government in Nanjing, 29 March 1941; a banner containing the portrait of Wang Jingwei is being hung.

3.2 Japan's relations with Europe, 1938–39

Hitler's annexation of Austria and Czechoslovakia between 1938 and 1939 violated the sovereignty of both countries, but the League of Nations failed to respond. The British and French policy of appeasement had now taken over from collective security. (In Case Study 2 you will analyse the European context of these events.) All these changes are very important for your understanding of Japan's decision-making in matters of foreign policy during this period. One reason that European affairs affected Japan so much was because of their impact on Britain (which had been Japan's greatest rival for influence in China) and on the Soviet Union (a neighbouring country which Japan had feared would expand into Manchukuo).

Japan and the Axis powers

In 1936, Mussolini and Hitler met and agreed to a pact of mutual understanding known as the Rome–Berlin Axis, from which the term **Axis powers** was derived. In 1938, Hitler issued instructions for all German advisors in China to return home and Germany formally recognized the state of Manchukuo. In 1939, the Pact of Steel was signed between Germany and Italy, making them military allies; Japan joined this alliance in September 1940. The growing ties between Germany and Japan greatly disappointed Jiang Jieshi. According to Rana Mitter, although 'there was no affinity' between China and Nazi Germany, Jiang had nonetheless hoped to 'persuade Germany to choose China and not Japan as its principal East Asian, anti-Communist partner' (Mitter, *China's War with Japan 1937–1945*, 2014, p. 163).

Hitler, however, had noticed how rapidly the Chinese army had retreated in 1937 and in turn noted Japan's greater potential as a powerful ally. It is also likely that, for

Hitler Youth members meeting Prime Minister Konoe Fumimaro on 27 August 1938.

61

An Italian delegation visits Japan in March 1938.

Hitler, an expansionist Japan would be a useful thorn in the side of both the Soviet Union and Britain, thus leaving Germany free to pursue its own expansionist policies in Europe (Crozier, *The Causes of the Second World War*, 1997, p. 208). In 1938, a group of Hitler Youth members visited Japan; they were photographed with Prime Minister Konoe. Representatives of Italy's Fascist government also made a visit, even visiting a Japanese temple. These were important indicators of Japan's growing affiliation for its co-signatories of the Anti-Comintern Pact.

The Nazi-Soviet Pact

Signed on 23 August 1939, the Nazi-Soviet Pact was confusing to most politicians and strategists outside of the chancellery in Berlin and the Kremlin in Moscow. Having spent most of the decade fulminating against each other, it was not expected that Stalin and Hitler should now sign a treaty that pledged ten years of non-aggression, secretly divided Poland, and later gave Stalin a free hand in the Baltic States and Bessarabia.

Later, in Chapter 6 of this book, you will assess the European response to the pact and the impact it had on the move to global war in the region. Historian AJP Taylor suggests that this was an 'epoch-making event', signifying Russia's 'return to Europe'. The Tianjin (Tientsin) Incident (for more, see page 64) had convinced Stalin that Britain would not stand up to Japan, so he felt he had better throw in his lot with Hitler. According to Taylor, 'the Soviet Union sought security in Europe, not conquests; and it is surprising that she did not seek it earlier by a deal with Germany' (Taylor, *The Origins of the Second World War*, 1962, p. 241).

Having signed the Anti-Comintern Pact, Japan had hoped for German support against the Soviet Union; the Nazi-Soviet Pact therefore came as a bitter disappointment, isolating Japan and further strengthening the supporters of a 'strike south'. Overall, the Nazi-Soviet Pact 'shook the basic foundation of Japan's earlier anti-Soviet, anti-Communist agreement with Germany'. According to Eri Hotta, Prime Minister Hiranuma Kiichirō (who had succeeded Konoe) was flabbergasted, saying, 'The European state of affairs is too complicated and bizarre' (Hotta, *Japan 1941*, 2014, p. 25).

Within Japan, opinions remained divided regarding the direction Japan's foreign policy should take. In the army, there was support for a military alliance with Germany. In the navy, there were concerns that such a step would further alienate Britain and the United States, causing them to draw closer and direct their enmity against Japan. Having said that, there were also groups within the navy that saw the benefits of calling for war against the United States, as this would justify increases in the budget for naval expenditure (Crozier, *The Causes of the Second World War*, 1997, p. 170). Despite the lack of a clear direction for Japanese foreign policy, events in Europe were heading towards war and so Japan had to prepare for the impact this would have on the Far East.

The outbreak of war in Europe and its impact on Japan

The invasion of Poland in September 1939 led to a six-month hiatus known as the **Phoney War**. Despite a declaration of war by Britain and France against Germany, Poland was quickly defeated. In the Far East, Japan was buoyed by the fall of France in June 1940 and the apparent isolation of Britain. This offered opportunities for Japan to expand in the Far East and it was able to apply pressure on Britain to close its supply route through Burma to China. Vichy France (the collaborationist regime established under the leadership of Marshal Pétain) would also be pressured into accepting Japanese control over Indochina. Japan set its sights on the Dutch East Indies with its valuable resources of oil, rubber, and tin. In this way, the German conquest of much of Western Europe opened up opportunities for Japan and – as mentioned earlier – despite the Nazi-Soviet Pact, brought Japan closer to a formal military alliance with the Axis powers.

In Japan, Konoe returned as prime minister in 1940; he brought into his cabinet Matsuoka Yōsuke as foreign minister, Tojo Hideki as war minister, and Yoshida Zengo as navy minister. With Germany winning the war in Europe, Matsuoka called for a military alliance that would, he was convinced, make the United States more 'respectful' of Japan. By mid-1940, several important decisions had been made to shape Japan's foreign policy with the following aims:

- to strengthen ties with Germany and Italy
- to create the New Order in Asia (to be known as the Greater Asian Co-Prosperity Sphere)
- to sign a non-aggression pact with the Soviet Union
- to bring the British, French, and Dutch colonies in East Asia under Japanese influence
- to reach an agreement with Jiang Jieshi and bring China into the New Order.

CHALLENGE YOURSELF

Thinking, research communication, and self-management skills ATL

Go back through this case study and, by making a note of each event that involved Japan and Russia/the Soviet Union, write an account of how and why their relationship changed up to 1941.

3.3 Japan's relations with the United States and Britain

Although Japan was very much affected by the turn of events in Europe, it was also preoccupied by its failure to bring the China Incident to a close, a situation which continued to seriously affect relations with Britain and the United States.

The Tianjin (Tientsin) Incident

One of the most significant events to impact Anglo-Japanese relations in 1939 was the Tianjin (Tientsin) Incident, an event that also fuelled Britain's fears that it would have to wage war against Japan in the Far East as well as against Germany in Europe.

An important Chinese centre for trade, Tianjin was home to around 3,000 British citizens, who lived in the British Concession. In April 1939, a Chinese national working as a Japanese bank manager was murdered; in June, demands were made by the Japanese authorities for the handover of four Chinese suspects residing in the British Concession. While the British ambassador to Japan advised that Britain comply with Japanese demands, the British ambassador to China argued that any British show of weakness should be avoided. The Japanese responded to this British non-compliance by imposing a blockade and humiliating British residents by strip-searching them as they travelled in and out of the concession. War could easily have broken out if Britain had retaliated, especially as Japan was applying pressure in Rome and Berlin for an outward show of support. After some careful diplomacy, Britain agreed not to undermine Japanese authority in occupied China, although it refused to relinquish its control of the British Concession to the Japanese police. Even so, they did eventually hand over the four suspects who were then executed.

The Tianjin Incident made it clear to Britain that it needed US support if it was to maintain its presence in China. While President Roosevelt of the United States did not send military aid, he did show support by announcing that he would abrogate the 1911 American–Japanese trade agreement within six months. According to Robert Dallek (Dallek, *Franklin Roosevelt and American Foreign Policy 1932–45*, 1981, p. 195), this had a triple effect:

- it encouraged Britain to respond more firmly to Japanese aggression
- it bolstered Chinese morale
- it met with widespread approval in the United States, affirming the popularity of a strong stand against Japan.

As we shall see, Japan's decision to sign the Tripartite Pact in 1940 and, the year after, to occupy all of Indochina prompted the United States to take the following actions:

- move its fleet to Pearl Harbor
- sign a lend-lease deal with Britain
- end the sale of aviation fuel and certain types of scrap metal to Japan, which was later extended to prohibit the sale of all scrap metal to Japan.

Meanwhile, for Japan, the New Order remained elusive, as did its conquest of China.

Scrap metal

Scrap metal is basically iron and any other metal that can be melted down and recycled. Towards the end of the 1930s, Japan needed sources of iron for shipbuilding, armaments, and so on. One major source was the United States, which sold 2 million tons of scrap metal to Japan in 1939. In March 1939, Chinese workers in Astoria, Oregon, picketed the sale of scrap iron to Japan. Their action was supported by the longshoremen (dock workers) and the protest then spread to Portland. By July 1940, the export of certain kinds of scrap metal was stopped; by September 1940 this extended to all types of scrap metal.

Source A

A photo taken on 8 December 1941, when the owner of this grocery store in Oakland California put up this notice. The newspaper that published the photo stated that he was a 'University of California graduate of Japanese descent'.

Source B

This captured image from April 1941 shows a Japanese man sitting on top of a heap of scrap metal to be recycled.

1. What are the messages conveyed by Sources A and B?

Student answer - Katherine

Source A is a photograph of a grocery store in California that was taken the day after Pearl Harbor. The big sign across the front of the shop is meant to tell customers that the owner is an American citizen, even though the store is called 'Wanto Co.', which they would probably have assumed was a Japanese (or Asian) name. It looks like the store has been sold so maybe the owner has to leave. The photo shows us that it didn't matter if you were an American citizen, you were still considered to be Japanese. It is interesting that the newspaper also mentioned that the store owner was a graduate of the University of California, probably so that readers could sympathise with him.

Source B is a 'captured picture' so it was probably not published in Japan. It shows how desperate the people were to collect all kind of metal things, some of them look like railings. The man is sitting on top, maybe he is guarding it, as it was of value.

Examiner's comments

In the Paper 1 exam, you will not be asked to comment on two photographs for part B of the first question, but it is quite useful here to see how Katherine has explained the message of the two sources.

For Source A she has picked up on signs in the store front and explained that they show how it didn't matter if you were an American citizen if you were also ethnically Japanese. She goes a bit further by referring to the way that the newspaper described the owner. You will not always be provided with this kind of detail but do remember to read all the information you are given about the source as it may help you to determine the message. Katherine also mentions the SOLD sign and suggests this may be connected to the theme of the picture. Overall, she has been quite thorough and certainly earned the full marks that would be awarded for this kind of question.

For Source B, Katherine describes the heap of scrap metal and suggests that all kinds of objects were being collected. She could have developed this by saying that it shows there was probably a desperate need for metal to make arms. Katherine does comment on the man and comments on why he may be sitting there. Again, she makes two points but could have developed them a little more.

The shortage of metal in Japan was acute and, by 1941, its use by civilians was greatly limited, with substitutes being used. Most notably, according to Eri Hotta, 'all metal buttons on school uniforms were confiscated and replaced by ones made of glass' (Hotta, *Japan 1941*, 2014, p. 109).

3.4 The signing of the Tripartite Pact

Although some degree of factionalism continued over foreign policy decisions, on 27 September 1940, Japan signed the Tripartite Pact with Germany and Italy. According to the pact:

• Germany and Italy recognized the leadership of Japan in Asia.
• Japan recognized the leadership of Germany and Italy in Europe.
• All agreed to support each other by all means (militarily, economically, and politically) if attacked by a power not 'involved in the European war or in the Sino-Japanese conflict'.

The unnamed power mentioned above was, of course, the United States. For Japan, the agreement would have alleviated its concern that Britain would move towards an accommodation with the United States (which would disadvantage Japan) in the event of defeat by Germany. For Germany, however, the pact was meant to dissuade the United States from aiding a 'soon-to-be-defeated' Britain (Crozier, *The Causes of the Second World War*, Blackwell, 1997, p. 170).

Map of Khalkhin-Gol.

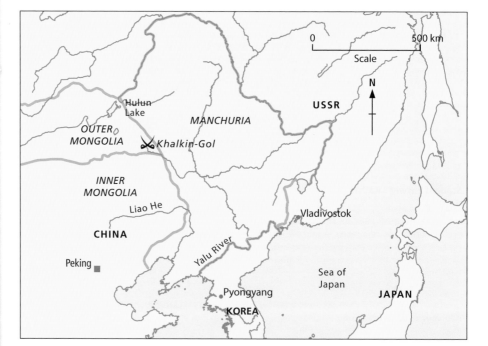

The border conflict between Japan and the Soviet Union

The establishment of the Second United Front led to a flow of aid from the Soviet Union to China, but relations between the two powers worsened in December 1939, when the Council for the League of Nations condemned the Soviet invasion of Finland. Known as the Winter War of 1939–40, this act of aggression led to the expulsion of the Soviet Union from the League. As a member of the Council of the League, China could have prevented this by meeting Stalin's request to use its veto to prevent the resolution from passing. Jiang, however, instructed the Chinese representative to abstain. Aware that this would damage relations with the Soviet Union and endanger the flow of further aid, Jiang was prepared to risk this rather than alienate the other members of the Council.

Besides, Jiang suspected that Stalin was less committed to helping China defeat the Japanese than to prolonging a war of attrition that reduced the risk of Japan launching a full-scale attack on the Soviet Union (Mitter, *China's War with Japan 1937–1945*, 2014, p. 214; Yu, *The Dragon's War: Allied Operations and the Fate of China, 1937–1947*, 2013, p. 30). For some time, there had been border skirmishes between Japan and the Soviet Union, and, in 1939, these became more serious, culminating in the Battle of Khalkhin-Gol (*Nomonhan* in Japanese) when over 20,000 Japanese troops died, not only on the battlefield but also from hunger, thirst, and disease. Along with the disappointment over the Nazi-Soviet Pact, the cost of this campaign in resources and lives convinced the Imperial Japanese Army to abandon the '**strike north**' strategy and to support the '**strike south**' strategy favoured by the Japanese navy (Buruma, *Inventing Japan 1853–1964*, 2004, p. 108).

The conflict with the Soviet Union rumbled on for the next two years. By April 1941, however, both the Soviet Union and Japan had more urgent threats to their own security. For the Soviet Union, relations with Germany were no longer as cordial as they had been; for Japan, the risk of war against Britain and the United States was increasing. With these factors in mind, the Soviet Union and Japan signed a neutrality pact that would last until August 1945. Soviet aid to China thus came to an end.

In a show of confidence, now that its northern border with the Soviet Union was secure, Japan moved to take over French Indochina. The closer Japan became to realizing its foreign policy aims, however, the further it moved away from any hope of improving relations with the United States.

> **'Strike north' and 'strike south'**
>
> 'Strike north' refers to a strategy popular with the Japanese army that favoured preparing for war against the Soviet Union. 'Strike south' was a strategy adopted in 1941, when the Imperial Japanese Army headed south into Indochina, Malaya, and the Dutch East Indies while the Imperial Japanese Navy headed into the Pacific.

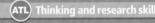

Activity 5   **ATL** Thinking and research skills

Below are the terms of the Soviet–Japanese neutrality pact signed in April 1941. (http://avalon.law.yale.edu/wwii/s1.asp)

ARTICLE ONE

Both Contracting Parties undertake to maintain peaceful and friendly relations between them and mutually respect the territorial integrity and inviolability of the other Contracting Party.

ARTICLE TWO

Should one of the Contracting Parties become the object of hostilities on the part of one or several third powers, the other Contracting Party will observe neutrality throughout the duration of the conflict.

ARTICLE THREE

The present Pact comes into force from the day of its ratification by both Contracting Parties and remains valid for five years. In case neither of the Contracting Parties denounces the Pact one year before the expiration of the term, it will be considered automatically prolonged for the next five years.

ARTICLE FOUR

The present Pact is subject to ratification as soon as possible. The instruments of ratification shall be exchanged in Tokyo, also as soon as possible.

In confirmation whereof the above-named Representatives have signed the present Pact in two copies, drawn up in the Russian and Japanese languages, and affixed thereto their seals.

Done in Moscow on April 13, 1941, which corresponds to the 13th day of the fourth month of the 16th year of Showa.

1. According to its origin, purpose, and content, what are the value and limitations of this source for historians studying Soviet-Japanese relations before and during World War II?

3.5 An overview of US foreign policy after 1936

During President Franklin D Roosevelt's first term in office (1933–37), US foreign policy was guided by isolationism. In part, this was a response to public opinion that was vehemently opposed to any further US involvement in European conflicts, fuelled by the work of revisionist historians such as Sidney B Fay, who argued that World War I was not solely Germany's fault. Furthermore, the Nye Committee hearings of 1934, led by Senator Gerald Nye, revealed huge profits made by US munitions manufacturers and financiers during World War I. The United States had already rejected membership of the League of Nations, but it also rejected membership of the International Court of Justice in 1926 (which isolationists feared would lead inexorably to membership of the League).

The Neutrality Acts of 1935–37 reflected US policy at the time by stipulating the following:

- The First Neutrality Act 1935: When a state of war existed, the president was required to declare an arms **embargo** against all belligerents and to warn American citizens not to travel on belligerent ships. (When the League imposed sanctions on Italy after its invasion of Abyssinia in 1935, the United States did not join in the sanctions, though Roosevelt did call for a 'moral embargo' – in other words, for American businesses to voluntarily refuse to trade with Italy.)
- The Second Neutrality Act 1936: The United States would refuse war loans and credits to belligerent nations.
- The Third Neutrality Act 1937: Travel on belligerent ships was now made unlawful. This act also brought in the 'cash-and-carry' rule, whereby the president could require belligerent nations to pay in cash for all purchases and to transport them on their own ships (Jones, *The Limits of Liberty, American History 1607–1992*, 1995, p. 488).

Although Roosevelt was not keen on the fact these acts didn't differentiate between belligerent countries, popular opinion made it impossible for him to oppose them. According to Maldwyn Jones, Roosevelt 'for the first time gave his undivided attention to foreign affairs' when Japan invaded China in 1937, though even then he did not apply the embargo on arms sales to China because there was no official declaration of war (Jones, *The Limits of Liberty, American History 1607–1992*, 1995, p. 489).

The Quarantine Speech

On 5 October 1937, in Chicago (a city considered to be at the heart of isolationism), Roosevelt gave a speech that indicated a shift in American policy. In what became known as the Quarantine Speech, Roosevelt spoke of a growing 'international anarchy and instability', suggesting that there was a need to quarantine aggressor nations. When asked whether or not this meant an imposition of sanctions, Roosevelt responded by telling the world that America was looking for a way to preserve peace. Even so, soon after the speech was made, the United States participated in the Brussels Conference of 1937 (see chapter 2, page 50).

Activity 6
 ATL **Thinking and communication skills**

Below is an extract from the Quarantine Speech given by President Roosevelt in Chicago on 5 October 1937. (http://millercenter.org/president/speeches/speech-3310)

> *War is a contagion, whether it be declared or undeclared. It can engulf states and peoples remote from the original scene of hostilities. We are determined to keep out of war, yet we cannot insure ourselves against the disastrous effects of war and the dangers of involvement. We are adopting such measures as will minimize our risk of involvement, but we cannot have complete protection in a world of disorder in which confidence and security have broken down. If civilization is to survive, the principles of the Prince of Peace [Roosevelt was referring to Jesus Christ] must be restored. Trust between nations must be revived. Most important of all, the will for peace on the part of peace-loving nations must express itself to the end that nations that may be tempted to violate their agreements and the rights of others will desist from such a course. There must be positive endeavours to preserve peace. America hates war. America hopes for peace. Therefore, America actively engages in the search for peace.*

1. According to its origin, purpose, and content, analyse the value and limitations of the source for historians studying Roosevelt's foreign policy.

Student answer – Jacob

The origin of this source is the Quarantine Speech given by President Roosevelt in October 1937, when the Spanish Civil War was taking place in Europe and the Sino-Japanese War was about to break out in China. Roosevelt gave this speech in Chicago. The purpose of the speech was to convey some idea of American foreign policy at this time. The value of the speech is that it is given by the president and so it tells us about US policy. Also, it says that America wants peace and that it hates war. There are limitations to the source because Roosevelt was giving a public speech and so may not have been expressing his real thoughts about this.

Student answer – Frederick

The origin of the source is the Quarantine Speech that Roosevelt gave in Chicago in October, 1937, when there was growing tension in Europe and in the Far East. The purpose of the speech was to reassure Americans that he was not intending to go to war. He says, 'America hates war', 'America hopes for peace', but he also says that 'peace-loving nations' have to be ready to say that they oppose war. So, one value of this speech is that it shows us how Roosevelt tried to reassure Americans that he would not take them into war, but, at the same time, that America must be aware of the dangers of war because 'war is a contagion' and so it can spread. Another value is that this is the president of the United States speaking and so this would be the policy of his administration. The limitations are that we do not know how people responded to this speech and whether they supported him. Also, Roosevelt had to try and persuade people to support him and so he cannot say just what he thinks. We can see this in how he doesn't come right out and say that America may have to go to war, he only very vaguely suggests this.

Examiner's comments

Both Frederick and Jacob refer to the origin, purpose, value, and limitations of the source and this is a good way to approach the question. They make it very clear that they have considered each part of the question, although Frederick is also very explicit about using the content and he uses it very effectively to support both a value and a limitation of the source. Jacob is a little more superficial in his answer, as he doesn't really develop the points that he makes. Jacob does give quite a lot of background to the origin of the speech by setting it in context, but you would not be expected to give this amount of detail and Frederick's comment that the speech was made when there was rising tension is quite sufficient to set the scene. Do make sure that you link the origin, purpose, and content to the value and limitations rather than just listing them separately.

Britain is often mentioned as the only country in Europe that was fighting the Axis powers by the summer of 1940; in fact, until its defeat in May 1941, Greece was still fighting Italy and then Germany.

Franklin D Roosevelt stood for a third term as president in 1940. Traditionally, it was possible, within the American constitution, for a president to stand for third or a fourth term. This finally changed in 1947, when the 22nd Amendment stated that a president could run for only two terms.

After the sinking of the USS *Panay* in 1937 (see Chapter 2, page 50), further pressure was applied to Roosevelt. Public reaction was muted, but isolationists seized the opportunity to put forward a constitutional amendment stating that the US Congress could declare war only after a national referendum had given approval. Roosevelt vehemently objected to this amendment, arguing that it would 'cripple any president in his conduct of our foreign relations' (Quoted in Jones, *The Limits of Liberty, American History 1607–1992*, 1995, p. 490). The amendment failed to pass through Congress by a very narrow margin of 188 in favour and 209 against.

Despite the worsening situation in Europe in 1938 and 1939, the United States remained tied to a policy of isolationism, although the Naval Expansion Act of May 1938 provided $1 billion for naval rearmament over the next decade. It was planned to build a navy equivalent in size to that of Germany, Italy, and Japan combined, a clear intent to match the capability of the Axis powers.

The end of American isolationism

In 1939, on the outbreak of war in Europe, the United States issued a Declaration of Neutrality, but it also passed another Neutrality Act in November that repealed the arms embargo and allowed belligerents to buy arms on the basis of paying in cash and carrying the arms in their own ships. It was understood that the customers for American arms would be Britain and France. For the majority of Americans, supplying arms to Britain and France (so they could do the fighting) would make it unnecessary for the United States to go to war. The events of 1940 proved this assumption to be erroneous as France surrendered in June. Even so, Britain had not yet fallen to the Axis, and Roosevelt was able to get approval from the Congress in 1941 for the transfer of 'surplus' planes, guns, and ammunition to Britain and to begin the Lend-Lease programme.

3.6 Final stages of the move to global war

According to Niall Ferguson, 'The sole obstacle to Japanese hegemony in South-East Asia was America' (Ferguson, *The War of the World*, 2006, p. 487). Indeed, by 1941, Japan's continued occupation of China, as well as its occupation of French Indochina, led to a worsening of relations with the United States. This was significant because Japan was short of resources with which to produce arms: around a third of its imports, including cotton, scrap iron, and oil, came from the United States. The Japanese army had supported a strategy of striking north against the Soviet Union but had been unable to secure a definite victory in the land war in China, so it depended on the Imperial Japanese Navy to secure control of the coastal cities. This had strengthened the influence of the navy over decision-making in Tokyo, while the Nazi-Soviet Pact made war against the Soviet Union unlikely. However, Japan still needed resources, and if these could not be secured through trade with the United States, then other sources had to be found in Asia, which would mean an extension of hostilities against the oil-rich Dutch East Indies.

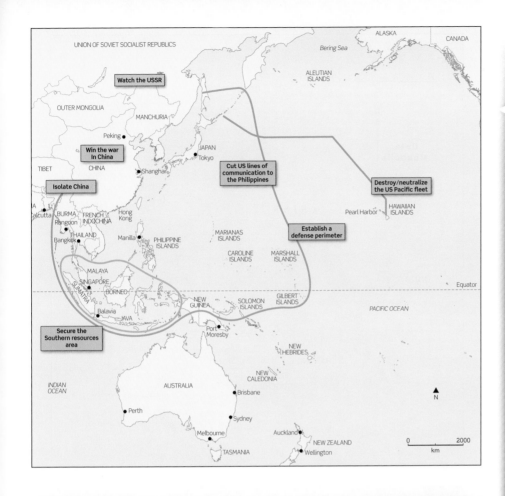

Map showing Japanese war objectives and planned opening attacks.

Operation Barbarossa, June 1941

The German invasion of the Soviet Union (codenamed Operation Barbarossa) changed everything, as it brought the Soviet Union towards an alliance with Britain and the United States. For Japan, this opened up the possibility of reviving the 'strike north' strategy. Prime Minister Konoe, however, was cautious and thought it wiser to look for improved relations with the United States, although he understood that to do so would require the abandonment of the New Order (or Greater Asian Co-Prosperity Sphere, as the New Order was now called), a policy that would be totally unacceptable to the army as it would entail retreating from China.

Meanwhile, the United States warned Japan not to invade the Soviet Union, as this would 'endanger peace in the Pacific'. Furthermore, by July, the United States was keeping itself well-informed about Japan's policies through *Magic*, the name given to its code-breaking device, which provided access to all encrypted Japanese diplomatic correspondence.

Richard Sorge, a German journalist working in Tokyo, was a spy for the Soviet Union and he sent many warnings to Moscow about the impending German attack on the Soviet Union. These, however, were dismissed by Stalin as 'untrustworthy'. Even so, once the invasion had begun, Stalin instructed Sorge to look for any information regarding Japanese troop movements on its border with the Soviet Union. He was arrested soon after giving Stalin assurances in September 1941 that Japan was not planning an invasion. He was executed in 1944 (Hotta, *Japan 1941*, 2014, p. 119).

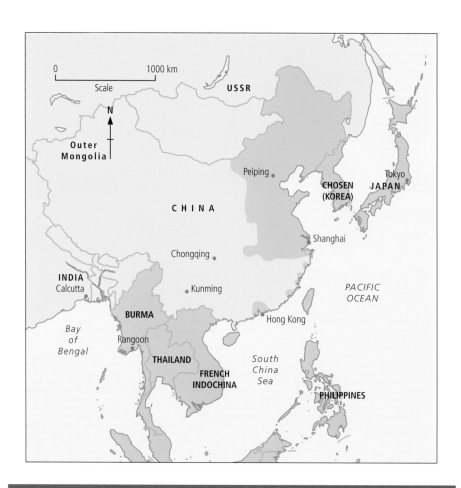

Map of Southeast Asia showing the extent of Japanese occupied territory (in orange) by 1942.

The emergence of the ABCD Bloc

Matsuoka Yōsuke, the Japanese foreign minister, spent much of the early part of 1941 coming to an agreement to end the long-running dispute over the border between Thailand and French Indochina. Japan offered itself as a mediator and a treaty was signed accepting a new border in May 1941. Akire Iriye suggests this event was an important one, because Japan was establishing itself as the dominant power in Southeast Asia in accordance with its aim of creating the Greater East Asian Co-Prosperity Sphere (Iriye, *The Origins of the Second World War in Asia and the Pacific*, 1995, p. 131).

The response to this agreement, however, came in the form of the ABCD Bloc, an alliance between the United States (A), Britain (B), China (C), and the Dutch government-in-exile (D). The idea was to apply economic pressure on Japan, supplementing it with the presence of the US fleet in the Pacific. Although this was only forward planning among military officers rather than a formal alliance, it established the basis for future cooperation. Throughout 1941, this alliance (especially between Britain and the United States) was further strengthened by the meeting between Churchill and Roosevelt off the coast of Newfoundland in August 1941 and the writing of the Atlantic Charter, which affirmed the common interests of the two nations. Akire Iriye notes that, inside Japan, this was seen as an ultimatum (it would be one of many) to either accept the status quo of the 'Anglo-American world view' or to oppose it (Iriye, *The Origins of the Second World War in Asia and the Pacific*, 1995, p. 156).

Niall Ferguson argues that Japan did not think it possible that the United States would be rash enough to declare war when Japan was allied to the seemingly victorious Italy and Germany, and when the Soviet Union had also stood alongside the Axis powers (Ferguson, *The War of the World*, 2006, p. 310). Furthermore, the American public seemed resolutely isolationist.

The strategists in the Japanese navy, nonetheless, planned for war: they believed that victory was possible, but only if a surprise attack on the US navy was carried out successfully – thus began Admiral Yamamoto's initiation of the plan to strike Pearl Harbor in April 1941.

Meanwhile, the Roosevelt administration was committed to peace and this had been the basis of the president's campaign for re-election in 1940 – and, indeed, plans were being made to delay, or even prevent, war in the Pacific by using economic sanctions and the build-up of the Pacific fleet to deter Japan from further aggression.

Indochina and the US embargo on oil, 1941

Indochina, made up of Laos, Cambodia, and Vietnam, had been a French colony since 1887. The Japanese occupation of this territory had been prompted in part by Operation Barbarossa, which made it less likely that a Japanese 'strike south' might result in a Soviet incursion into Manchuria. At first, Vichy France resisted Japanese demands to take over Indochina but it acceded to these on 22 July 1941. Eri Hotta notes that control over Indochina gave Japan access to tin, rubber, and other raw materials, as well as eight air bases and two ports (Hotta, *Japan 1941*, 2014, p. 143).

The United States responded to this further expansion of Japanese occupied territory by freezing all Japanese assets held in the United States. On 1 August, it applied an embargo on the sale of oil. For the Japanese army and navy this was 'tantamount to an act of war', making the 'strike south' seem a matter of survival, as it was feared that unless the embargo was lifted, oil supplies would begin to run out by December that year (Crozier, *The Causes of the Second World War*, 1997, p. 221). Admiral Yamamoto, the Japanese naval chief of staff, still hoped that war would not be necessary if oil supplies were resumed. For the army, however, war was seen as inevitable as the United States would surely demand the withdrawal of Japan from China and Southeast Asia, something Japan would consider non-negotiable.

According to Eri Hotta, some compromise was reached between the war and peace factions by September 1941, as outlined in the Guidelines for the Implementing National Policies that stated:

- Japan should be ready for war by the end of October
- negotiations with the United States would proceed, but if these were unsuccessful by mid-October, war would follow (Hotta, *Japan 1941*, 2014, p. 171).

For Japan, 'successful' negotiations would include the end of all Anglo-American aid to China, no further increase in Anglo-American military strength in Southeast Asia, and the end of economic sanctions against Japan.

Activity 7

This American cartoon, published in 1941, illustrates Japanese expansion into Indochina.

Source: Special Collections Research Center, The George Washington University

1.   What is the message conveyed in this source?

CHALLENGE YOURSELF

ATL Thinking and research skills

Based on what you have read so far, how likely was it that Japan's negotiations with the United States, as outlined in the guidelines, would be successful? Give reasons for your answer.

The failure of diplomacy

Negotiations between Japan and the United States took place all through the autumn of 1941; however, Cordell Hull, the US secretary of state, made it clear to Nomura Kichisaburō, the Japanese ambassador, that any agreement would have to be supported by Britain and China – something Japan knew was going to be unlikely. Japan's naval minister Oikawa Koshirō remained opposed to war as he knew the navy would bear the brunt of the fighting against the United States. However, for Tojo Hideki, a general of the Imperial Japanese Army and minister of war, military action was inevitable, and the sooner it happened the better given his belief that a delay would favour the United States. Having failed to persuade Roosevelt to engage in direct talks, Konoe resigned as prime minister and was replaced by Tojo on 1 November. The newly appointed prime minister set 30 November as the absolute final deadline for negotiations to succeed or fail, a fact known to the United States due to its interception of Japanese diplomatic correspondence. Furthermore, with no progress being made, Prime Minister Tojo ended up sending Kurusu Saburō, a more experienced diplomat, to support Ambassador Nomura in the negotiations.

In Washington, the unexpected arrival of Kurusu was seen as a positive indication of Japanese desire to reach agreement. Together, Kurusu and Nomura met with President Roosevelt on 17 November. Among other things, Kurusu was asked to discuss the possibility of Japan leaving the Tripartite Pact. Knowing full well that Prime Minister Tojo would never consent to this, Kurusu declined to do so. According to Hotta, this was a decision that Kurusu would come to 'regret deeply', as events soon spiralled out of control (Hotta, *Japan 1941*, 2014, p. 252). By 20 November, the Pearl Harbor task force was ready to sail; a final note for consideration was presented to Cordell Hull, but the United States insisted that Japan withdraw from China (including Manchuria) and Indochina.

Kurusu Saburō

As former Japanese ambassador to Germany, Kurusu had signed the Tripartite Pact. He was not a supporter of the Nazis, however, and had been dismayed by his posting to Berlin in 1936. Kurusu's arrival in the United States in November 1941 was seen, at first, as a positive move but was later interpreted as part of an elaborate deception woven by Japan as it prepared for war. Eri Hotta refutes this and argues that Kurusu had always been of the utmost sincerity in looking for a diplomatic solution.

(*left to right*) Nomura, Hull and Kurusu arrive at the White House for a conference in November 1941.

The Hull Note

An important stage in the countdown to war was the Hull Note presented to Ambassador Nomura on 26 November 1941, which stipulated that Japan should withdraw from Indochina and China as the first step to any easing of the embargo. In fact, the previous day, Hull had written a different note proposing that Japan withdraw its troops only from southern Indochina, reduce its troops in northern Indochina to 25,000, and, in return, the United States would lift some economic sanctions. According to Eri Hotta, the earlier note was cancelled because the United States had found out that Japan had mobilized troops in Taiwan and in the South Seas (Hotta, *Japan 1941*, 2014, p. 265). So, when Tojo read the final version of the Hull Note, he interpreted it as a declaration of war by the United States.

General Tojo Hideki, Japanese minister of war (1940–41) and prime minister (1941–45).

 Activity 8 — **ATL** **Thinking and communication skills**

Source A

Below is an extract from *The Cambridge History of Japan, Volume 6: The Twentieth Century* (Cambridge UP, 1995, p. 338), edited by Peter Duus, an American historian who specializes in the history of Japan.

> As a basis for Japanese–American agreement, it [the Hull note] listed such terms as a complete withdrawal of Japanese military, naval, air and police forces from China and Indochina; a mutual surrender of extraterritorial rights in China; and recognition of only the Nationalist government. Nomura and Kurusu told Hull that they found the note unacceptable. In Tokyo the crestfallen Togo [foreign minister] conferred immediately with the prime minister and his stupefied colleagues, who all agreed that there was nothing further to do. Many of the army and navy leaders were elated by the Americans' uncompromising attitude.

Source B

Below is an extract from *Japan 1941* (2014, p. 269) by Japanese historian Eri Hotta.

> The Hull Note did not impose a specific deadline, but it was taken as an ultimatum when it reached the Japanese government around noon on November 27. Togo was shocked by its content. 'I was struck by despair,' he later recalled. 'I tried to imagine swallowing whole [the demands], but there was no way to force them down my throat.' He felt the note rejected wilfully and categorically all the efforts that the two countries had been putting into their discussions, as though they had never taken place. For those restlessly itching for military action, the note was 'nothing short of a miracle!' noted one bakuryo [a word used to describe an officer whose task it was to plan for war] officer on the Army General Staff. It now seemed that no diplomatic settlement was possible.

1. Compare and contrast the views expressed in Sources A and B in relation to the Hull Note of November 1941.

Student answer – Mei

In both sources, it is stated that the Hull Note was taken as a step towards war; in Source A, it says 'there was nothing further to do' and in Source B that 'it was taken as an ultimatum'.

Also, both sources agree that Togo was affected by the note – in Source A, he is described as 'crestfallen' and in Source B as 'struck by despair'. In addition, both sources mention that some of the Japanese were pleased with the note, as it meant they would go to war. In Source A, it says, 'the army and navy leaders were elated' and in Source B that 'for those restlessly itching for military action, the note was 'nothing short of a miracle'.

The two sources are also different in some ways. Source A outlines what the note demanded but Source B mentions only that the note was written as though discussions 'had never taken place'. Also, Source B only mentions that a 'diplomatic settlement' was not possible, while Source A states that 'there was nothing further to do'.

Student answer – Karl

Source A makes a list of what the United States wanted Japan to do, but Source B does not do this. Also, Source A says that the Hull Note did not impose a deadline, but Source B does not mention any deadline. They do say some similar things, however. Source A and Source B agree that this note was like a declaration of war for the Japanese. Also, that Togo was unhappy when he received the note. In addition, some people supported the note, because they wanted to go to war with the United States.

Examiner's comments

Both Karl and Mei organize their answers well by comparing and contrasting the sources. It is a good idea to employ a comparing-and-contrasting method here as it helps the examiner to see the points they are trying to make. They both use quite appropriate phrases, such as 'both sources' to indicate a comparison, and 'Source A says... but Source B says...' to make it clear that they are pointing out a contrast.

However, notice how Karl resorts to saying, 'Source A says... but Source B does not...' Try to avoid doing this, as it doesn't develop your point sufficiently. Mei develops her points more effectively and includes short phrases from each source as supporting evidence. For example, she mentions how Source B says that a 'diplomatic settlement' was not possible, and then contrasts this with Source A where, instead of mentioning a 'diplomatic settlement', it just says that 'there was nothing more to do'. By doing this, Mei shows that she has understood the sources.

If you look at the markbands that examiners use for the third question in the paper (see chapter on exam tips, page v) where do you think Mei's and Karl's answers belong? What marks would you give them?

The descent into war

On 29 November 1941, Emperor Shōwa (Hirohito) was told that war was inevitable, and on 1 December, the Japanese naval force was informed that the attack on Pearl Harbor was to take place on 7 December. The United States knew by then an attack was imminent but didn't know where or when it would take place; President Roosevelt made one last effort at peace by sending a message to Tokyo on 6 December asking for the withdrawal of Japanese troops from Indochina.

Eri Hotta notes how, due to the censorship now imposed on all incoming telegrams, the Japanese emperor did not receive Roosevelt's message until 3 p.m., by which time the task force could not be recalled. Likewise, because of the time taken to decipher and rewrite the declaration of war against the United States, Nomura and Kurusu were not able to deliver it, as planned, to the White House 30 minutes before the attack on Pearl Harbor but did so 50 minutes after the attack had started, at 1:50 p.m. As such, Nomura and Kurusu were unaware that the attack had already started until they returned to the Japanese Embassy where angry crowds had already gathered to protest (Hotta, *Japan 1941*, 2014, p. 280). According to Hotta, neither Kurusu nor Nomura knew about the Japanese deadline of 30 November and Prime Minister Tojo had not told them about the fleet sailing for Hawaii. If this was indeed the case, then Kurusu and Nomura could not be accused of duplicity, despite Roosevelt's feeling that the 'stealth of the Pearl Harbor strategy and the accompanying use of diplomacy as its cloak were the most abominable part of Japan's conduct' (Hotta, *Japan 1941*, 2014, p. 283).

On 8 December 1941, as a result of the invasion of Malaya, Singapore, and Hong Kong, Britain declared war on Japan. On the same day, the government of the Netherlands (in exile) also declared war on Japan. This was followed, on 11 December, by a declaration of war on the United States by Germany and Italy.

According to Niall Ferguson, the US aircraft carriers were away from their base in Pearl Harbor on 7 December but the following were put out of action as a result of the attack: 8 battleships, 3 destroyers, 3 light cruisers, 3 auxiliaries, and 177 aircraft; 3,297 Americans lost their lives. The Japanese, on the other hand, lost 29 aircraft and 55 men (Ferguson, *The War of the World*, 2006, p. 492).

Activity 9   **ATL** Thinking skills

Source A

Below is an extract from a statement made by US secretary of state Cordell Hull in response to the declaration of war.

> I must say in all my conversations with you [Ambassador Nomura] during the last nine months I have never uttered one word of untruth. This is borne out absolutely by the record. In all my fifty years of public service I have never seen a document that was more crowded with infamous falsehoods and distortions on a scale so huge that I never imagined until today that any Government on this planet was capable of uttering them.

From Andrew Crozier, *The Causes of the Second World War*, Blackwell, 1997, p. 224, quoting R.C. Butow, 'Tojo and the Coming of War', p. 125

Source B

Here is an anti-US propaganda poster published in Japan in 1941.

Source C

This is an anti-Axis propaganda poster published in the United States in 1943.

Source D

Here is a Chinese poster from 1944 showing an American airman stamping on a Japanese soldier.

1. According to its origin, purpose, and content, analyse the value and limitations of Source A for historians studying the outbreak of war between the United States and Japan. Why was Cordell Hull so angry?

2. What is the message conveyed in Source B?

3. What is the message conveyed in Source C?

4. What is the message conveyed in Source D?

TOK

 Thinking and communication skills

Propaganda was used extensively during World War II in order to motivate the civilian population to support the war effort. Study Sources B to D in Activity 9 and discuss how they differ in terms of content and style. What kinds of emotional response were they intended to trigger in the people who saw them? What are the ethical limits to what can be portrayed in propaganda?

An American cartoon published on 19 October 1941. The caption reads: 'The old daisy game'.

Source: Special Collections Research Center, The George Washington University

  Thinking, research, and self-management skills

Now that you have read through this final chapter, draw up a table (like the one below) that shows how events in Europe and Asia affected the United States in the run-up to World War II.

Date	Events in Europe	Events in the Far East	Response of the United States
1937	• Hossbach Memorandum • Italy signs Anti-Comintern Pact	• Marco Polo Bridge Incident • Tianjin Incident	• Quarantine Speech

3.7 Historiography – different interpretations of the outbreak of war

Many reasons have been suggested to explain the outbreak of war in the Far East. They include the following:

- Japan wanted to establish a system that would allow it to be the dominant economic power in China and the Far East, and was willing to go to war to achieve this.
- Japan wished to end European imperialism in Asia.
- Japan was pushed to go to war because the US trade embargos were crippling its economy.
- Japan was concerned that the longer it delayed going to war, the more time the United States would have to arm itself.
- Events in Europe and Operation Barbarossa made Japan more confident about waging war with the United States.
- Roosevelt imposed trade restrictions on Japan, even though he knew these would greatly harm Japan.
- Roosevelt insisted that Japan withdraw from China but must have understood that this was would be seen as an ultimatum and thus lead to war.

Below are the views of a number of historians regarding the main factors of war during this period:

- **Rana Mitter** is a British historian and professor of history. He argues that the United States' insistence in 1941 that Japan withdraw from China was a crucial factor. He considers that a diplomatic solution could have been reached if Konoe had remained prime minister of Japan but that his successor, General Tojo Hideki, was already planning war and thought it was 'inevitable' (Mitter, *China's War with Japan 1937–1945*, 2014, p. 235).
- **Ian Buruma**, a writer who specializes in the Far East, states that Tojo grasped the Hull Note as a pretext for war, but that 'the Hull Note was just an excuse. The plan for the attack on Pearl Harbor had already been made' (Buruma, *Inventing Japan 1853–1964*, 2004, p. 119).
- **Robert Dallek**, an American historian and professor of history, argues that the surprise attack on Pearl Harbor 'greatly distressed' Roosevelt, but 'it also relieved him' because he no longer had to make decisions as 'Japan had now made the decision for him' (Dallek, *Franklin Roosevelt and American Foreign Policy 1932–45*, 1981, p. 311).
- **Antony Best**, a British historian, argues that Britain has to take some responsibility for war, because it wanted to maintain its authority in the Far East and chose to ignore the rise of Japan as a regional power. In particular, he notes that 'the sheer complexity of the events… shows that the idea of Japanese guilt is hard to apply in the Pacific War – it was rather a never-ending struggle between those who "have" and those who "have not"' (quoted in Crozier, *The Causes of the Second World War*, 1997, pp. 247–48).
- **Andrew Crozier**, a British historian, suggests that Japan and the United States had a 'mutual misunderstanding' that resulted in 'mutual underestimation'. Crozier maintains that while 'the causes of the war in Europe can be studied virtually without reference to the Pacific war, the causes of the war in the Pacific cannot be treated in isolation from Europe' (Crozier, *The Causes of the Second World War*, 1997, p. 256).

• **Niall Ferguson** is a British historian and a professor of history in America. His view is that Japan went to war because it believed it was better to 'gamble on immediate war, rather than submit to relative decline in the near future' (in other words, to risk being dominated by the United States) (Ferguson, *The War of the World*, 2006, p. 490).

CHALLENGE YOURSELF

 Thinking and research skills

Read both lists above. See if you can match up the historians' interpretations (list two) with the reasons given for the outbreak of war (list one).

> **TOK**
>
> You may recall that, near the start of Chapter 2, there is a TOK box that discusses the use of the term 'incident' (as in Manchurian Incident) to describe the conflict in 1931. It asks you to consider the significance of how we name wars.
>
> Now that you have read more about the naming of World War II in Japan, do you think this knowledge affects the way you respond to the question on page 33?

In Japan, World War II has many names. In 1990, Bandō Hiroshi from the National Committee of Japanese Historians wrote an article in which he pointed out how, in 1956, Japanese historian Tsurumi Shunsuke referred to this period as the Fifteen-Year War (1930–45) comprising the Manchurian War, the China War, and the Asia-Pacific War. According to Bandō, Shunsuke had argued that '[they] were not incidents unrelated to each other' and that each war was fought because of Japanese imperialism (*Historical Studies in Japan (VII): 1983–1987*, 1990). This claim is supported by other Japanese historians who claimed that the Tanggu Truce, intended to end the Manchurian Incident in 1933, was referred to by sections of the Japanese army as the North China Truce, meaning that it applied only to part of the conflict that had started in 1931. Another compelling argument is that 41,000 Chinese were killed in battles fought between 1933 and 1936, suggesting that this was, indeed, a time of continual (if not continuous) warfare. During the war itself, the name used in Japan was Greater East Asian War, but this was prohibited by the US authorities who occupied Japan in 1945, stating that the correct (and only) name for the conflict was the Pacific War.

> **TOK**
>
> The 70th anniversary of the Japanese surrender was commemorated on 15 August 2015. In his speech, Prime Minister Abe Shinzō expressed 'deepest remorse' and 'sincere condolences' to Japan's wartime victims. However, he added:
>
> 66 *We must not let our children, grandchildren, and even further generations to come, who have nothing to do with the war, be predestined to apologise. Even so, we Japanese, across generations, must squarely face history. We have a responsibility to inherit the past, in all humbleness, and pass it on to the future.*
>
> Commenting on Abe's speech, President Park Geun-hye of South Korea said the following:
>
> 66 *It is hard to deny that Prime Minister Abe Shinzō's statement of yesterday, marking the 70th anniversary of the end of the war, did not quite live up to our expectations. History cannot be hidden, but rather lives on through the testimony of surviving witnesses.*
>
> Whose view do you agree with? Do you think it is better to draw a line under the past and to move forward, or is it more important to remember?

A review of Chapter 3

This chapter completes Case Study 1: Japanese expansionism in East Asia, 1931–41. As with the previous chapters, the focus of this chapter has been on linking events in the Far East to those in Europe. We have seen how Japan responded to the outbreak of European war in September 1939 and also how Europe and the United States responded, in turn, to events in the Far East. The events in China had significant repercussions on both British and American policy with decisions having to be made on how best to support China. Meanwhile, the failure of Japan to swiftly and irrevocably end the war in China dragged it into further clashes with the Soviet Union and, most likely, with Britain and the United States. Japan desperately wanted to secure China under its control but Chinese resistance, supported by Britain and the United States, prevented this. For Japan, the choice quickly became whether to abandon its desired New Order (hegemony over China) or accept the challenge of war against the emerging ABCD Bloc. At the heart of this dilemma was whether the United States had the will to fight: if it didn't, Japan could dominate the Far East; if it did, war would be a huge gamble. As we saw, there were competing forces within Japan calling, on the one hand, for a pre-emptive attack on the United States and, on the other, for a negotiated peace. In the end, both gambits were tried but war was the outcome.

Activity 10	**Thinking, research, self-management, and communication skills**

Now that you have read through this chapter, answer the following question:

Using the sources and your own knowledge, to what extent would you agree that Japan attacked Pearl Harbor because of the trade embargo imposed by the United States?

! This question is typical of the fourth question you will get in the Paper 1 exam. You can check back to the end of the previous chapters to see the suggestions for how best to approach this kind of mini essay. Don't forget: although it may be tempting to answer this question first (because it carries the most marks), you are better off working through each question in order as this will help you think about what may or may not be relevant for the fourth question. As long as it isn't during the five-minute reading time, you could also highlight possible quotations as you come across them in the various sources.

This particular question asks about the reasons that Japan went to war. The command term is 'to what extent', so you need to consider not just the impact of the trade embargo on Japanese policy, but also other reasons that may have been relevant. For example, did Japan intend to expand its empire into Southeast Asia and the Pacific, and use the trade embargo as an excuse to go to war? Was Japan genuinely intending to 'liberate' Asia from the grip of European colonialism and ready to risk war for this? Don't forget to plan your answer and to time how long you spend on it. You have only one hour to answer all four questions so estimate around 20 minutes for this.

 To access websites relevant to this chapter, go to www.pearsonhotlinks. com, search for the book title or ISBN, and click on 'Chapter 3'.

CASE STUDY

2

GERMAN AND ITALIAN EXPANSION, 1933–40

GERMAN AND ITALIAN EXPANSION, 1933–40

The end of the Great War in 1918 produced a brief period of peace in Europe. The Versailles Peace Settlement of 1919 strived to solve the many problems that had caused the outbreak of war in 1914. Despite the attempts to promote open diplomacy and collective security, Europe – and then the world – became involved in World War II (1939–45) only 20 years later.

The rise of Benito Mussolini in Italy and of Adolf Hitler in Germany are key to explaining the events leading to World War II. Their ideologies defended military expansionism as a right of their countries as well as a method of addressing postwar economic and geopolitical issues.

This case study examines the contributions of German and Italian expansionism between 1933 and 1940 to the move to global war. It is broken down into three chapters:

- Chapter 4 focuses on the causes of Italian expansion under Mussolini, and the international response to Italian aggression.
- Chapter 5 analyses the causes of German expansion under Hitler, challenges to postwar settlements, and the international response to German aggression.
- Chapter 6 examines German and Italian foreign policies from 1938 onwards, the international response to the actions of Hitler and Mussolini, and the extent to which events during this period contributed to the outbreak of World War II.

Key concepts:

The case study analyses all these decisive actions within the rapidly evolving context of international events during the period 1933–40. As you read through the three chapters, consider the following key concepts we use when studying history and how they apply to this case study:

- **Change:** This period saw significant changes in the diplomatic relations in Europe. What factors contributed to these changes? For example, did the changes respond to ideological factors? Did economic problems, like the Great Depression, play a role? Did they relate to issues arising from the Versailles Peace Settlement?

- **Continuity:** Consider the extent to which the aims of Hitler's and Mussolini's foreign policies were similar to the ones of the governments that ruled their countries after 1919. Think, for example, of their views on the Versailles Peace Settlement or on the fear of Bolshevism.

- **Causation:** Think about the reasons that can explain the outbreak of war in 1939. Why had war not broken out before the German invasion of Poland? Why couldn't war be averted?

- **Consequence:** This case study assesses the international response to German and Italian aggression. What were the consequences of their actions? Did they help or hinder German and Italian expansion?

- **Significance:** This case study addresses some domestic aspects of Fascist Italy and Nazi Germany such as their economic policies. How significant was the impact of domestic economic issues in explaining the expansionist foreign policies of Hitler and Mussolini?

- **Perspective:** As you work though the case study, try to come up with your own explanation as to how important German and Italian expansionist policies were to the move to global war. What role did other factors, such as the failure of collective security, play? Do you consider some of these causes more important than the others? Why?

1915

- Italy enters World War I as an ally of France and Britain.

1919

- The Treaty of Versailles is signed.

1922

- Mussolini is appointed prime minister of Italy.

1923

- French occupation of the Ruhr.
- Mussolini orders the occupation of Corfu.

1924

- Mussolini seizes Fiume.
- The Dawes Plan is signed.

1925

- The Locarno Pact is signed with Germany as a signatory nation and Italy as one of its guarantors.

1926

- Albania becomes an Italian protectorate.
- Germany joins the League of Nations.

1928

- The Briand–Kellogg Pact is signed.

1929

- The Young Plan is signed.
- Wall Street Crash.

1933

- Adolf Hitler is appointed chancellor of Germany.
- Italy, Britain, Germany, and France sign the Four-Power Agreement.
- Germany abandons the League of Nations and the World Disarmament Conference.

1934

- German–Polish Non-Aggression Pact signed.
- Mussolini mobilizes the Italian army to the Austrian border after the assassination of the Austrian chancellor Engelbert Dollfuss.
- The Soviet Union becomes a member of the League of Nations.

1935

- The Saar plebiscite takes place.
- Hitler announces rearmament and the reintroduction of conscription in Germany.
- The Stresa Front between Italy, Britain, and France is signed.
- Britain and Germany sign the Anglo-German Naval agreement.
- Italy invades Abyssinia (Ethiopia) and the League of Nations imposes sanctions.

1936

- German remilitarization of the Rhineland.
- Mussolini and Hitler sign the Rome–Berlin Axis.

1936–39

- Italy and Germany become involved in the Spanish Civil War.

1937

- Italy and Britain sign the 'gentleman's agreement'.
- The Hossbach Conference takes place in Germany.
- Italy becomes a member of the Anti-Comintern Pact.
- Italy abandons the League of Nations.

1938

- The Anschluss (German annexation of Austria) takes place.
- The Manifesto on Race, revoking citizenship to Italian Jews, is passed.
- The Munich Agreement is signed.

1939

- Hitler marches into Bohemia and Moravia.
- Mussolini occupies Albania.
- Hitler denounces the Anglo-German Naval Agreement.
- Italy and Germany sign the Pact of Steel.
- Germany and the Soviet Union sign the Nazi-Soviet Pact.
- Germany invades Poland.
- Britain and France declare war on Germany.
- Italy declares herself non-belligerent.

1940

- German occupation of Denmark and Norway.
- The fall of France. Occupation of Belgium, Luxembourg, the Netherlands.
- The Battle of Britain.
- Italy enters World War II and invades southern France, Egypt, and Greece.
- Germany, Italy, and Japan sign the Tripartite Pact.

CHALLENGE YOURSELF

 Thinking, self-management, social, communication, and research skills

In preparation for this case study, let's start by looking at some of the issues arising from the Paris Peace Conference of 1919.

Europe in 1919

Study the map below, which shows the territorial divisions in Europe after the Paris Peace Conference.

In groups, answer the following.

1. Compare the map above with a map of Europe in 1918 (see if you can find one from the internet or a book). What significant territorial changes can you see on the 1919 map?

2. Using both maps, plus any previous knowledge you may have, evaluate the territorial losses suffered by Germany as a result of the Treaty of Versailles. How significant were these losses for the German economy? What were the German government's major objections to the territorial changes?

3. Using both maps again, assess the impact that the territorial changes had on Italy. Find out why Italy was dissatisfied with these changes.

Europe in 1940

This is a map of Europe in 1940.

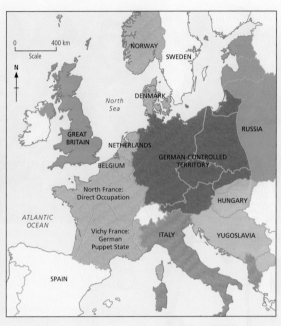

Study this map and the map of Europe in 1919. In groups, answer the following.

4. What were the most significant territorial changes in Europe between 1919 and 1940?

5. Assess the extent of German territorial changes between 1919 and 1940. What do these changes reveal about German foreign policy? Which countries were affected by German expansion?

6. Compare Germany's territorial changes with those of Italy between 1919 and 1940. Is there anything about these changes you find worth noting?

04

Chapter 4: Italian expansion and its consequences

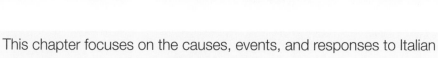

This chapter focuses on the causes, events, and responses to Italian expansion up to 1937. In particular, it will:

* examine the reasons why Italy had ambitions for new territory
* assess the impact of Italy's foreign policy on European diplomacy and on the move to global war.

4.1 Causes of expansion

When World War I (1914–18) broke out, Italy was a relatively new European country facing many challenges; the concept of national identity was still in the making and Italians were more loyal to their regions than to their new country. There was conflict between the Catholic Church and the national government: as a result of the annexation of the Papal States to Italy in 1870, the pope refused to recognize the legitimacy of the Italian state. Italian Catholics, a vast majority of the population, saw themselves torn between political citizenship and their religious beliefs. Industrial centres had developed in the north, but agriculture continued to be the main economic activity in the south, where the levels of poverty, illiteracy, and malnutrition were high. In order to gain access to more raw material and markets, Italy tried to colonize parts of Africa before World War I but was limited to Libya, Eritrea, and part of Somaliland. None of these territories provided Italy with relevant resources or with prestige.

As a treaty partner of the **Central Powers** at the time of the outbreak of World War I, Italy remained neutral in the conflict until it joined the side of the Allies in 1915, under the Treaty of London (also known as the London Pact). The treaty had promised Italy territories including South Tyrol, Istria, Trentino, Trieste, part of the Dalmatia coast, plus indemnities corresponding to war efforts, and possible gains in Africa. Although Italy did receive a big part of what had been agreed upon in 1915, the **Treaty of St Germain** (1919) made Dalmatia a part of the Kingdom of Yugoslavia. Furthermore, although Germany was stripped of its colonies, none went to Italy. This lack of colonial gains and the loss of Dalmatia became main sources of frustration for Italians, who were dissatisfied with the treaty and claimed they had 'won the war but lost the peace'.

After the war, Italy demanded territories, such as the port of Fiume, which had not been included in the Treaty of London. In protest against the postwar settlement, Gabriele D'Annunzio led a group of war veterans to occupy Fiume by force in 1919, thus sparking a wave of nationalism.

Gabriele D'Annunzio and the Blackshirts

Gabriele D'Annunzio was an Italian nationalist who opposed the postwar territorial arrangements for Italy, and who referred to the situation as a 'mutilated peace'. It was also D'Annunzio who seized Fiume with Italian volunteers wearing black shirts, an event that inspired the paramilitary group that came to be known as the Blackshirts. The Blackshirts eventually played a part in bringing Benito Mussolini to power. The occupation of Fiume was short-lived, however, as D'Annunzio was forced to abandon it in January 1921.

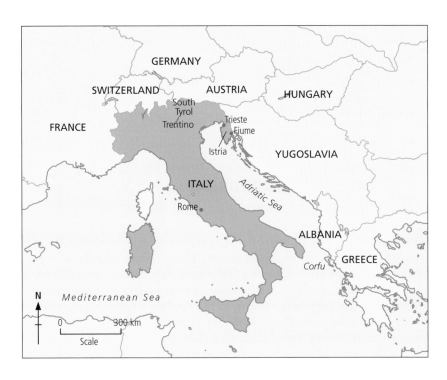

A map of the Kingdom of Italy in 1919 and its surrounding states.

Postwar Italy faced a number of other problems:

• *Economic issues*: Italy owed large sums of money to Britain and the United States – money used to finance the war effort. Inflation and unemployment caused much unrest across the country.

• *Social issues*: There were repeated workers' strikes and riots as well as peasants' attempts to take over land in the south.

• *Political issues*: As a country with limited democratic experience, the coalition governments that ruled Italy after the war were inefficient. Industrialists and landowners feared the influence of **Bolshevism** and turned to paramilitary organizations, offering them financial support in exchange for protection from left-wing groups.

The period between 1919 and 1920 was a violent one in Italy. Former soldiers, who, like D'Annunzio, were discontented with the results of the war for Italy, organized themselves to intimidate communists and socialists. One of these groups in Milan was led by Benito Mussolini, who was appointed prime minister in 1922 for the National Fascist Party (*Partito Nazionale Fascista*, PNF) under the principles of 'order, discipline, hierarchy'.

The name of the National Fascist Party was inspired by ancient Roman history. The term 'Fascist' derives from the word *fasces*, meaning a bundle of rods tied about a lictor's axe, a symbol of Roman authority. A bound bundle is also a symbol of strength through unity, given that the rods would be much stronger when bundled together. Mussolini's vision of an ideal Italy was said to be inspired by the ancient Roman Empire at the height of its prosperity and glory.

CHALLENGE YOURSELF

ATL Thinking, research, and social skills

Now that you have an understanding of Italy's situation after World War I, carry out some research in groups to find out how and why Mussolini came to power. You may wish to consider the following questions: How did Mussolini propose to solve the problems facing Italy after the war? Which social groups felt represented by the Fascists and why? Explain how Mussolini came to power by analysing the events leading up to his appointment as prime minister in October 1922, including the March on Rome.

Impact of Mussolini's Fascism on Italy's foreign policy

As you work through this next section, analyse the continuity and change in Italian foreign policy under Mussolini. To what extent were such changes a response to Mussolini's pragmatic considerations? What elements of continuity can you identify?

In order to understand the impact of Mussolini's Fascist ideology on his foreign policy, you should first analyse what Italian **Fascism** stood for. It is difficult to provide a single, accurate definition of Italian Fascism from its establishment in 1922 to its collapse in 1945. Mussolini himself considered Fascism a movement and a concept that was constantly changing. In the same way Fascism moved from being anti-monarchic to working with the monarchy, or from being liberal to becoming highly protectionist; in foreign policy Italy experienced dramatic changes as Mussolini refused to compromise to any set principle, acting at times as an 'honest broker' and at others like a 'mad dog'.

Many children joined the Fascist group *Balilla*. This photograph shows a group of children in Rome, attending a speech by Mussolini. What does this image say about the significance of war to Fascist ideology?

Ideologically, war was considered a necessary stage in the development of great nations. Mussolini himself claimed that,

> War alone brings to its highest tension all human energy and puts a stamp of nobility upon the peoples who have the courage to meet it [...] Thus a doctrine which is founded upon this harmful postulate of peace is hostile to Fascism.

> **My Autobiography**, Dover Publications, 1996, p. 230

But Mussolini was also a pragmatic leader whose foreign policy was shaped by considerations relating to domestic issues as well as changes in the international situation.

Activity 1
ATL Thinking and research skills

Source A

Below is an extract from a speech delivered by Benito Mussolini in the Chamber, 16 November 1922.

> The fundamental principle upon which our foreign policy is based is that treaties of peace, once signed and ratified, must be carried out, no matter whether they are good or bad. A self-respecting nation cannot follow another course. Treaties are not eternal or irreparable; they are chapters and not epilogues in history; to put them into practice means to try them. If in the course of execution they are proved to be absurd, that in itself constitutes the possibility of a further examination of the respective positions.

> Our foreign policy, which aims at the protection of our interests, respect of treaties and the settling of our position in the Entente, cannot be described as adventurous and imperialist, in the vulgar sense of the word. We want to follow a policy of peace that will not, however, be at the same time suicidal.

Source B

Christopher Duggan is a British historian specializing in Italian history. Below is an extract from his book *Fascist Voices. An Intimate History of Mussolini's Italy.*

> After the March on Rome, Mussolini was careful to indicate that he did not intend to embark on any new or independent path in foreign policy. He had no experience on the international stage [...] He talked repeatedly of the need for overseas 'expansion' in order to meet the requirements of Italy's fast- growing population. He denigrated the recently constituted League of Nations as little more than a 'Franco-British duet' [...] And on the few occasions that he travelled abroad, he made it clear that he was determined to uphold Italy's right to be regarded as a great power.

> **Christopher Duggan**, *Fascist Voices*, 2012, Vintage Books, pp. 73–74

1. In Source A, what is the meaning of the sentence 'we want to follow a policy of peace that will not, however, be at the same time suicidal'?
2. With reference to its origin, purpose, and content, analyse the value and limitations of Source B for a historian studying the aims of Mussolini's foreign policy.

> Question 2 asks you to analyse the value and limitations of a source by referring to three elements: its origins, purpose, and content. An effective structure for this question is to treat the value and limitations separately and link each of these to the origins, purpose, and content.

Activity 2

Look at the following question:

Compare and contrast what Sources A and B in Activity 1 reveal about the aims of Mussolini's foreign policy.

Below is an extract from a sample answer.

Student answer – Jane

Both sources show that Mussolini considered Italy to be a great power. In Source A he acknowledged Italy to have a 'place in the Entente' and Source B says 'he was determined to uphold Italy's right to be regarded as a great power'. Also, both sources show a certain readiness to cooperate at an international level. This is shown when Source B mentions that Mussolini did not intend to embark on any new or independent foreign policy, which is consistent with the message in Source A about Italy following a policy of peace.

However, Source B states that Mussolini denigrated the League of Nations, and Source A shows him very willing to cooperate in the peaceful solutions of conflicts that may arise from treaties. Also, Source B mentions Mussolini's desire to expand overseas, while in Source A Mussolini seems to be more interested in a peaceful revision of treaties that do not work.

Examiner's comments

Jane makes some explicit comparisons and contrasts between the sources. She has written two paragraphs: one for comparisons and one for contrasts. It is an effective way to show the examiner she has approached both parts of the question. Also, see how her points are supported with specific reference to each source, either by briefly quoting from a source or by paraphrasing it.

However, Jane's answer does not contain enough comparisons and contrasts to obtain full marks (6 marks). To gain full marks, you need to identify six points about the sources: you may include three points for comparisons and three for contrasts, though if you find more of one than the other that would be fine.

Now, complete Jane's answer by addressing any other comparisons and contrasts that have not yet been mentioned. Once you have done this, find a partner and swap your answers. Mark each other's work using the markbands for the third question on page xv.

An expansionist foreign policy – a right and a necessity

It could be argued that Mussolini saw an expansionist foreign policy both as a *right* and a *necessity*.

It was considered a right because of the following:

- Echoing the feelings of many Italians, Mussolini saw a need to revise the postwar treaties in order to revert to the 'mutilated peace' of 1919.
- Mussolini believed in Italy's 'imperial destiny': as heir of ancient Rome, Italy had a historical right to the Mediterranean region.
- As his rule progressed, Mussolini defended Italy's right to claim more territories with racial arguments.

It was considered a necessity because of the following:

- Given that propaganda was an important characteristic of Fascism, territorial expansion was used to increase Italy's prestige and to enhance the cult of the leader.
- Mussolini claimed Italy needed colonies to provide arable land in order to expand the economy as well as new territories to resettle a growing Italian population.
- As Mussolini's regime met increasing challenges at home, a successful foreign policy was sought as an opportunity to move attention away from his domestic policies.

How did Mussolini plan to achieve these aims?

Although Mussolini was appointed head of a coalition government, he obtained dictatorial powers very quickly by using methods such as coercion and intimidation of the opposition. He founded a secret police, implemented censorship, and reformed the state with the aim of having direct control over all areas. By 1925, formal opposition to Fascism was banned and Mussolini began to rule by decree the following year. Known as Il Duce (meaning 'The Leader'), Mussolini became the centre of a personality cult campaign that encompassed education, propaganda, and indoctrination.

In the background of this propaganda poster of the *Fasci di Combattimento* you can read the Fascist motto 'Believe, Obey, Fight'. What do you think the significance of this poster was in terms of communicating Mussolini's aims?

Impact of domestic economic issues on Italy's foreign policy up to 1929

Mussolini understood that, until Italy's economic issues were solved, opportunities for an aggressive foreign policy were limited. The Italian economy was relatively small and depended on imports. When Mussolini came to power, Italy was burdened by unemployment, a huge gap between the agrarian countryside and the industrial north, and a dependency on foreign products.

Until 1925, Mussolini had implemented liberal economic policies to encourage private investment and the reactivation of the economy. By 1925, unemployment had dropped from 500,000 to 122,000, and Italy even enjoyed a budget surplus. After 1925, the Italian economy became **protectionist**. Here, Mussolini's aim was to make Italy self-sufficient (that is, to achieve **autarky**) and not depend on imports. With the aim of increasing national production, he placed import duties on many goods. He also introduced the Battle for Grain and the Battle for the Lira. The Battle for Grain aimed at increasing the production of cereals to achieve self-sufficiency; although Italy did achieve self-sufficiency in wheat, it was at the expense of other agricultural products: the exports of traditional Italian products, such as wine and olives, dropped. The Battle for the Lira revalued the currency to increase Italian prestige, which also worked as propaganda. While imports benefited from the new terms of trade, exports suffered as they became more expensive to other countries. This contributed to a decline of Italian exports and of tourism.

Activity 3

 ATL Social, thinking, and communication skills

Source A

This is an extract from a public speech by Mussolini in Pesaro, 1926.

> We will conduct the economic battle for the defense of the lira with the utmost resolve. From this square to the entire civilized world I say that I will defend the lira to the last breath, to the last blood... The Fascist regime is ready, from its leader to its last follower, to require all the necessary sacrifices needed. Our lira, the symbol of our nation, the mark of our wealth, the symbol of your struggles, our efforts, our sacrifices, our tears, our blood, must be defended and will be defended.

Source B

John Pollard is a British historian. Below is an extract from his book *The Fascist Experience in Italy* (1998).

> What Fascist foreign policy lacked in the 1920s was not ambitious aims but the means and, above all, the opportunity to achieve them [...] Economic difficulties also played a part. Until the 1930s, Italy was too closely tied into the world economic system, and in particular too dependent on other powers, notably the United States and Britain, for its financial stability, to be able to indulge in military adventures. Above all, until the early 1930s, the international situation was not conducive to the success of Fascism's ambitious, expansionist foreign-policy aims. Thanks to American isolationism, the international boycott of Soviet Russia and the weakness of Weimar Germany, Britain and France ruled the international roost, dominating European affairs and effectively controlling the League of Nations; hence Mussolini's suspicion, sometimes hostility, towards that organisation. Forced to continue playing the junior partner to the Western powers, Mussolini had little room for diplomatic manoeuvre or to flex his international muscles.

1. What does Source A say about the reasons for the revaluation of the Lira?
2. With reference to its origin, purpose, and content, analyse the value and limitations of Source A to a historian studying Mussolini's aims.
3. In pairs, identify the reasons provided in Source B to explain why Mussolini did not execute an aggressive foreign policy in the 1920s.

 Question 1 is the type of question you will get as the first to answer in your exam. It is worth 3 marks. Find three points that could be made about the source in relation to the question and state them briefly. You will not receive any marks for outside knowledge, so limit yourself to the material within the source.

CHALLENGE YOURSELF

ATL Research and social skills

In groups, find more information about the Italian economy and Mussolini's policies up to 1929. In particular:

· What did Italy import and what did it export? How does this information help you understand the challenges of the Italian economy?

· Consider other battles, such as the Battle for Land and the Battle for Births. What were their aims and results?

· What was the 'corporate state'? To what extent did it contribute to the organization of the Italian economy?

ATL Commununication skills

Think of other examples you have studied that proposed an expansionist foreign policy to solve their economic problems. For example, what did you learn in Case Study 1 about the relations between the Japanese economy and its foreign policy? What are the similarities and differences between what happened in Japan and what happened in Italy?

Mussolini's Italy never became self-sufficient. This was partly due to a combination of both the nature of the Italian economy and Mussolini's policies. Later in this chapter, you will analyse the influence of another important event on Italy's economy and foreign policy: the Great Depression of the 1930s.

4.2 Italian expansion and international response

In the previous section you have studied Mussolini's aims in foreign policy. You have also read about the methods he implemented to consolidate power, and the ways in which the economic policies of Italy related to Mussolini's foreign policy. This section analyses Mussolini's foreign policy and assesses the responses of the international community. As you work your way through it, think of the key concept of *significance*. Which events in this section do you consider as having contributed the most to the move to global war? Also, consider the key concept of *perspective*. How far did the changes in the diplomatic alignments respond to Mussolini's foreign policy? What other explanations have you been able to find?

Italian foreign policy between 1922 and 1933

Although the case study focuses on events from 1933, it is useful to have some background information on Italy's foreign policy in the 1920s. Mussolini had limited opportunities to expand before the 1930s, but he attempted to gain some territory in the Mediterranean by attacking Corfu (1923) and Fiume (1924). As mentioned in the previous section, Mussolini believed Italy had a right to control the Mediterranean Sea; he therefore challenged Britain and France, which also had interests in the region.

The Corfu Incident, 1923

In 1923, Mussolini blamed Greece for the murders of four Italian diplomats working for the **Conference of Ambassadors** on the Greek–Albanian border. When Greece refused to offer official apologies and pay economic compensations to Italy, Mussolini bombarded and invaded the Greek island of Corfu. The League of Nations attempted to settle the dispute but its terms were rejected by Mussolini, who threatened to leave the organization if his demands were not met. The Conference of Ambassadors then ruled that Greece had to pay reparations to Italy, and, after threats of intervention by the British, Mussolini finally withdrew from Corfu. Although the invasion was advertised in Italy as a huge success, the country was forced to withdraw from Corfu; relations with Britain and France were damaged.

Activity 4 — ATL Thinking, communication, and social skills

Source A

Here is an extract from a speech by Mussolini to the Italian Senate, November 1923.

> You must not believe that the occupation of Corfu was carried out only as a sanction; it was also carried out to increase the prestige of Italy... Italians have never been much interested in the League of Nations; they believed it was a lifeless academic organization of no importance... In point of fact, the League is an Anglo-French duet... Italy's position so far has been one of absolute inferiority.

Source B

The following cartoon was published in *Punch*. It shows Mussolini setting foot on Corfu. The caption reads: 'The Latest Caesar. Sig. Mussolini (a bit above himself). "I do bestride the narrow world like a colossus." After *Julius Caesar*, Act 1, Scene 2.'

1. What is the message of Source B?
2. To what extent does the message in Source B support the view in Source A?

PUNCH, OR THE LONDON CHARIVARI.—September 13, 1923.

THE LATEST CÆSAR.

Sig. MUSSOLINI (a bit above himself). "I DO BESTRIDE THE NARROW WORLD LIKE A COLOSSUS."

After JULIUS CÆSAR, Act. 1., Scene 2.

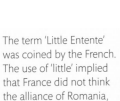

A cartoon caption can offer much valuable information to help you understand the message of the cartoon. Make sure you consider the captions when answering cartoon-based questions. In pairs, explain the meaning and significance of this particular caption. Discuss how it relates to the cartoon. Then write up your answers individually.

The term 'Little Entente' was coined by the French. The use of 'little' implied that France did not think the alliance of Romania, Czechoslovakia, and Yugoslavia was as strong as the Triple Entente, an association between France, Russia, and Britain formed before World War I.

Fiume, 1924

Earlier in the chapter you have read about the Italian claims to Fiume, a territory under Yugoslavia, and about Gabriele D'Annunzio's brief occupation of it. Shortly after the Corfu Incident, Mussolini invaded Fiume. The king of Yugoslavia handed over Fiume to Italy and signed the Pact of Rome with Mussolini. Both countries promised mutual neutrality in case of an attack by a third party.

France disliked Mussolini's intimidation of Yugoslavia and how he tried to expand in the Balkans. In the 1920s, France signed military and political agreements with the members of the Little Entente – a defensive alliance between Romania, Czechoslovakia, and Yugoslavia – to prevent them undermining the Paris Peace Settlement in the Balkans. Britain, for its part, did not want Mussolini to extend his influence in the Mediterranean. Mussolini kept Fiume, but clashes with France and Britain over the Mediterranean and the Balkans were to continue.

Italy and collective security in the 1920s

In the mid-1920s, the European nations came to the conclusion that it was impossible to expect the postwar treaties to be upheld by the use of force. Consequently, they promoted international treaties to maintain **collective security**. Several treaties were signed to guarantee the frontiers established at Versailles, and to reject using war as a means to solve conflicts. Mussolini, aware of the alarm raised in Europe by his attacks on Corfu and Fiume, chose this opportunity to show himself as a more conciliatory character.

There were two reasons why Mussolini became more conciliatory after Fiume:

• Joining the efforts of collective security was perceived as a good way of diffusing British and French suspicions.
• Neither the Italian economy nor the Italian armed forces were ready to engage in an armed conflict.

The Locarno Pact, 1925

The Locarno Pact was a series of treaties signed in 1925 by France, Germany, Britain, Belgium, and Italy. The pact guaranteed the frontiers between Germany, France, and Belgium as set up by the Treaty of Versailles. Britain and Italy acted as the underwriters, agreeing to defend any signatory that became the victim of a violation of the terms of the pact. Although Italy was able to sit at the high table among the great powers, Locarno was not the diplomatic success Mussolini had hoped for: since the pact did not guarantee Germany's eastern frontiers, it did not allay Italy's concerns over a potential expansion of Germany into neighbouring Austria.

The treaties signalled the beginning of a decade in which Mussolini appeared to behave as a 'good European': in 1928, he signed the Kellogg–Briand Pact to ban war as an instrument to resolve conflicts. However, while promoting collective security in Europe, Italy secretly supported separatist forces in the Balkans, such as the Croats in Yugoslavia, in stirring up unrest among the Little Entente members and, consequently, offsetting French influence.

Activity 5 — (ATL) Thinking and communication skills

The paragraph below tells us Mussolini's view of the Locarno Treaty.

> It would have been a colossal blunder not to have underwritten the Locarno guarantees. Had we abstained, we should have had no part in the agreement which is at the basis of the relations between the great European Powers. In the second place, we should have been isolated. In the third, we should have lost an opportunity to put ourselves on an equal footing with England on a memorable occasion.

From Gaetano Salvemini, *Prelude to World War II*, Gollancz, 1953, p. 67.

1. According to the source, why did Italy sign the Locarno Treaties?
2. What does the source reveal about a) the aims and b) the methods of Mussolini's foreign policy in the late 1920s?

Student answer to Question 1 – Rhidian

Italy signed the Locarno Treaties firstly to be part of the great European powers; secondly, to avoid Italian diplomatic isolation; thirdly, so it could be on an equal footing with England.

Examiner's comments

Rhidian has identified three reasons why Italy signed Locarno. The answer is brief but addresses the question effectively. The reasons are clearly signposted, using linking words like 'secondly' and 'thirdly'. This is an effective way of showing you are addressing different points.

Italian foreign policy in the 1930s

The 1930s saw a series of significant changes in European relations – changes that influenced Italy's foreign policy and accelerated the move to global war.

Firstly, Europe was hit by the **Great Depression**. This world economic crisis had a negative impact on international trade, affecting Italy and cutting its access to foreign loans. In an attempt to solve economic problems, Mussolini's foreign policy became more aggressive than it had been in the 1920s. A second factor that modified the European state of affairs was the rise of Adolf Hitler in Germany in 1933. Even though Hitler and Mussolini were to fight on the same side in World War II, Hitler – at the time of his appointment as German chancellor – was viewed by Mussolini with much suspicion; the latter had feared that Germany would try to revise the Treaty of Versailles, in particular with regard to Germany's ambition to unite with Austria, Italy's neighbour.

Italian foreign policy in the 1930s could be roughly divided into two periods, with 1935 as the turning point. Before 1935, Italy continued to show some cooperation with Britain and France. In 1935, its foreign policy became openly aggressive and the country remained in a state of constant war until the end of World War II.

The impact of the Great Depression on Italy's economy and foreign policy

The Italian economy was already experiencing some difficulties as a result of Mussolini's policies (such as the revaluation of the Lira), when the Great Depression created an additional burden. International trade was severely affected and Italian exports were no exception. Like the rest of Europe, Italy lost international financial support from the United States. Mussolini first saw the crisis as an American problem and considered that Italian policies aiming at autarky would protect his country from the Depression. But the revaluation of the Lira, as well as high levels of public spending, had not prepared the Italian economy well. With a decrease in international demand, industrial production fell by 25 per cent between 1929 and 1932. This had a negative impact on wages and employment levels: by 1932, unemployment had reached 1 million.

Mussolini responded to the effects of the Depression by increasing state intervention. He introduced policies to limit unemployment, such as the expansion of public works and rearmament. The navy and the air force rapidly expanded as a result. Mussolini also saw the Depression as an opportunity for expansion since the foreign powers were preoccupied with finding solutions to overcome the crisis. He believed that a successful revision of the postwar treaties – by expanding Italian territory – could help mitigate the effects of the Depression on Italy; additionally, short and successful wars could divert attention away from Italy's domestic problems.

Activity 6
 **ATL Thinking and social skills**

The following extract is from a speech by Mussolini addressing the workers of Milan in 1934. It highlights the relationship between a Fascist economy and a Fascist foreign policy.

> *This is not a crisis in the traditional sense of the term. It is the passage from one phase of civilization to another. It is no longer an economy aiming at individual profit, but an economy concerned with collective interests [...] The future cannot be planned like an itinerary or a timetable. One must not take out a mortgage too long into the future. Indeed, as we have said before, we are absolutely convinced that fascism is bound to become the standard type of civilization of our century for Italy and for Europe.*

1. What does this source reveal about Mussolini's views of the 1930 crisis?
2. With reference to its origin, purpose, and content, analyse the value and limitations of this source for a historian studying the impact of the Great Depression on Mussolini's foreign policy.

Below is an answer to Question 2 from Jim. Read it and see what you think.

Student answer – Jim

This is a contemporary source as it is from a speech by Mussolini to Italian workers given in 1934. It is therefore a useful document in providing insight into the impact of the Depression in Italy. It shows Mussolini is aware that the crisis imposes the need to make changes in Italian foreign policy. It demonstrates his ambition to expand Fascism beyond Italy. Because he is addressing Italian workers, it also shows he is aware of the need to have the support of Italian men if Italy is to embark on a more aggressive policy.

However, because this is a public speech, it may be intended as propaganda and may not reveal Mussolini's real plans for Italy after the Depression. It does not offer any indication of the reactions of the workers or of foreign countries to the speech. Additionally, Mussolini does not explain how he intends to bring about the necessary changes. Finally, because the speech is from 1934, it can only focus on the short-term effects of the Depression on Italian foreign policy.

3. In groups, discuss the strengths and weaknesses of Jim's answer above.

The rise of Hitler in Germany

Hitler's appointment as chancellor of Germany in 1933 contributed to a number of changes in diplomatic alignments in Europe. Many nations reacted to the rise of Hitler by reinforcing collective security. In order to curb Hitler's ambitions, Mussolini proposed a treaty between Italy, Germany, France, and Britain in June 1933. The Four-Power Pact, an agreement of understanding and cooperation, was signed to promote collaboration and maintenance of peace. Although the pact contributed to the cult of Mussolini as a successful international leader within Italy, it did not last long. In October that year, Hitler withdrew Germany from the League of Nations and the Disarmament Conference; cooperation between the four countries thus became more difficult to sustain.

Activity 7 Communication and thinking skills

This is a cartoon published by *Punch* in 1933. The caption reads: 'Dealing with Gulliver. The Leading Lilliputians (all at once): "Now, boys, if the Geneva strings burst before we've finished with him we'll use this rope to tie him down."'

DEALING WITH GULLIVER.

THE LEADING LILLIPUTIANS (*all at once*). "NOW, BOYS, IF THE GENEVA STRINGS BURST BEFORE WE'VE FINISHED WITH HIM WE'LL USE THIS ROPE TO TIE HIM DOWN."

1. What is the message conveyed by this source?

As mentioned earlier, Mussolini had concerns over Hitler's intentions in Austria. South Tyrol, formerly part of the Austro-Hungarian Empire, was handed to Italy in 1919 under the terms of the Treaty of St Germain. Although the union between Germany and Austria (known as **Anschluss**) was banned under the terms of the Treaty of Versailles, nationalism was strong and the rise of Hitler in Germany was becoming a

Thinking and research skills

What other examples in history in which a group tried to impose its beliefs on others are you familiar with? Can you think of a contemporary example of this? What is your reaction to these events? How far can the study of history contribute to the protection of cultural diversity?

threat to Italy's authority in South Tyrol. During the 1920s, Mussolini tried, with limited success, to 'Italianize' this largely German-speaking territory by banning the use of the German language and promoting the migration of Italians to the region.

In July 1934 Austria's chancellor, Engelbert Dollfuss, was murdered by Nazi agents in an attempt to bring about an Anschluss between Austria and Germany. Italy quickly threatened to intervene in defence of Austrian independence by mobilizing troops to the Austrian border, the Brenner Pass. Germany, not yet strong enough to face Italy, backed down. This was a great triumph for Italian diplomacy and served to put forward the idea of a strong Italian military. However, the murder of Dollfuss demonstrated the vulnerability of Austrian independence. When Hitler introduced conscription and announced rearmament in 1935, Mussolini proposed a conference with Britain and France to discuss ways to control German revisionism. The three countries signed the Stresa Front by which they reinforced their commitment to the 1925 Locarno Pact of preserving the 1919 German western frontiers. They also pledged to consult each other if the independence of Austria was threatened.

Activity 8 Communication and social skills

Professor A William Salomone was a specialist in modern Italian history. Below is an extract from his published work *Readings in Twentieth-Century European History* (1950).

> At the beginning of 1935, despite the lack of any formal diplomatic agreements, there existed among France, Great Britain, and Italy a certain solidarity of views in regard to the 'German Problem.' […] The Nazi Putsch in Vienna in July, 1934, was checked by Italy's quick and perhaps decisive reaction through the dispatch of Italian divisions to the Brenner. On September 27, 1934, had come the Three Power Declaration reasserting 'the common policy' of France, Britain, and Italy 'regarding the necessity of maintaining the independence and integrity of Austria.' The question, however, remained for Italy: when would the next step of a German drive for the Alpine frontier and Southeastern Europe come and for how long could Mussolini alone stand in Hitler's path? Germany seemed at present occupied with European territorial questions. But for Britain the query was: when would naval and colonial problems assume the form of a threat against her supremacy? […] The Stresa Conference of April, 1935, proved decisive but not as expected.

1. According to this source, why were Italy and France worried about Germany in 1935?
2. In pairs, study the map of Europe in 1919 on page 90. Identify the countries that would have felt threatened by the political changes taking place in the 1930s.

Similar to the fate of the Four-Power Pact, the Stresa Front – the last attempt by Europe to use collective security against German revisionism – collapsed. The failure of Stresa can be attributed to the fact that by 1935 national interests were put above collective security: for even before Stresa, Mussolini had started to mobilize troops in his African colonies in preparation for an invasion of Abyssinia (see next section); as for Britain, it actually helped Germany break the Treaty of Versailles by signing the Anglo-German Naval Agreement in June 1935, which allowed the German navy to be one-third of the size of Britain's (see page 129). France and Italy were outraged by the fact that Britain did not consult them before signing the agreement.

Activity 9 — ATL Thinking and communication skills

Here is an extract from a speech by Mussolini to the Italians, 11 October 1935.

> *For the past thirteen years I have been asking, begging, threatening so that the Italian people get their own place within lawful boundaries. I want the Italians to be able to earn their own bread and to be liberated from having to work for starvation wages at the arbitrary wishes of foreign powers [...] What I could achieve on Italian soil by improving this earth, I have already done. This cannot be forced any further [...] We need territories, otherwise we shall explode [...] We shall do everything in our power, we shall sacrifice everything we must, but we shall not surrender our aims!*

1. What does the source reveal about the relationship between domestic economic issues and foreign policy in Italy in 1935?
2. What did Mussolini consider to be 'Italy's lawful boundaries'? On what grounds did this include Abyssinia?

Italian expansion in Abyssinia, 1935–36

Abyssinia (known today as Ethiopia) was an independent monarchy located between the Italian colonies of Eritrea and Somaliland. Attempting colonial expansion, Italy invaded Abyssinia towards the end of the 19th century; it was defeated in 1896 at the Battle of Adowa, during the First Italo-Ethiopian War. The 'Adowa scar' became a source of national humiliation for Italians. Haile Selassie, who became emperor of Abyssinia in 1930, ruled the country as an absolutist. The country's constitution, drafted after the model of the Japanese one, declared the emperor sacred. Haile Selassie wanted to modernize his empire and initiated reforms such as the building of railways. After the Great Depression, he strengthened trade with Japan.

Both Abyssinia and Italy joined the League of Nations after World War I. Article six of the League Covenant had stated that, should any member declare war on a member state, it would be treated as an attack on the entire organization requiring collective action. Additionally, Italy and Abyssinia had signed the Italo-Ethiopian Treaty of Friendship and Arbitration in 1928, declaring that territorial disputes between the two countries would be solved by impartial arbitration. However, neither the Treaty of Friendship nor the League of Nations prevented Italy's annexation of Abyssinia in 1935.

Activity 10 — ATL Thinking and research skills

Here is a map of Abyssinia in 1934.

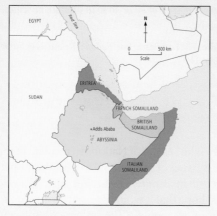

1. What can the map reveal about the reasons behind Mussolini's interest in Abyssinia?

Why did Italy invade Abyssinia in 1935?

- *Historical factors*: Mussolini had an ambition to redress the humiliation of Adowa and conquer an empire for Italy.
- *Economic factors*: Mussolini hoped that Abyssinia would provide access to raw materials and markets, as well as creating new territory for a growing Italian population. Evidence showing that plans to attack Abyssinia were ready as early as 1929 seems to support this argument. Also, the effects of the Great Depression had put Italy under additional pressure to lift itself out of an economic crisis.
- *Political factors*: A successful campaign in Abyssinia would divert the attention of Italians away from the economic problems and affirm Mussolini's image as a successful leader.
- *The 'Abyssinian' factor*: According to Piers Brendon (for more information, see page 103), Mussolini viewed Abyssinia's attempts at modernization with suspicion. He feared that unless he moved immediately, a modern Abyssinia could become a threat to the Italian colonies of Eritrea and Somaliland. It is also true that that Mussolini criticized the feudalism of Abyssinia and, above all, the prevalence of slavery.
- *International factors*: Mussolini thought Britain and France would give him a free hand to do as he pleased in Abyssinia, as a way of keeping on good terms with Italy in view of German rearmament. Also, given that Italy felt threatened by German ambitions in Austria, a victory over Abyssinia would show the Germans the strength of the Italian military.

This is an official stamp from 1975 with the image of Emperor Haile Selassie.

The invasion

In December 1934, Italian troops provoked Abyssinia into a border clash with Italian Somaliland near the Walwal oasis. These borders had never been clearly set. Both Italian and Abyssinian nationals were killed in the confrontation and, like with Corfu, Mussolini began preparations for an invasion and demanded compensation for the Italian casualties as well as formal apologies from the Abyssinian government.

Often, a memorandum can offer a more personal (or revealing) view on an event or a situation than a public speech. In this specific source, Mussolini explains to his chief of general staff that Italy needs to move against Abyssinia immediately, for he is worried about the speed at which Abyssinia's forces are growing and developing. It is unlikely that Mussolini would have used this argument to justify the invasion before the Italian citizens. Therefore, we may say that the purpose of a source (in this case, to whom it is directed) conditions its content and affects its value and limitations.

Activity 11   (ATL) Thinking and communication skills

This is an extract from a memorandum by Mussolini to Marshal Badoglio, Italian chief of general staff, 30 December 1934.

> ❝ I decide on this war, the object of which is nothing more nor less than the complete destruction of the Abyssinian army and the total conquest of Abyssinia. In no other way can we build the Empire […] For our arms to achieve a rapid and decisive victory, we must deploy on a vast scale the mechanised forces, which are now at our disposal, and which the Abyssinians either do not possess at all or do so in insufficient degree, but which they will possess within a few years…

Anthony Adamthwaite, *The Lost Peace: International Relations in Europe 1918–1939*, The Camelot Press, 1980, p. 165

1. According to the source, why did Mussolini decide to provoke Abyssinia in December 1934?
2. With reference to its origin, purpose, and content, analyse the value and limitations of the source for a historian studying the causes of Italian expansion.

Haile Selassie appealed to the League of Nations to mediate in the conflict, but the League refused to discuss issues of sovereignty as the borders between Abyssinia and Italian Somaliland were still in dispute. The League agreed to place an arms embargo on both countries in the hope that it would prevent an armed escalation of the conflict while a diplomatic solution was sought. The embargo significantly affected Abyssinia as it deepened the gap with Italy, a country that was able to produce most of its armaments at home.

In October 1935, Italian forces launched an invasion of Abyssinia. Partly because of its economic limitations and partly because of the arms embargo, Abyssinia could not confront the Italian army and air force. Once again, Haile Selassie appealed to the League of Nations, this time demanding the arms embargo to be lifted for his country so that his troops could obtain weaponry to fight the Italian advance. He was unsuccessful.

Despite the Italian forces being technologically superior (as shown by the use of tanks and aircrafts), they still employed illegal fighting methods, such as attacking civilians and ambulances and using chemical weapons against the Abyssinian population. The League formed a special committee to investigate the use of chemical weapons but claimed to be unable to reach a verdict; Britain and France never confronted Italy about this issue.

TOK

In his account of the Abyssinian crisis, historian Piers Brendon notes how, in 1934, Haile Selassie asked Germany for supplies of conventional and chemical weapons, and how Hitler sent him rifles and machine guns. How does knowing that Haile Selassie tried to obtain chemical weapons from Hitler influence the way you evaluate this event? To what extent does the rightness of an action depend on the context? What does this reveal about the role of emotions in the study of history?

CHALLENGE YOURSELF

(ATL) **Research and self-management skills**

Both Italy and Abyssinia signed the 1925 Geneva Protocol, which prohibited the use of poisonous gas and other bacteriological methods of warfare. Find out why this protocol was signed, and how it proposed to deal with members breaking it.

Activity 12
(ATL) **Thinking and communication skills**

This is an illustration depicting the Battle of Amb Aradam (1936) by Achille Beltrame. It was published in the Italian weekly newspaper *La Domenica del Corriere* on 1 March 1936.

La disastrosa ritirata dei guerrieri di Ras Mulughietà, dopo la battaglia dell'Amba Aradam. Soldati in rotta, animali in fuga; e qualche isolato supremo tentativo di resistenza contro gli stormi di aeroplani che gettano tonnellate di esplosivi. (Disegno di A. Beltrame)

1. What message is this source trying to convey?
2. With reference to its origin, purpose, and content, analyse the value and limitations of this source for a historian studying the nature of warfare in Abyssinia between 1935 and 1936.

Ending the conflict

In an attempt to end the conflict between Italy and Abyssinia, the international community implemented two methods: economic sanctions and diplomacy.

Economic sanctions

After the invasion, the League declared Mussolini an aggressor and imposed a series of economic sanctions on Italy to force him out of Abyssinia. However, the sanctions were ineffective for the following reasons:

- The sanctions, which did not include trading of coal, oil, and steel (essential to the Italian economy and war effort), took a long time to implement
- When finally implemented, the sanctions only lasted from November 1935 to June 1936 – not long enough a period to have a significant impact on Italy
- At the time, Britain's naval priorities were focused on the protection of British possessions against Japan in the Far East. Britain did not want to engage in a conflict in the Mediterranean and, therefore, did not close the Suez Canal. This allowed Italy to continue to send forces and supply the troops in Africa.

Activity 13  **(ATL) Thinking and communication skills**

This is a Fascist poster against the sanctions imposed by the League of Nations, 18 November 1935, following Italy's invasion of Abyssinia. The poster reads: 'November 18: Sanctions. Italians, remember!' (translated by author).

1. What is the message of this source?
2. To what extent can this poster be considered as propaganda? How far can it be viewed as government information?

Without the full commitment of non-member countries like the United States, Japan, and Germany to economic sanctions, it was very difficult to cripple Italy's economy. Given the size of the Italian army and the resources it had access to, Italy would have defeated Abyssinia regardless of the sanctions. The closure of the Suez Canal, on the other hand, would have had a more immediate impact on the Italian supply lines.

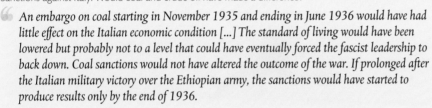

Activity 14   Thinking and communication skills

Source A

Cristiano Andrea Ristuccia is an economics professor. This is an extract from his article entitled '1935 Sanctions against Italy: Would coal and crude oil have made a difference?'

> *An embargo on coal starting in November 1935 and ending in June 1936 would have had little effect on the Italian economic condition [...] The standard of living would have been lowered but probably not to a level that could have eventually forced the fascist leadership to back down. Coal sanctions would not have altered the outcome of the war. If prolonged after the Italian military victory over the Ethiopian army, the sanctions would have started to produce results only by the end of 1936.*

Source B

Here is an extract from a speech made to the House of Commons in May 1936 by Anthony Eden, British secretary of state for foreign affairs.

> *There was only one sanction that could be immediately effective and that sanction was to deny to Italy the use of the Suez Canal. That sanction must have inevitably entailed military action; there is no doubt of it. That military action must, in my judgement, have led to war [...] We imposed sanctions that could not be immediately effective, and we knew it; but if the war had lasted a year they would certainly have played their part in the final settlement. If Honourable Gentlemen wish to take military action I must warn them that you cannot close the Canal with paper boats.*

> **From Steven Morewood, *The British Defence of Egypt, 1935–1940: Conflict and Crisis in the Eastern Mediterranean*, Frank Cass, 2005, p. 80**

1. Why, according to Source A, were the sanctions imposed by the League of Nations inefficient?
2. What is the meaning of 'you cannot close the Canal with paper boats' in Source B?
3. Compare and contrast what Sources A and B reveal about the effectiveness of economic sanctions on Italy.

 Question 3 asks that you focus on the views expressed in the sources. Do not compare and contrast issues related to the origins and purpose of the sources but on the content of the sources.

Diplomatic negotiations

Acting independently of the League of Nations, Britain and France opened negotiations with Italy to end the conflict by making territorial concessions in Africa. This decision was due to a number of factors.

Firstly, as shown with the crisis following the murder of Austrian chancellor Dollfuss in 1934, Italy had become strategically more important to Britain and France as Hitler rose to power in Germany. By 1935, the German economy was recovering very quickly and Hitler reintroduced conscription. In 1936, while the Abyssinian crisis was taking place, Hitler remilitarized the Rhineland, alarming France and Britain. Good relations with Italy ensured that France could assist the Little Entente allies quicker through Italian territory, and could guarantee safety for the French Mediterranean coast. Also, in the event of war against Germany, a neutral Italy would not require France to protect the Alps.

Secondly, the willingness of these two countries to negotiate with Italy behind Abyssinia's back was in part a response to British and French public opinion, since significant numbers of their citizens had refused to go to war for a country so removed from what they considered their national interests.

The Hoare–Laval Pact

In December 1935, British Foreign Secretary Samuel Hoare and French Prime Minister Pierre Laval proposed to offer Mussolini two-thirds of Abyssinia, partly through direct political control and partly through economic influence. Abyssinia would also gain some land from British Somaliland that contained an outlet to the sea. Before negotiations began, however, details of the pact were leaked by the French press. This caused a political crisis, one that forced Samuel Hoare to resign.

Activity 15 — ATL Thinking and social skills

Here is a map outlining the proposed territorial division by the Hoare–Laval Pact.

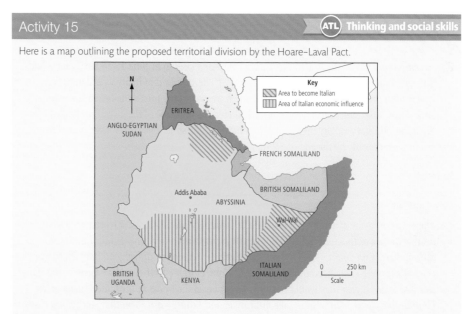

1. In groups, study the map and compare it with the map of Abyssinia in 1934 on page 101. Discuss the potential impact of the Hoare–Laval proposal on both Italy and Abyssinia.

Impact of the invasion

Effects on Abyssinia and Italy

Abyssinia was devastated by the Italian campaign and eventually surrendered in 1936. In May that year, Haile Selassie went into exile in Britain, from where he continued to campaign for the liberation of his nation. Two months later, the League abandoned its economic sanctions on Italy.

Activity 16 — ATL Thinking and communication skills

Here is an extract from a speech by Emperor of Abyssinia Haile Selassie to the League of Nations, 30 June 1936.

> The very refinement of barbarism consisted in carrying ravage and terror into the most densely populated parts of the territory, the points farthest removed from the scene of hostilities. The object was to scatter fear and death over a great part of the Ethiopian territory. These fearful tactics succeeded. Men and animals succumbed. The deadly rain that fell from the aircraft made all those whom it touched fly shrieking with pain. All those who drank the poisoned water or ate the infected food also succumbed in dreadful suffering. In tens of thousands, the victims of the Italian mustard gas fell [...] I... come myself to bear witness against the crime perpetrated against my people and give Europe a warning of the doom that awaits it, if it should bow before the accomplished fact.

1. With reference to its origin, purpose, and content, analyse the value and limitations of this source for a historian studying the effects of the invasion of Abyssinia on its population.

The Italian occupation had a significant impact on Abyssinia. Resistance groups fought the Italian forces with guerrilla tactics and the fighting extended throughout the country, impacting on the lives of Abyssinian civilians. Italy opened concentration camps for the prisoners of war, which also kept opponents to Italian rule. Consistent with the introduction of racial policies in Italy, Abyssinia became a racially segregated country.

When Italy entered World War II in June 1940 it began attacking British colonies in Africa but its success was short-lived; Abyssinia was liberated from Italian rule in 1941.

As for Italy, in May 1936, King Victor Emanuel III was proclaimed emperor of Abyssinia. Abyssinia, Eritrea, and Italian Somaliland became known as Italian East Africa. Although Abyssinia provided Mussolini with a domestic triumph, the cost of war had an impact on the Italian economy; Italian troops continued to clash with the guerrillas and were unable to go home; Abyssinia did not offer Italy the raw materials it had been after; and the resettlement projects failed: disappointed by the conditions in Abyssinia, many Italians soon returned home.

Effects on international relations and the Spanish Civil War

The invasion of Abyssinia proved that collective security was ineffective against international aggression, and it confirmed that the League of Nations was unable to solve disputes involving the bigger nations. Britain and France no longer perceived Mussolini as a leader who could be trusted, and Italy sank into a kind of diplomatic isolation. That being said, German–Italian relations developed: partly as a response to Italy's isolation, Mussolini drew closer to Hitler and both leaders signed the Rome–Berlin Axis in October 1936 (for more, see page 131). In 1936, Italy and Germany both intervened in the Spanish Civil War on the side of the Nationalists.

Haile Selassie returned to Abyssinia after the country was liberated by the British in 1941. He ruled his country with mixed results, attempting to modernize it but refusing to grant citizens political rights. In 1974, a *coup d'état* ousted Haile Selassie from power. He died, in rather unclear circumstances, the following year.

The Spanish Civil War

The Spanish Civil War (1936–39) started as a military revolt against the Popular Front coalition government by General Francisco Franco, who led the Nationalists against the Republicans. Both groups appealed to foreign help for their cause. The Nationalists were supported by Nazi Germany and Fascist Italy, while the Soviet Union supported the Republicans who were also aided by foreigners joining the International Brigades. The war came to an end with a Nationalist victory in March 1939.

This poster from 1937 reads: 'Stand up against the Italian invasion of Spain!'

CHALLENGE YOURSELF

 Research, social, and self-management skills

1. Divide the class into groups. Each group should make a brief presentation on one of the causes leading to the outbreak of the Spanish Civil War:
    a. The weakness of the Republicans
    b. The role of the Spanish army
    c. The role of the Church
    d. Economic causes
    e. Regionalism

2. Each group should find out about the role of one the following in the conflict:
    a. Italy
    b. Germany
    c. France
    d. Britain
    e. The Soviet Union
    f. The International Brigades

3. Discuss the reasons why the Spanish Civil War is often referred to as a 'dress rehearsal for World War II'. To what extent do you consider this civil war a contributing factor to the move to global war?

This photograph shows Mussolini on board a train, bidding farewell to Hitler after a meeting in 1937. By then, both leaders had become allies through the Rome–Berlin Axis and the Anti-Comintern Pact.

An Italian parade welcoming Mussolini after an official visit to Germany. You can see a banner in the background that reads: 'Europe will be Fascist'. What is the message of this image?

Changing diplomatic alliances

Despite supporting opposing sides in the Spanish Civil War and despite Italy allying with Nazi Germany, an opportunity to improve Italo-British relations after Abyssinia arose. Throughout the 1930s, Britain was reluctant to fight against Italy, given that Germany and Japan were both viewed as more significant threats to British interests. Under the Gentlemen's Agreement of January 1937, Italy and Britain pledged themselves to maintain the territorial status quo in the Mediterranean.

Later that year, however, Italy made a number of decisions that contradicted the Gentlemen's Agreement:

- Mussolini increased Italy's military presence in Africa, threatening both British and French colonies as well as Spain. Moreover, he announced that he would not withdraw from Spain until Franco defeated the Republicans. This was a source of concern as it threatened to change the status quo in the Mediterranean.
- Mussolini made another attempt to approach Germany by joining the Anti-Comintern Pact (1937), an anti-communist alliance.
- Italy left the League of Nations by the end of the year.
- Italy signed another treaty of economic cooperation with Yugoslavia that guaranteed mutual neutrality in case of a conflict. This treaty threatened France, which had been up until that point the leading great power in the Balkans through its alliance with the Little Entente countries.

Russian writer Leo Tolstoy believed that great men did not shape history according to their own will; rather, he thought their actions were shaped by the course of history. In what ways does Tolstoy's view shape our thinking on the changing diplomatic alignments in Europe between 1936 and 1937? For example, were Mussolini's decisions in this period led by his political views, or was he responding to an international context beyond his control? What are the implications of Tolstoy's view for the study of history?

To find out more about the works of Tolstoy and the circumstances in which he made the point above, see *Building Tomorrow's Leaders Today: On Becoming a Polymath Leader* by Michael A. Genovese, Routledge, 2014, p. 7.

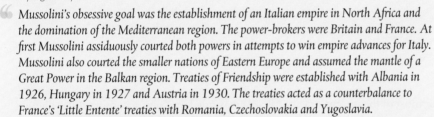

Activity 17

ATL Thinking, research, and social skills

Source A

The extract below is taken from Reynolds M. Salerno's book, *Vital Crossroads: Mediterranean Origins of the Second World War, 1935–1940* (2002). In order to produce this work, the author carried out extensive research in 28 archives in five different countries.

> *Italy's new relationship with Yugoslavia, however, represented an overt attempt to install Italian preeminence in the Adriatic region at France's expense. The potential loss of Yugoslavia as a French ally meant not only the sudden evaporation of France's influence in the Balkans but also the beginning of the end for France's network of central European allies and the eastern front – one of the most important deterrents to German aggression. By defecting from the French-sponsored Little Entente, Yugoslavia could indirectly destroy France's relationship with Czechoslovakia and Romania.*

Source B

Here is an extract from *The Second World War: Ambitions to Nemesis* (2004) by educator and writer Bradley Lightbody.

> *Mussolini's obsessive goal was the establishment of an Italian empire in North Africa and the domination of the Mediterranean region. The power-brokers were Britain and France. At first Mussolini assiduously courted both powers in attempts to win empire advances for Italy. Mussolini also courted the smaller nations of Eastern Europe and assumed the mantle of a Great Power in the Balkan region. Treaties of Friendship were established with Albania in 1926, Hungary in 1927 and Austria in 1930. The treaties acted as a counterbalance to France's 'Little Entente' treaties with Romania, Czechoslovakia and Yugoslavia.*

1. In groups, find out why the Balkans was strategically important to France.

2. Chose one country in the Balkans and research its situation in 1937. For example: What type of ruling government did it have? What political and social issues did it confront? Why was this country viewed as an important strategic ally to the West?

3. Why, according to Source A, were Italy's relations with Yugoslavia a source of concern for France?

4. Compare and contrast what Sources A and B reveal about relations between Italy and France before the outbreak of World War II.

The invasion of Albania, 1939

In 1912, Albania declared its independence from the Ottoman Empire. However, after World War I many Albanians continued to live outside the borders of their own country (in Greece, for example). Albania had limited arable land but had some valuable resources, such as oil and minerals. Albania attracted the interest of a number of countries: Yugoslavia and Greece, two neighbours that shared borders with Albania, were both keen to expand their territories into Albania; France and Italy, two rival powers in the Balkans, were aware of the importance of Albania for the control of the Mediterranean. Unsurprisingly, Albania was involved in several border clashes with both Yugoslavia and Greece. It was the conflict with the latter that led to the Corfu Incident, as manipulated by Mussolini (see page 95).

Mussolini wanted to control Albania for a number of reasons:

• He wanted control of the oil and mineral deposits to assist in his policy of autarky.
• Albania had access to the Mediterranean Sea, which he saw as his 'Italian lake'.
• Control of Albania would give Italy a foothold in the Balkans and would keep Yugoslavia in check.

A map of the Balkans in 1920.

For most of the interwar years Albania was ruled by Zogu, a conservative chieftain who, with Mussolini's assistance, became King Zog I of Albania in 1928. Since 1925, Mussolini had exercised a policy of economic and political penetration of Albania that ended with its annexation in 1939.

In 1926 and 1927, Italy and Albania signed the Treaties of Tirana, establishing Italy's political influence over Albania in exchange for Italian economic assistance that contributed to keeping Zogu in power. Italy gained access to Albanian minerals, founded the Albanian national bank, and controlled several areas of the transport industry. According to the pact of 1927, Italy also gained control over the Albanian armed forces which continued to grow into the next decade.

During the Great Depression, Mussolini applied pressure on Albania to further increase Italy's control of the country. In the 1930s, Italy gained further access to the much-needed Albanian oil and, in exchange, gave King Zog new loans. In 1934, Mussolini even sent warships into Albania to pressure King Zog into accepting further demands – a potential crisis that was averted with help from Britain: wishing to keep in good terms with the British, Mussolini withdrew his navy.

Finally, in April 1939, Mussolini ordered the invasion of Albania and the deposition of King Zog (who fled the country). King Victor Emmanuel of Italy succeeded Zog as the new king of Albania.

Reasons for Mussolini's invasion of Albania

Mussolini had a number of reasons to invade Albania in 1939. Firstly, he wanted a military alliance with Hitler, and saw the situation with Albania as an opportunity to showcase the strength of the Italian military (even though, as with Abyssinia, the Albanian forces at the time were no match for the Italians anyway). Secondly, by the time of the invasion in 1939, Hitler had regained control of the Rhineland, annexed Austria, received part of Czechoslovakia at the Munich Conference, and moved into the Czech provinces of Bohemia and Moravia (you will find out more about these events in later chapters) – Mussolini was therefore determined to demonstrate that he could also build a Mediterranean empire. Thirdly, the fact that the world's eyes were on Hitler's movements and the growing tensions between Germany and Poland meant Mussolini could invade Albania without much intervention from the other nations.

Activity 18   (ATL) Thinking and communication skills

Source A

This photograph shows Italian military troops entering Tirana, the capital of Albania, in April 1939.

Source B

Laura Fermi (1907–1977) was an Italian-born writer and political activist. Below is an extract from her book *Mussolini* (1966).

> The reaction of the Western democracies to the Albanian coup was mild, as was to be expected after the moderate reactions to German action in Bohemia and Moravia. Mussolini took upon himself the task of reassuring Greece and England. In his early years in government he had once shelled and occupied the island of Corfu. Now both Greece and her ally, England, feared that the occupation of Albania meant a second occupation of Corfu, if not an invasion of Greece. Furthermore, the British thought the occupation of Albania a breach of promise, for with a gentlemen's agreement in January, 1937, and an Easter pact in the spring of the following year, Italy and England had pledged to respect the status quo in the Mediterranean. The foreign office, however, seemed to be satisfied with Mussolini's explanation that since Albania had been in the Italian sphere of influence for many years, occupation had not changed matters at all.

Source C

Zara Steiner is a British historian specializing in 20th-century European and US histories. Below is an extract from her book *The Lights That Failed: European International History, 1919–1933* (2005).

> [Austen] Chamberlain accepted Mussolini's 1926 treaty with Zogu, the crafty Albanian leader, preferring the Italians to the Yugoslavs as underwriters in Albania. There were, however, limits to his willingness to countenance Italian revisionism. Chamberlain's first loyalty was to Briand, and he had no wish to see major conflicts in the Balkans. He took umbrage [offence] at the second Treaty of Tirana in 1927 and the reduction of Albania to the status of an Italian protectorate [...] Chamberlain's relations with the Duce turned cool. There was an attempted reconciliation between the two men, but Anglo-Italian relations were not restored to their former standing before the Labour victory in London in 1929.

Extract from Zara Steiner, *The Lights That Failed: European International History, 1919–1933*, Oxford University Press, 2005, p. 499

1. To what extent can Source A help you to understand why it took Italy a week to take total control of Albania?

2. Compare and contrast what Sources B and C reveal about Britain's reaction to the Italian invasion of Albania.

Results of the invasion

As you have seen, Italy had already had access to minerals, oils, and other Albanian resources since the late 1920s, so in this regard, the invasion did not make a significant contribution to the acquisition of resources for Italy. However, Mussolini did have fortifications built on Albanian territory. These came into use when, in October 1940, he launched an invasion of Greece from Albania – an attack that turned out to be a disaster for Italy.

A review of Chapter 4

This chapter has focused on Italian expansion up to 1937. It has discussed the effects of World War I and the peace treaties on Italy, and the rise to power of Benito Mussolini and the Fascist Party, including the aims of Mussolini's foreign policy. It has also analysed the methods used to achieve these aims, including the role played by domestic policies as well as the international response to events in Europe.

Activity 19   (ATL) **Self-management and communication skills**

Now that you have read through this chapter, answer the following question:

Using the sources in this chapter and your own knowledge, evaluate the contributions of Mussolini's foreign policy to the move to global war between 1930 and 1937.

This is very similar to the kind of mini essay that you would get asked to write in the fourth question of the Prescribed Subject exam paper. It isn't a good idea to try and start your exam by answering this question first (even though it carries the highest marks). Always answer the questions in the order they are written in the exam: in other words, start with the first question and work your way through to the fourth. By doing so, you become familiar with the sources and are better prepared to tackle this mini-essay question. Don't forget that the question asks you to include references to the material in the sources as well as your own knowledge. To write a good answer, you need to include references to all the sources (there are always four sources included in the exam), and use your own knowledge as well as the sources to support your argument. You can use your own knowledge to either support the message of a particular source, to argue against it, or even to start a new argument. Allow yourself around 20 minutes of the exam time to answer the fourth question – and don't forget to plan your answer before you start writing. Always include a brief introduction and conclusion that address what the question is asking.

Remember, your answer should only focus on the specific time period of the question. For this particular question, a discussion on Corfu and Fiume is therefore not relevant. You will not have time to discuss everything you have studied in this chapter, but here are some relevant points you may wish to focus on:

• Mussolini's aims in foreign policy
• Italy's diplomatic alliances and treaties signed
• the invasion of Abyssinia and Italy's withdrawal from the League of Nations
• the invasion of Albania.

Are there other points you could add to this list?

To access websites relevant to this chapter, go to www.pearsonhotlinks. com, search for the book title or ISBN, and click on 'Chapter 4'.

05

Chapter 5: German expansion and its consequences

When Adolf Hitler came to power in 1933, Germany had been forced to accept responsibility for the outbreak of World War I and to sign the Treaty of Versailles (1919); the country suffered territorial losses, it was asked to pay a colossal amount in reparations, and it had been disarmed. By 1940, however, Hitler had violated most of the terms of the treaty; Germany was in control of Denmark, Norway, France, Belgium, Luxembourg, and the Netherlands.

This chapter focuses on the causes, events, and responses to German expansion between 1933 and 1940. In particular, it examines:

- the aims of Nazi foreign policy and their impact on domestic issues
- German expansion and the international response between 1933 and 1937.

Adolf Hitler was a charismatic leader with a notable talent for public speaking. These qualities proved crucial in helping him gain support for his rule of Germany. In what ways do you think such qualities may have also helped increase support for his foreign policy?

5.1 Causes of German expansion, 1933–37

In order to understand how and why Germany contributed to the move to global war between 1933 and 1940, we need to return to the end of World War I and look at the impact of the Treaty of Versailles on Germany.

Historical background

In 1914, Germany was preparing to fight a short and successful war in order to expand its territory and consolidate its position as the most powerful country in continental Europe. However, the war shattered these plans and Germany emerged from it not only defeated but also transformed. Kaiser Wilhelm II abdicated, a democratic republic was proclaimed, and Germany signed an armistice ending the war on 11 November 1918. In January 1919, the Paris Peace Conference was convened with the aim of addressing both the problems that had led to the outbreak of war as well as those created by its effects. The peace treaties imposed a series of territorial changes that affected most of Europe, with the collapse of the Russian, German, Austro-Hungarian, and Turkish empires leading to the creation of a number of multi-racial nations, such as Czechoslovakia, Poland, and Yugoslavia.

Germany's grievances related to the Treaty of Versailles

The Germans initially thought that the peace treaty would be based on **Wilson's Fourteen Points**, which had constituted the basis for negotiations leading to the armistice. However, Germany was presented with a peace treaty that made it fully responsible for the war; the treaty took away territory both in Europe as well as overseas; it limited the size of German military forces. How and why did this happen?

The widespread opinion outside Germany in 1919 was that responsibility for the start of the war rested with Germany and its allies. This was also the view adopted at the

Peace Conference: holding Germany responsible for the start of the war provided the legal argument to make Germany pay for its cost. However, because the final figure for this was only decided in 1921, Germany claimed that it had been made to sign a **'blank cheque'** when it signed the Treaty of Versailles in 1919. By holding Germany responsible, the conference also stripped away the rights of the German delegates to take part in the treaty negotiations. The Germans therefore felt that the Treaty of Versailles was a 'dictated peace'.

Other decisions made during the treaty negotiations included the following:

- Germany was disarmed to the lowest point compatible with internal security. It was allowed to keep six battleships (made obsolete by the new dreadnought battleships) and 100,000 soldiers. German **conscription** was banned.
- Germany was forbidden from creating a union (Anschluss) with German-speaking Austria, which was now a separate nation from Hungary.
- Germany lost all of its overseas colonies as well as its trading rights in China and Egypt.
- Germany's frontiers in Europe were adjusted.

Activity 1

 Social, research, self-management, and communication skills

Divide the class into groups. Using the map of Europe in 1919 on page 90, each group should pick a country from the list below, to find out its status in 1914 and how it had been affected by the peace treaties by 1919.

- Alsace and Lorraine
- The Rhineland
- The Saar
- The Polish corridor
- Danzig
- East Prussia
- Eupen-Malmedy
- Upper Silesia
- Northern Schleswig
- Memel

Now read the following sources and answer the questions.

Source A

Below is an extract from *The Origins of World War II*, a book by Keith Eubank, a US professor of history.

> *Thus, the treaty of Versailles, contrary to the beliefs of early critics, left Germany's potential strength virtually untouched. In population, resources, and size, Germany was still the largest nation in Central Europe, except for the Soviet Union. And the war had not turned its soil into a wasteland as it had with French and Belgian land. Germany remained the industrial powerhouse of Europe despite the loss of iron ore from Lorraine and Saar coal. Although defeated, Germany suffered less damage in economic and human resources than the other major European belligerents. In spite of defeat, Germany remained the greatest economic power in Europe.*

Keith Eubank (ed.), *The Origins of World War II*, 3rd ed., Harlan Davidson, 2004, p. 12

Source B

John Hiden is a British historian. The following is an extract from his book on the history of the Weimar Republic and the Third Reich.

> Germans felt that their territorial losses were harsh. As a result of the Treaty of Versailles more than 6 million Germans were left outside the new borders of the Weimar Republic. In the process 65,000 square kilometers of land were lost to the new Germany. The fact that union between Germany and Austria was expressly forbidden by the Treaty of Versailles was also regarded with great bitterness since popular opinion in both countries was then running in favour of Anschluss. Territorial debits were completed with the loss of Germany's colonies […] To the reparations burden must be added the depletion of Germany's economic base through the loss of territories and possessions. A calculation of lost resources would include 14.6 per cent of Germany's arable land, 74.5 per cent of its iron ore, 68.1 per cent of its zinc ore, 26 per cent of coal production, as well as the potash mines and textile industries of Alsace.

John Hiden, *Republican and Fascist Germany: Themes and Variations in the History of Weimar and the Third Reich, 1918–45*, Longman, 1996, p. 15

1. According to Source A, what was the impact of the Treaty of Versailles on Germany?
2. According to Source B, why did the Germans think their territorial losses were harsh?
3. Compare and contrast the two sources in terms of what they reveal about the impact of the Treaty of Versailles on Germany.

It was not only the German citizens who were outraged at the terms of Versailles. Even within the new government there were disagreements among its members as to whether Germany should sign. In the end, on 28 June 1919, Germany signed the Treaty of Versailles, though this affected the new republic negatively in many ways: a large part of the German population felt disillusioned and did not support the new regime; the government was held responsible for accepting what was considered a humiliating peace, one that few were prepared to abide by.

Some sources (such as Source B) offer many relevant points. However, since you are working within a time limit, you cannot mention all of them; instead, you need to be selective about which points to mention in your answer. One way of deciding how many points to include is to consider the marks available for the question. In the cases of Questions 1 and 2 in this activity, they are similar to what you get in part A of the first question in your exam paper, which means they are worth 3 marks each.

Activity 2   (ATL) Thinking skills

This photo shows a mass demonstration taking place in Berlin on 3 August 1919. The placard reads 'down with the violence of peace'. It was organized by the Independents and the Communists against the peace terms of the Treaty of Versailles.

1. What does this image reveal about the Germans' feelings towards the treaty?

CHALLENGE YOURSELF

 Social, research, and thinking skills

1. In groups:
   a. find out who the 'November criminals' were and why they were called that.
   b. explain the origins and significance of the 'stab-in-the-back' myth.
2. Divide the class into two groups. One group should argue that the Treaty of Versailles was too harsh on Germany. The other group should argue that Germany was not completely weakened by the treaty.

CHALLENGE YOURSELF

 Research and communication skills

In pairs, find out about the main political parties in Germany after World War I. Which ones were the most committed to democracy? Which ones challenged the system? Provide one example of an uprising from the right and one example of an uprising from the left. Show how the Weimar Republic dealt with these challenges.

This German housewife is using millions of deutsche marks (the German currency at the time) to light a stove in 1923. What does this image tell you about the problems of living under hyperinflation?

The Weimar Republic and the rise of Hitler

The Treaty of Versailles was not the only challenge facing the Weimar Republic. There were also other problems in Germany at the end of the war. The change of political system from monarchy to republic did not come about as a result of the German population's desire, but was decided by politicians. In November 1919, the kaiser abdicated and left the country. Almost overnight, Germany became a democratic republic as a result of a 'revolution from above'. The republic had an elected president who was the head of state. He commanded the army and could appoint or dismiss the chancellor. In emergencies, the president could suspend the constitution and rule by decree.

The Weimar constitution was very democratic in theory but this made it difficult to have political stability. Members of the Reichstag (parliament) were elected by universal suffrage. The multi-party democracy meant that no single party ever gained a majority of votes in the Weimar Republic. Coalitions were formed but were unstable and quickly dissolved over disagreements on policies.

Attempts to bring down the republic came both from the left and the right. The influence of the Bolshevik Revolution and the rise of unrest from the left took the form of waves of strikes and violent protests, some of which threatened to overthrow the republic. Opposition from the right came from the armed forces resenting the peace treaties, and the industrialists who complained about economic instability and who, like landowners, considered the government was not doing enough to control the left. They were joined by the *Freikorps*. The challenges from both left and right contributed to a negative perception of the republic's ability to deal with crisis situations. However, at the time neither the right nor the left were strong enough to overthrow the republic by themselves.

In 1923, Germany ceased the payment of reparations. France and Belgium invaded the Ruhr to extract payment in kind. The German government called for **passive resistance**. This meant that the workers in the Ruhr went on a general strike and production came to a halt. The government continued to pay the workers' salaries and compensated the industrialists for the loss. These decisions put the economy under great pressure and led to **hyperinflation.** The crisis was blamed on the French and Belgian occupation, the Treaty of Versailles, and reparations, but also on earlier governments' overspending and budget deficit.

When the Wall Street Crash hit the United States in 1929, Germany lost access to US loans and investments. The Great Depression caused massive unemployment in the country. Agricultural prices collapsed and producers went bankrupt. Unlike 1923, the main problem was not inflation but unemployment. But, like in 1923, the crisis showed that the German government could not respond effectively and that politicians were divided as to how best to tackle such problems. By the time the government began to take measures to promote employment, one of every three German workers was already out of work.

It is very difficult to say whether the Weimar Republic collapsed as a result of the economic crisis, which had deepened the political and social problems, or whether it would have been able to survive – like in 1923 – had Adolf Hitler not entered the political scene.

Impact of Nazism on Germany's foreign policy

Adolf Hitler began his political career after fighting for Germany in World War I. Infuriated by the armistice and the Treaty of Versailles, he joined the newly formed German Workers' Party in 1919 and became its leader in 1921. By then, the party was known as the Nationalist Socialist German Workers' Party and had made public a 25-Point Programme which combined nationalist and socialist principles with a strong element of anti-Semitism.

Activity 3	(ATL) Thinking and communication skills

Source A

This 1920s Nazi Party election poster is entitled 'One Can Only Combat Terror from the Left with Sharper Terror'.

 Prescribed Subject 3 does not specifically focus on the Treaty of Versailles and the Weimar Republic period. However, you may find the above section useful when answering the fourth question in the paper, as this question usually focuses on the key concepts in history (for example, causation, continuity, and change) that require your understanding of the background to the move to global war.

Hitler making a public speech.

 The Nazi Party had approximately 55,000 members in 1923. It had within it a paramilitary organization called the *Sturmabteilung*, which engaged in violent clashes with members of parties of the left and was used to intimidate opponents.

Source B

Below is an extract from the Nazi 25-Point Programme.

1. *We demand the unification of all Germans in the Greater Germany on the basis of the right of self-determination of peoples.*

2. *We demand equality of rights for the German people in respect to the other nations; abrogation of the peace treaties of Versailles and St Germain.*

3. *We demand land and territory (colonies) for the sustenance of our people, and colonization for our surplus population.*

1. Study Source A. To whom do you think the poster appealed and why?

2. With reference to its origin, purpose, and content, analyse the value and limitations of Source B for a historian studying the aims of Nazi foreign policy.

3. Find out which territorial clauses of the Treaty of St Germain the Nazis were opposed to and why.

 Thinking skills

Go back to the section in this case study that addresses Mussolini's March on Rome. To what extent could it be claimed that the Beer Hall Putsch was inspired by Mussolini's March on Rome in 1922?

Following the invasion of the Ruhr, Hitler tried to seize power in what became known as the Munich Putsch or Beer Hall Putsch. The aim was to seize control of the local government and then march to Berlin. The Putsch failed and Hitler was tried and sentenced to prison. It was during his sentence that he wrote *Mein Kampf*, a book that recorded his aims, particularly in foreign policy. Like the 25-Point Programme, *Mein Kampf* included strong elements of nationalism, anti-Semitism, and contempt for the peace treaties.

This photo shows Adolf Hitler (to the left of the image, standing higher up than the other onlookers) in 1926 reviewing *Sturmabteilung* (SA) troops carrying a banner reading 'Death to **Marxism**'. Who do you think SA parades appealed to and why?

After the failure of the Putsch, Hitler decided he would try to rise to power using the parliamentary system of the republic. But if the Nazis were to be voted into power, then they had to extend their basis of support by becoming more pragmatic and flexible. Hitler claimed he would end unemployment and re-establish law and order. He promised to return to German traditional national values, protect Germany from Bolshevism, and end the Treaty of Versailles.

CHALLENGE YOURSELF

(ATL) Thinking, research, and social skills

You now have some background on Germany's problems after World War I. In groups, research how and why Hitler came to power. You may wish to consider some of the following questions:

1. How did Hitler propose to solve the problems facing Germany after World War I?
2. Which social groups felt represented by the Nazis and why?
3. Explain how Hitler came to power by analysing the events leading up to his appointment as chancellor in January 1933.

What did Nazism propose in foreign policy?

Both the 25-Point Programme and *Mein Kampf* can help historians understand the Nazis' aims in foreign policy. To what extent are these documents useful for understanding Hitler's aims? (Later in this chapter you will have the opportunity to study another relevant historical document, the Hossbach Memorandum of 1937.)

Some historians, like K Hildebrand, have argued that Hitler had a plan, and that documents such as *Mein Kampf* are the blueprint (see *The Foreign Policy of the Third Reich*, 1973). AJP Taylor, on the other hand, believed that Hitler's foreign policy had not been planned in advance and that it was the result of different internal pressures, such as those created by the German economy. He also claimed Hitler took advantage of opportunities presented to him by external factors, such as the role played by other statesmen (see *The Origins of the Second World War*, 1961). Somewhere in between these interpretations we find Allan Bullock's explanation stating that Hitler had set out his aims in *Mein Kampf* but that he also used opportunist methods to achieve them (*Hitler: A Study in Tyranny*, revised edition, 1962, p. 315).

As you work through this chapter, think of these different interpretations. Which one do you consider best explains Hitler's foreign policy?

What were Hitler's aims?

Hitler was determined to make Germany a great power again. To do this, he believed he had to achieve the following:

Overthrow the Treaty of Versailles

Like many Germans, Hitler considered the Treaty of Versailles a humiliation and was determined to have it repealed. But this was impossible as long as Germany continued to be disarmed. One of the aims in Nazi foreign policy was therefore to rearm Germany so that it could regain any territory lost as a consequence of Versailles.

A 'Greater Germany'

The Treaty had left Germans living outside its borders, in countries such as Austria, Czechoslovakia, and Poland. The incorporation of these into the Third Reich would create a 'Greater Germany', formed only by those of common Aryan origin.

Lebensraum

Nazism did not only want to restore the map of Germany to its pre-1918 frontiers. *Lebensraum* (meaning 'living space' in English) was based on the assumption that post-war Germany was overpopulated and would not be able to feed its own people in the short term. Hitler therefore aimed to gain more 'living space' by expanding towards Eastern Europe and into the Soviet Union. This would also help to achieve the destruction of Bolshevism, an enemy of Nazism.

Lebensraum was also based on the idea that the Aryan race was superior to other races, such as the Slavs and the Jews. Hitler claimed that, as a master race, the Aryans had a right to more territory and resources at the expense of what he called 'subhuman' races.

Activity 4

 **ATL** **Research and social skills**

1. In pairs, find out more information about the racial beliefs of Nazism in 1933. How did they influence the aims of Nazi foreign policy?

How did Hitler plan to achieve these aims?

Germany was in no condition to challenge the Treaty of Versailles by force in 1933. In order to achieve his aims, Hitler needed to consolidate his power, strengthen the economy, and rearm the country.

He destroyed German democracy by suspending constitutional civil rights with the Decree for the Protection of the People and State. He was given the right to pass decrees under the terms of the Enabling Law, which meant that he could bypass the Reichstag and introduce laws without its approval. When President Hindenburg died in 1934, Hitler combined the offices of president and chancellor and took on the title of führer (leader).

With the policy of *Gleichschaltung* (coordination), Hitler consolidated his power further. All political parties except the Nazis were declared illegal and Germany became a single-party state. Trade unions were dissolved and were replaced by the Nazi German Labour Front. New local governments were set up and Germany became a centralized regime with no local elections. German organizations such as the Hitler Youth were created to work for the Nazi cause.

In order to eliminate critics and consolidate his rule, Hitler purged the army as well as the SA which, as you may remember, had been formed during the early days of the Nazi Party. On the death of President Hindenburg in August 1934, the army was made to swear a new oath of allegiance directly to Hitler rather than to Germany. A Ministry for Public Enlightenment and Propaganda was created and controlled the media. Education was reformed on Nazi principles and children were indoctrinated. Mass rallies were frequently used by Hitler to show strength and encourage a personality cult.

Nazi Germany became a police state. The *Schutzstaffel* (more commonly known as the SS), which had started as Hitler's personal protection force, and the *Gestapo* (secret police) were used for the repression of political opponents. People were encouraged to denounce each other. Concentration camps were created for political prisoners and other 'enemies of the state' such as Jews.

Activity 5 — ATL Thinking skills

Source A

This photo shows Hitler and members of his paramilitary forces attending a Nazi event in 1933.

Source B

This is a propaganda poster for the Nazi Germany Labour Service. The text reads: 'We equip body and soul'.

1. Study Source A. What is the message conveyed by the image?
2. Study Source B. What is the message conveyed by the poster?

Impact of domestic issues on Germany's foreign policy

Hitler wanted the rearmament of the country. However, in 1933, the most urgent problem was that of unemployment. As a result of the Great Depression, millions of German citizens were out of jobs. It became a priority of the Nazi government to solve this situation and ensure political stability. To reduce unemployment, the Nazis executed a large programme of public works funded by the government and served by the National Labour Service. This organization provided work for unemployed men who were transferred around the country and were subjected to military discipline. Public projects such as the renovation of the city of Berlin and irrigation works in the countryside were executed. But one of most significant features was the building of new motorways to connect the German territory more efficiently. During the war, they ensured the quick transfer of troops across the German territory.

This photograph, taken in 1938, shows Hitler inspecting the new Volkswagen Beetle, which he called the 'Strength-through-Joy Car' ('*Kraft durch Freude-Wagen*'). The man standing beside Hitler is the car's designer Ferdinand Porsche.

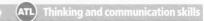

TOK

ATL **Thinking and communication skills**

Official statistics claimed unemployment decreased from 5.6 million (before the rise of the Nazis) to 1.6 million in 1936. These figures were used to show the success of the Nazis in addressing unemployment. However, unemployment figures in Nazi Germany did not include the Jews who had lost their jobs as a result of anti-Semitic policies. Nor did they include the communists and other opponents of the regime who had also lost their jobs. Unemployment figures were also reduced by the reintroduction of conscription in 1935 as many unemployed joined the armed forces. The creation of a vast state bureaucracy also contributed to reducing unemployment figures.

1. Is there any relationship between statistics and emotions? For example, how would you have interpreted these figures if you had been a newly employed German at the time? What would your opinion had been if you had been one of the 1.6 million who were still unemployed in 1936? How would you have interpreted them if you had been part of the 'invisible unemployed', those who were not included in statistics?
2. What do the above reflections say about the value and limitations of statistics for historians?

The Volkswagen Beetle, the people's car, was designed to become an affordable car for the average German citizen, who could purchase one by putting money into a government saving scheme. However, no one received their Beetle in the end and the money was put into the armament industry. What does this tell you about the relationship between domestic economic factors and German foreign policy?

Although unemployment was drastically reduced, this didn't necessarily lead to an improvement in the living standards or in the protection of workers' rights. Industrial production was centrally planned and factories were required to meet production targets. After 1935, the armament industry became a priority. If Germany was to expand, the country had to be prepared for war. As the Nazi government put it, guns were more important than butter and citizens were expected to make sacrifices.

In 1936, Hitler demanded that the economy be ready for war in four years. This four-year plan called for increased government planning and control of the economy. Hitler believed that if Germany had to fight a war, it had to become self-sufficient. The sanctions against Italy following the invasion of Abyssinia (see page 102) convinced Hitler that Germany needed to produce substitutes for any products that could be cut off by a blockade.

Activity 6

Source A

The following is an extract from Larry Leu's article 'Economic Policy in Nazi Germany: 1933–1945', published in the *Penn History Review*, October 2013.

> *From an economic point of view, the preparations for war practically meant that more resources should flow not toward consumption goods to raise the overall standard of living of the Germans, but to military production in order to be ready for the war. Hitler also made it clear that the private sector had to submit to the direct order of the economics ministry in order to fulfill his armament goal. In order to prevent a negative fallout of trade blockades resulting from war, Hitler also thought it was crucially important to build up domestic production and quickly conquer central and eastern Europe to take advantage of their raw materials.*

Source B

Here is Richard Overy, writing in the academic article 'An economy geared to war', published in *History Today*, November 2001.

> *Hitler's commitment to excessive levels of war preparation stemmed from his desire to turn Germany into a military and economic superpower before the rest of the world caught up. In 1938 and 1939 he authorised new military production programmes which were intended to achieve the superpower status he wanted. In 1939 the German economy was not yet ready for a major war. Germany was, of course, much more heavily armed in 1939 than in 1936, and was capable, as it turned out, of defeating Poland and France and expelling Britain from Europe in 1939 and 1940. But the large programmes of war production were not yet complete, some barely started.*

1. Compare and contrast what sources A and B reveal about the influence of Nazi foreign policy on the economy of Germany.

Student answer – Tim

Both sources state that Germany was preparing for war. Both sources indicate that she was doing this by increasing military production. Both show Hitler in command of the German economic plans.

However, Source A says that resources were not to be used to raise the living standards of the Germans while Source B states that Germany was not ready for war and continues to explain the impact this had on the Second World War.

Examiner's comments

Tim has identified similarities and differences between the sources but has not expanded on them. He offers three comparisons but does not use the sources as supporting evidence. It is good practice to show where in the sources you have identified the similarities you refer to. Think of how you would do that for this answer.

Contrasts in this answer are less clear and Tim seems to be referring to two different issues. Perhaps he could have argued, for example, that Source A states Germany needed to become self-sufficient in order to be prepared for war, whereas in Source B the German preparation for war seemed to have been limited to rearmament.

Activity 7

You now know about the causes of German expansion. Compare them with the causes of Italian expansion you have read about in Chapter 4. How similar are they? Where are the differences between the two sets of causes? As you move to the next section, consider whether or not German and Italian aggressive policies between 1933 and 1937 also show similarities.

5.2 German challenges and international response, 1933–37

This image shows Austrian citizens in Salzburg celebrating the Anschluss in March 1938. Many Germans living outside the borders of the Third Reich desired to be incorporated into Nazi Germany. However, there were also those who resisted it.

The League of Nations and the World Disarmament Conference

The League of Nations, together with Britain and the United States, set up a World Disarmament Conference (which first met in 1932) with the aim of promoting international disarmament to guarantee peace. Germany was a member of the conference and had also joined the League of Nations in 1926. However Hitler withdrew Germany from both organizations within months of becoming chancellor. How and why did this happen?

Germany had violated the disarmament clauses of Versailles even before Hitler came to power. In the 1920s, there were satellite armament production centres in the Netherlands and Sweden, which manufactured artillery and tanks for Germany. Also, by a secret clause in the 1922 Treaty of Rapallo between Germany and the Soviet Union, the latter had provided weapons and facilities for German military training in exchange for German army training of Soviet troops.

Hitler's stance at the conference was that the disarmament of Germany was unfair because it was the only disarmed nation, which put it in a vulnerable position. Germany's neighbours, such as France and Poland, had offensive weapons while Germany was not even permitted to build fortifications on its borders. Hitler claimed that Germany would continue to support disarmament if its neighbours also disarmed; if they refused to do so, then Germany should be allowed 'equality', that is, to rearm until parity with the rest of Europe was reached. When it became clear that neither of these options would be supported, Hitler, arguing that Germany had not been treated as an equal nation, announced the withdrawal from the Disarmament

Treaty of Rapallo

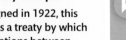

Signed in 1922, this was a treaty by which relations between Germany and the Soviet Union were re-established. It stated that both nations would renounce all the territorial and economic claims of World War I.

Conference and from the League of Nations. He had this decision ratified by 95 per cent of the German citizens in a **plebiscite**.

 Activity 8   (ATL) **Thinking and communication skills**

Below is an extract from an interview with Adolf Hitler in the British newspaper *The Daily Mail*, 19 October, 1933.

 We are manly enough to recognize that when one has lost a war, whether one was responsible for it or not, one has to bear the consequences. We have borne them, but it is intolerable for us as a nation of sixty-five millions that we should repeatedly be dishonoured and humiliated. We will put up with no more of this persistent discrimination against Germany. So long as I live I will never put my signature as a statesman to any contract which I could not sign with self-respect in private life. I will maintain this resolution, even if it means my ruin! For I will sign no document with a mental reservation not to fulfil it. What I sign, I will stand by. What I cannot stand by, I will not sign.

1. With reference to its origin, purpose, and content, analyse the value and limitations of this source for a historian studying Hitler's attitude towards the Disarmament Conference.

International response and early changing diplomatic alliances

Hitler's withdrawal from the Disarmament Conference and the League of Nations was a clear indication of his decision to rearm in the near future. Even though Hitler did not express this publicly in 1933, it was a decision that had been anticipated by other European countries – an eventuality they had to start preparing for.

The Four-Power Agreement to promote international cooperation, which in June 1933 had brought together Britain, France, Italy, and Germany (see page 99), ended. However, Britain could to some extent understand Germany's demands for equal treatment because both countries took the view that some revision of the Treaty of Versailles would be required to maintain peaceful relations in Europe. Moreover, Hitler's early successes in dealing with political and economic problems were interpreted as a sign that Nazi Germany could act as an effective barrier against the expansion of Bolshevism – which at the time was seen as more dangerous.

Poland – encircled by Germany and the Soviet Union, both of whom had claims on its territory – entered into a 10-year non-aggression pact with Germany in 1934. Both countries promised to solve their disputes peacefully. Poland temporarily eased its encirclement. Additionally, the pact helped to show Hitler as a statesman willing to work for peace. France feared German rearmament but could not find the support to prevent it in the international community. The non-aggression pact between Germany and Poland further weakened France's alliance with Poland of 1921. As for the Soviet Union, it suddenly found itself faced with the risk of a joint German–Polish attack. Stalin therefore responded by signing treaties of mutual assistance against German aggression with both France and Czechoslovakia in 1935.

  Thinking skills   (ATL)

Referring to Case Study 1, can you think of any other international event that influenced Germany's withdrawal from the League of Nations and the Disarmament Conference? Consider, for example, what was happening with the Japanese expansion in East Asia at the time. How, if at all, do you think these events influenced Hitler's policies as well as the international response to them?

> When analysing the content of a source, it may be useful to think not only in terms of *what* the source says, but also about *how* it says it. In the source above, Hitler's tone plays an important part in the ways the message is transmitted. How would you describe the tone? In what ways does considering the tone help you assess the value and limitations of the source?

A 1935 Nazi propaganda poster against French presence in the Saar. It reads: 'Get away from the German Saarland'. What is the message of this poster?

The Saar

The Saar was a German area rich in coal that France demanded to exploit in 1919 as reparations for its damaged mines in the north. Because it had a German population, the Saar was placed under the control of the League of Nations. A plebiscite for the population to decide whether they wanted to be French or German was held in January 1935. Ninety per cent of the Saar electorate voted for a return to Germany. Although this result had been expected given that the population was German, it was interpreted in Germany as an overwhelming success for Hitler.

In 1934, prior to the plebiscite, a book called the *Saaratlas* was published in Germany. It included facts and figures to support the idea that Germany was the dominating cultural and historical force in the Saar. For example, it showed the railway network extending into Germany but not France. What do you think was the message of this? How useful do you think this book would have been to a) people travelling there at the time and b) to historians today?

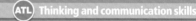

Activity 9   **ATL** **Thinking and communication skills**

Dr Michael Zalampas is an American historian. The following is taken from his book *Adolf Hitler and the Third Reich in American Magazines, 1923–1939*.

> *American magazines were divided in their interpretation of the events following the plebiscite. Newsweek reported Hitler was 'elated' by the election results. In 'a voice choked with emotion' Hitler had broadcast a speech thanking the Saar for its loyalty, expressing his appreciation to the League for its impartiality, and hinting that Germany might return to the League if given 'equality of armaments.' [...] Time, on the contrary, reported the Saar was in a turmoil. On January 28, Time reported Saarlanders were in 'a mad rush' to export French francs to the Netherlands, Switzerland, and France. In one week, 1,650,000,000 francs were shipped out of the Saar to avoid their conversion into marks. Time also asserted 'Saar Jews and other Saarlanders' were emigrating to France 'at a rate of one every 30 seconds.' Most of these refugees 'told tales of terrorism which could not be checked' as all non-Nazi newspapers had ceased publication.*

> **Dr Michael Zalampas, *Adolf Hitler and the Third Reich in American Magazines, 1923–1939*, Bowling Green State University Popular Press, 1989, p. 65**

1. What does this source reveal about the international response to events in the Saar?
2. With reference to its origin, purpose, and content, analyse the value and limitations of this source for a historian studying the United States' reaction to events in Europe.

Student answer - Mariko

The origin of this source is valuable in that it has been written by an American historian in 1989. The content of the book focuses on the Third Reich in American magazines and offers specific information on the US reaction to events in Europe, so it is valuable. It states that there were differing opinions regarding the events in the Ruhr and that can help a historian. The purpose is valuable because it aims at analysing the reaction of the US press in detail.

The limitation of the source is that the historian does not offer his own opinion and that it only focuses on the reaction of the press and not on US society. Also the book focuses only on the period up to 1939, so we do not know how US opinion may have changed after the outbreak of war.

Examiner's comments

Mariko's answer looks at the value of the source in more depth than its limitations. It is clear from the first paragraph that she has attempted to discuss the origin, purpose, and content. However, more detail is expected in the answer to this type of question. She could have explored further the value of studying a source that was published in 1989 (as opposed to contemporary accounts), for example, by considering the extent to which the writer would have benefited from hindsight and from gaining access to information that wouldn't have been available back in the 1920s and 1930s.

Furthermore, the limitations of the source are not discussed in depth. The only area Mariko has focused on is the content; she needs to be more explicit in her evaluation in terms of the source's origin and purpose.

German rearmament and international response

Encouraged by the success in the Saar plebiscite in 1935, Hitler declared that Germany would no longer observe the disarmament clauses imposed in 1919. Among the measures that followed, he introduced conscription and increased the budget for the military. The German aerial branch of the armed forces, the Luftwaffe, was created and quickly became the most modern in Europe.

Alarmed by Hitler's rearmament, Britain, France, and Italy formed the **Stresa Front** to resist potential German challenges to the European frontiers (see page 100). However, the Stresa Front was short-lived, as Britain entered a naval agreement with Germany that same year. Britain's partners in the Stresa Front interpreted the naval agreement as a betrayal of Britain's international commitments in exchange for its domestic security.

Anglo-German Naval Agreement

Under the terms of the Anglo-German Naval Agreement of June 1935, Germany was permitted to build a navy up to 35 per cent the size of the British Royal Navy. With this agreement, the British government aimed at allowing a revision of the terms of the Treaty of Versailles on German rearmament, while guaranteeing that the British navy would always be larger than the German navy. The agreement also showed that, at the time, Britain's priority was to obtain security without increasing armament spending.

Activity 10				ATL	Thinking, social, and research skills	

This table is taken from a book by John F Kennedy called *Why England Slept* (1940). It shows the defence expenditures in Europe between 1931 and 1936. Figures are indicated in millions of US dollars.

	1931	1932	1933	1934	1935	1936
France	694.8	509.2	678.8	582.7	623.8	716.4
Great Britain	449.9	426.1	455.5	480.6	595.6	846.9
Italy	272	270.6	241.2	263.7	778.1	870.8
USSR	280.8	285.5	309.5	1000	1640	2936.1
Germany	246.8	253.5	299.5	381.8	2600	2600

1. What does this source reveal about European rearmament between 1931 and 1936?
2. In groups, choose one of the countries in the source other than Germany and find out additional information as to how they responded to German rearmament. Share your findings with the rest of the class.

The remilitarization of the Rhineland

The Rhineland was an industrial area of German territory that became permanently demilitarized under the Treaty of Versailles. This meant that the Germans were forbidden to station military forces there, and a barrier was formed between France and Germany to protect the former. The Locarno Pact of 1925, which guaranteed the frontiers between France, Belgium, and Italy, reinforced these provisions (see page 96). Although Germany had agreed to respect the demilitarization of the Rhineland, in 1936 Hitler decided to reoccupy the area. There were a number of reasons why he felt this was necessary and why the time was right for him to do this:

Most exam papers include cartoons and photographs as their non-written sources. However, you should also be prepared to analyse and interpret statistical tables and graphs. When answering the question, it is important that you support every argument with specific examples drawn from the source. For instance, if you wanted to argue that the Soviet Union and Germany were the countries that increased their military defence the most, then you should make specific reference to the 1931 and the 1936 figures for both countries and compare them.

- Hitler's aim was to regain control of the Rhineland to secure the borders with France and protect the Ruhr, vital for German war supplies.
- Hitler had 'tested the waters': not only had he successfully announced rearmament he had also obtained British endorsement for the increase in the size of the German navy. By 1936, Hitler had also seen Japan and Italy successfully defy the League of Nations – he was therefore confident that the League would not intervene.
- Early attempts to control Hitler through international understandings, such as the Stresa Front, had collapsed, and Western nations were reluctant to go to war. Moreover, Britain and France were undergoing a tense period in their relations as a result of differences regarding Mussolini's invasion of Abyssinia.
- At a domestic level, Hitler wanted to exploit another international success.

To justify marching into the Rhineland, Hitler argued that the 1935 Franco-Soviet alliance – signed as a consequence of the non-aggression pact between Poland and Germany – had already broken the terms of Locarno and threatened Germany with encirclement. He therefore claimed that Germany was justified in seeking greater security for itself. At the same time, Hitler offered Belgium and France non-aggression pacts with Germany. This advocated the British view that Hitler was moving into Germany's own back garden and had no intentions to start a war. France, alone and with upcoming elections, did not resist either.

On 7 March 1936 Hitler sent a force of 20,000 men into the Rhineland.

German soldiers marching across the Cologne bridge, March 1936.

The remilitarization of the Rhineland was a huge success for Hitler. It was, however, another blow against Versailles and left France more exposed to German aggression. Hitler interpreted French inaction as tacit permission for Germany to move against France's allies in Eastern Europe. After all, if France had been unwilling to protect the Rhineland, how likely was it that it would protect its Eastern European allies?

TOK

Historical accounts of the events in the Rhineland are controversial. The most commonly held view is that Hitler had ordered his troops to retreat if their advance was met with resistance. However, Keith Eubank states that this was not the case and that Hitler had no intention of calling the German troops back if they were attacked (*The Origins of World War II*, 3rd ed., Harlan Davidson, 2004, p. 61).

Think of how historians work with conflicting interpretations. What type of research would help you find out which of these views is true?

Activity 11 **(ATL) Social, communication, and self-management skills**

Organize a class debate to discuss the question: *'Could Hitler's remilitarization of the Rhineland have been stopped?'*

Divide the class in two groups. Each group should find supporting evidence for their claim. The first group should argue that the Rhineland represented an opportunity for Britain and France to use force to intimidate Hitler and prevent further German aggression. The second group should support the idea that it was unfeasible to stop Hitler in 1936 because both Britain and France were undergoing national crises and were unable to risk war with Germany.

Changing diplomatic alignments in Europe – Mussolini and Hitler

Mussolini had already been in power for more than 10 years when Hitler became chancellor. There were many similarities between these two statesmen:

- They were both hostile to democratic systems and ruled as authoritarian leaders.
- They were both anti-communist.
- Mussolini was known as Il Duce and Hitler as Führer – terms that emphasized their belief in strong leadership.
- In foreign policy, they both desired a revision of the Treaty of Versailles.

Despite their ideological coincidences, their relationship started on cold terms. For instance, Hitler's early admiration for Mussolini was not reciprocated at first.

One reason for Mussolini's initial mistrust of Hitler was that he was suspicious of Hitler's intentions in Austria. An Austrian by birth, Hitler aspired to lead the Anschluss and integrate the German-speaking Austrians into the Reich. The murder of Dollfuss in 1934 (see page 100) brought Hitler and Mussolini into confrontation over the issue. As you may remember, Mussolini had mobilized his troops to the Brenner Pass to prevent a possible German advance. His decisive action gained him the respect of Britain and France. However, Mussolini's invasion of Abyssinia in 1935 (see page 102) and Hitler's invasion of the Rhineland significantly changed the diplomatic alignments in Europe.

Events in Abyssinia had led to tensions between Italy, Britain, and France; Hitler benefited from these as they ended the diplomatic encirclement of Germany. He was also quick to recognize Italian rights over Abyssinia, which helped improve relations between Germany and Italy. However, it was the Spanish Civil War (see page 107) that offered Germany and Italy the opportunity to work alongside one another for the first time in support of Franco's forces. Both countries agreed to oppose communism in Spain and to recognize Franco as the rightful head of the Spanish government.

Germany entered the Spanish Civil War for several reasons: First, it provided an opportunity to test the strength of its armed forces, especially the Luftwaffe. Second, if Franco won the war with Hitler's support, Germany would gain a new ally against France, which would then be encircled by Germany, Italy, and Spain. Third, the isolation of France was an important condition for a Nazi expansion into Eastern Europe as an isolated France would find it difficult to honour her alliances in the East. Finally, Spain's mineral resources (especially iron) could contribute to Germany's war efforts.

The Rome–Berlin Axis, a name coined by Mussolini for the alliance between Nazi Germany and Fascist Italy, was formally announced on 1 November 1936. This alliance recognized mutual Italian and German spheres of influence. For Italy, this was the Mediterranean Sea; for Germany, it was Central and Eastern Europe. The axis was followed by the **Anti-Comintern Pact**, which aimed to prevent the expansion of communism outside the Soviet Union. On page 47 you have read about the reasons why Japan signed the Anti-Comintern Pact with Germany in 1936. Italy joined the pact in 1937. In Europe, the pact was a way for Hitler and Mussolini to show themselves as protectors against communism, which was to be broken by Germany in 1939.

This is a watercolour drawing, entitled 'To Another – Asia and the Pacific Ocean!', of the US filmstrip *The Fruits of Aggression*. It depicts the Axis leaders dividing the world. What does this image suggest about the nature of the Anti-Comintern Pact?

1937 – A year of awareness?

On 5 November 1937, Hitler called for a secret meeting in which he presented his military leadership with what he considered should become the next steps in German foreign policy. We know about this meeting because of a document, the Hossbach Memorandum, written by Colonel Hossbach five days after the event, based on his personal records of the meeting. The memorandum revealed Hitler's concerns about Germany's need for *Lebensraum* and his decision to move against Austria and Czechoslovakia as well as into Eastern Europe at the expense of fighting a war against Britain and France. According to Hossbach, Hitler saw a need for Germany to act quickly due to concerns about its rivals catching up in terms of military development.

The Hossbach Memorandum has been used to support the idea that Hitler had a detailed plan for war; it seemed to suggest that Germany would no longer limit its foreign policy to the reversal of the Treaty of Versailles.

Activity 12 **Thinking and communication skills**

In pairs, read the three views below on the Hossbach Memorandum. Are these views in agreement regarding the value of the memorandum as a historical source? What arguments have been used to question its usefulness and reliability?

Source A

The following extract is from *Nazism 1919–1945, A History in Documents and Eyewitness Accounts, Volume II* by Jeremy Noakes (a professor of history) and Geoffrey Pridham (a professor of politics).

 1937 was also a 'year of awareness' in the sense that by the autumn Hitler appears to have concluded that time was not on Germany's side and that she must go onto the offensive sooner rather than later. For the problem was that, by embarking on a massive rearmament programme Germany had started an arms race. Moreover, because of her limited resources by comparison with her rivals it was a race she was bound to lose if she went on for any length of time. She thus came under growing pressure to act quickly, using her temporary superiority to expand her resources by plundering her neighbours.

Jeremy Noakes and Geoffrey Pridham, *Nazism 1919–1945, A History in Documents and Eyewitness Accounts*, Volume II, University of Exeter, 1988, p. 675

Source B

Here is an extract from *The Rise and Fall of the Third Reich. A History of Nazi Germany* by historian William Shirer.

 As evening darkened Berlin on the autumn day of November 5, 1937 – the meeting broke up at eight fifteen – the die was cast. Hitler had communicated his irrevocable decision to go to war. To the handful of men who would have to direct it there could no longer be any doubt. The dictator had said it all ten years before in Mein Kampf, had said that Germany must have Lebensraum in the East and must be prepared to use force to obtain it.

William Shirer, *The Rise and Fall of the Third Reich. A History of Nazi Germany*, New York, Simon and Schuster, 1960, p. 307

Source C

Below is an extract from *The Origins of the Second World War* by historian AJP Taylor.

 The memorandum tells us what we knew already, that Hitler (like every other German statesman) intended Germany to become the dominant power in Europe. It also tells us that he speculated how this might happen. His speculations were mistaken. They bear hardly any relation to the actual outbreak of the war in 1939…

Hitler did not make plans – for world conquest or for anything else. He assumed that others would provide the opportunities, and that he would seize them.

AJP Taylor, The Origins of the Second World War, Penguin Books, 1961

1. According to source A, why was 1937 a year of awareness?

2. What evidence from your own knowledge can you provide to support the view in Source A that by 1937 'Germany had started an arms race'?

3. Compare and contrast what Sources A and B reveal about Hitler's foreign policy up to 1937.

4. With reference to its origin, purpose, and content, analyse the value and limitations of Source C for a historian studying the significance of the Hossbach Memorandum.

A review of Chapter 5

This chapter has focused on German expansion up to 1937. It has discussed the effects of World War I and various peace treaties on Germany, and the rise to power of Adolf Hitler and the Nazi Party, including the aims of Hitler's foreign policy. It has also analysed the methods used in achieving these aims, including the role played by domestic policies, as well as the international response to events unfolding in Europe.

Activity 13	**(ATL)** Thinking, research, self-management, and communication skills

Now that you have read through this chapter, answer the following question:

With reference to the sources and your own knowledge, discuss the extent to which you agree with the view that Hitler's foreign policy between 1933 and 1937 was more speculation than planning.

This question is typical of the fourth question you will get in the Paper 1 exam. Always answer the questions in the order they are written in the exam: in other words, start with the first question and work your way through to the last. By doing so, you become familiar with the sources and are better prepared to tackle this mini-essay question. Don't forget that the question asks you to include references to the material in the sources as well as your own knowledge. To write a good answer, you need to include references to all the sources (there are always four sources included in the exam paper), and use your own knowledge as well as the sources to support your argument. Allow yourself around 20 minutes of the exam time to answer the fourth question – and don't forget to plan your answer before you start writing.

In order to approach this specific question successfully, start by defining what it means to understand Hitler's foreign policy as a product of speculation and what it means to view it as a product of planning. You could support these explanations with reference to some **historiography**, but what is essential here is that you draw on supporting evidence for each of these views from events between the years 1933 and 1937 only. To achieve a balanced answer, analyse interpretation using both source material as well as your own knowledge before you state your conclusion.

To access websites relevant to this chapter, go to www.pearsonhotlinks. com, search for the book title or ISBN, and click on 'Chapter 5'.

06

Chapter 6: International responses
to Italy and Germany, 1938–40

By analysing the German and Italian foreign policies from 1938 onwards, the final chapter of this case study explores how and why war broke out in Europe in September 1939. Topics to be investigated in this chapter include:

- the international response to the policies and actions of Hitler and Mussolini, and the extent to which this contributed to the outbreak of war
- the first stages of World War II, from Hitler's invasion of Poland to the end of 1940
- a historiography focusing on various interpretations of the outbreak of war.

This photograph shows Neville Chamberlain (left) and Benito Mussolini (right) at the Munich Conference in 1938. It had been Mussolini who proposed the conference to determine the fate of Czechoslovakia. What does this photo reveal about the international responses to Italian and German aggression?

6.1 Moving closer to war

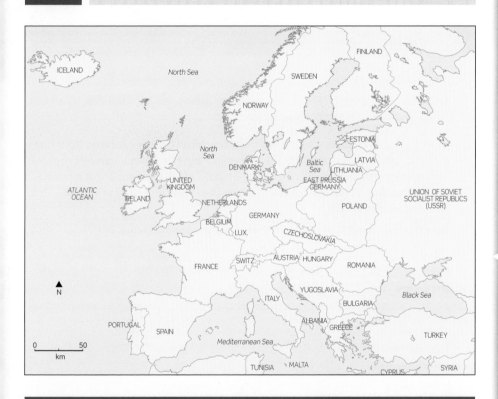

Map of Europe, 1938.

The Anschluss

In the previous chapter you have seen the direction Hitler's foreign policy was moving in up until 1937. Whether he had a calculated plan or was just seizing opportunities presented to him, the truth is that the year 1938 saw Germany executing a much more aggressive foreign policy.

The changes in the diplomatic alignments after Abyssinia and the Rhineland enabled Hitler to make plans for the Anschluss. He had considered it unlikely that either Britain or France would enter a conflict against Germany to defend Austria; the Rhineland episode had proved him right. Besides, Mussolini was now Hitler's ally and, in exchange for Hitler's recognition of the Italian Abyssinian Empire, the Italian leader stopped opposing the Anschluss. The fact that Austria included ethnic Germans who spoke German was only one of the reasons why Hitler demanded the Anschluss. German control of Austria also opened the way to Czechoslovakia and Eastern Europe.

The Nazi movement in Austria, funded by Germany, had been working to destabilize the government since 1934. Due to the increasing political influence gained by the Austrian Nazis, Kurt Schuschnigg, the Austrian chancellor, played a very careful game to avoid giving Germany an excuse to intervene directly. In 1936, as part of his policy, Schuschnigg agreed to sign an Austro-German agreement that demanded that Austria carried out its foreign policy in conformity with the 'leading principles corresponding to the fact that Austria regards herself as a German State'.

Despite this, German pressure on Austria increased in 1938 as Schuschnigg was summoned to meet Hitler, with the latter presenting the former with a list of demands that included the appointment of an Austrian Nazi, Arthur Seyss-Inquart, as **interior minister**; a number of other Nazi Party members were also given roles in the Austrian government.

Activity 1

ATL Thinking and communication skills

This is an extract from a conversation between the Austrian chancellor Kurt Schuschnigg and the German chancellor Adolf Hitler on 12 February 1938, as recorded by Schuschnigg from memory.

> *Schuschnigg: 'Naturally I realise you can march into Austria, but, Mr. Chancellor, we are not alone in this world. That probably means war.'*
>
> *Hitler: [...] 'Don't believe that anyone in the world can hinder me in my decisions. Italy? I am quite clear with Mussolini. England? She will not lift a finger for Austria. France? Well, two years ago we marched into the Rhineland with a handful of battalions and at that moment I risked a great deal. If France had marched then, we should have been forced to withdraw... but for France it is now too late.'*

From Winston Churchill, *The Gathering Storm*, Houghton Mifflin, 1948, p. 263

1. With reference to its origin, purpose, and content, analyse the value and limitations of this source for a historian studying the international response to German aggression.

Student answer – Jack

This source is valuable because it has been produced by a participant in the interview. However, given the events, it may be limited. Schuschnigg's aim was to record the conversation for the future but we don't know when he wrote it and how well he remembered it. The content tells us what Hitler expected the international response to have been but it does not show us whether that is what he really thought.

Examiner's comments

Jack's answer attempts to cover all the elements involved in the evaluation of sources. However, he does not do so in depth. It is important that you state the origins and purpose of a source *before* you actually explain how they contribute to its value and limitations. Although an examiner may understand what Jack meant by the phrase 'given the events, it may be limited', Jack needs to expand on this in order to be awarded more marks. For example, he could argue that Schuschnigg was put under significant pressure at the time and, therefore, may only have had partial recollection of what happened.

How would you have responded to this question?

Unable to deal with the internal unrest promoted by the Nazi party, Schuschnigg announced a plebiscite to be held on 13 March for the Austrian citizens to decide whether they wanted an independent Austria. Despite many Austrians having German roots, Schuschnigg assumed that many of them would not want to live under Nazi rule. At the same time, Hitler encouraged Seyss-Inquart to promote political violence while ordering preparations for the invasion of Austria. Unable to control the unrest and having no foreign support with which to oppose the Nazis, Schuschnigg resigned.

On 12 March, the day before the plebiscite, the German army triumphantly marched into Austria. The plebiscite was held as planned and, with 99 per cent of the votes in favour of the Anschluss, Austria became a province of the Third Reich.

'Austrian Homecoming', the title of a 1938 poster welcoming Austria into the Reich. What is the message conveyed by this source?

Activity 2 — (ATL) Thinking and communication skills

Source A

This photograph shows German tanks entering Vienna in March 1938.

Source B

Below is an extract of a speech by Benito Mussolini, from 16 March 1938.

> *To those more or less official circles beyond the Alps which ask why I did not intervene to 'save' the independence of Austria, I reply that I had not assumed any obligation of the kind, either direct or indirect, written or verbal. The Austrians, I feel bound to state, have always had the comprehensible modesty not to ask for forcible acts to defend the independence of Austria, for we should have answered that an independence which needs the help of foreign troops, even against the majority of the nation itself, no longer deserves the name. Everyone who is acquainted with the Austrians knows that they themselves would have been the first to resist any intervention of ours. Italy had an interest in the independence of the Austrian Federal State, but it was obviously based on the assumption that the Austrians, or at least a majority of them, desired independence; but what has happened in the last few days on Austrian territory shows that the profound aspiration of the people was for the Anschluss.*

From A William Salomone, *Readings in Twentieth-Century European History*, ed. Alexander J. Baltzly, Appleton-Century-Crofts, 1950, p. 428

1. What is the message of Source A?
2. Why, according to Source B, did Mussolini not intervene to prevent the Anschluss?

Student answer to Question 2 – Tomas

Mussolini refused to intervene in Austria because Italy had never assumed any type of obligation to do so. He also claimed Austria would have resisted Italian intervention. Finally, Mussolini claims Italy did not intervene because the Austrians wanted the Anschluss.

Examiner's comments

Question 2 of this activity is a typical Paper 1 question; it is worth 3 marks. Here, Tomas offers three clearly distinct and relevant reasons. He signposts them so that the examiner can clearly identify them. It is important that you do not use too much of your time in this question. Remember: the fourth question in the exam is always in the style of a mini essay, and so you should allow about 20 minutes for it.

The Sudeten crisis

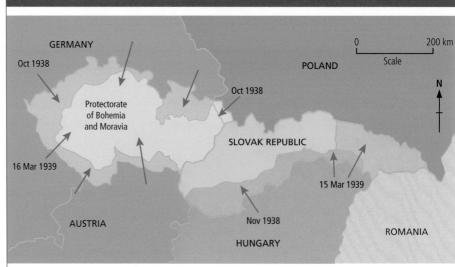

This map depicts the sequence of events following the Munich Agreement.

KEY
1. October 1938: Germany occupied the Sudetenland.
2. October 1938: Poland annexes Zaolzie, an area with a Polish plurality, over which the two countries had fought a war in 1919.
3. November 1938: Hungary occupies border areas (southern third of Slovakia and southern Carpathian Ruthenia) with Hungarian minorities in accordance with the First Vienna Award.
4. 15 March 1939: During the German invasion of the remaining Czech territories, Hungary annexes Carpathian Ruthenia (which had been autonomous since October 1938).
5. 16 March 1939: Germany establishes the Protectorate of Bohemia and Moravia with a puppet government.
6. At the time of Germany's invasion of Czech territories, a pro-Hitler Catholic–Fascist government splits off the remaining territories of Czechoslovakia and declares the Slovak Republic an Axis client state.

Czechoslovakia

Founded in October 1918, Czechoslovakia comprised the territories of Bohemia, Moravia, parts of Silesia, Slovakia, and Ruthenia. It included industrial areas that produced armaments, cars, and chemicals among others. It adopted a parliamentary democratic system that enjoyed relative political stability.

Like the Austrian Republic, Czechoslovakia was born out of the 1919 peace treaties (see Treaty of St Germain). As a multi-racial state, it faced tensions with its neighbours Poland and Hungary. (The map above shows the regions in dispute.) There were also approximately 3 million citizens of German ethnic origin living on the borders of Bohemia and Moravia, in a region known as the Sudetenland. It was rich in natural resources and Hitler wanted to incorporate it into Germany.

The Anschluss made Czechoslovakia more vulnerable. Even if Czechoslovakia had possessed an efficient army and border protections, like Austria's, it would have been difficult for it to resist a German invasion alone. But, after the Rhineland and the Anschluss, there was limited hope that France would honour their alliance and defend Czechoslovakia.

As with Austria, Germany funded the Czech Nazi Party in the Sudetenland and encouraged unrest. Leaders of the party demanded special rights and autonomy for the German minority in the Sudetenland. They claimed that the Germans were mistreated and, although there was some element of truth in this, incidents were also manipulated to support the claim for autonomy.

The May crisis

Political agitation increased between March and May 1938 owing to rumours that Germany was making military preparations to move against Czechoslovakia. Some skirmishes took place near the German border, while Britain and France warned Hitler against intervention and stated that if Germany attacked, France would defend its ally. Although Hitler had not finalized plans to march on Czechoslovakia, the French and British warning had made it look as if he had backed down. He was outraged by this and increased the pace of military preparations.

Violence continued after the May crisis. Britain and France put pressure on the Czech government to negotiate autonomy for the Sudetenland. In September, Czech president Edvard Beneš granted the German Sudeten their autonomy, together with the control of communication centres and industries. Despite this, Hitler broke off diplomatic relations and mobilized troops to the Czech border. He also encouraged agitation from other ethnic minorities in Czechoslovakia, such the Slovaks, to the point that the Czech government was forced to introduce martial law in some districts.

Both the violence in Czechoslovakia and Hitler's reaction prompted British Prime Minister Neville Chamberlain to fly to meet Hitler in order to find a solution to the problem. The French endorsed Chamberlain's mission to escape their obligations towards Czechoslovakia. Chamberlain agreed to Hitler's demand on the Sudetenland and the proposal was put forward to the Czechs. President Beneš was worried that the handover of the Sudetenland to Germany could set a precedent for other nations, such as Hungary and Poland, to demand territory on the grounds of their nationals living within Czech borders; also, while the Sudetenland's handover could lead to the dismemberment of the country, refusal to comply could mean war against Germany. Britain guaranteed the integrity of the rest of Czechoslovakia, and President Beneš agreed to cede the Sudetenland.

However, by then, Hitler wanted more. He demanded the inclusion of the Polish and Hungarian claims to Czech territory in the settlement of the dispute. It now appeared as if Hitler's aim was not to solve the problems of the German minorities in the Sudetenland but to have points of contention with Czechoslovakia to justify an invasion of the country.

Back in Britain, public opinion was divided between those supporting the defence of the integrity of Czechoslovakia and those, like Chamberlain, who were prepared to compromise with Hitler. Czechoslovakia was also unwilling to accept Hitler's increasing demands and, by the end of September, it looked as if war was unavoidable.

Activity 3 — ATL Thinking and communication skills

Study this source. It is an extract from a radio broadcast by Neville Chamberlain, 27 September 1938.

> How horrible, fantastic, incredible it is that we should be digging trenches and trying on gas masks here because of a quarrel in a far-away country between people of whom we know nothing. It seems still more impossible that a quarrel which has already been settled in principle should be the subject of war. [...] However much we may sympathize with a small nation confronted by a big, powerful neighbor, we cannot in all circumstances undertake to involve the whole British Empire in a war simply on her account. If we have to fight, it must be on larger issues than that.

Keith Eubank (ed.), *The Origins of World War II*, 3rd ed., Harlan Davidson, 2004, p. 111

1. What does this source reveal about the British response to Nazi foreign policy?

The Munich Conference

Mussolini, unwilling to enter a war he was unprepared to fight, offered to mediate in the conflict and proposed a four-power conference to Hitler. The Munich Conference of 29 September 1938 was attended by the British Prime Minister Chamberlain; the French Prime Minister Édouard Daladier; Hitler; and Mussolini. Neither the Czechs nor their allies, the Soviets, were represented.

At the conference, an agreement was reached:

- Germany was allowed occupy the Sudetenland sooner than had previously been agreed.
- Polish and Hungarian claims to Czech territory were to be settled, and the Czech borders determined by an international committee.
- The integrity of what remained of Czechoslovakia was to be guaranteed by the Four Powers.

In addition, Chamberlain and Hitler signed a separate declaration of friendship and pledged to resolve any conflict between them by diplomatic consultations.

Activity 4　(ATL) Thinking and communication skills

Source A

This is a Soviet cartoon from 1938 by Kukryniksy, entitled 'Munich Betrayal'; it shows Western powers handing over Czechoslovakia, on a plate, to Hitler. The inscription on the flag reads: 'To the East!'

Source B

Below is an extract from *Europe of the Dictators, 1919–1945* (Fontana Press, 1970, p. 147), a book by journalist and historian Elizabeth Wiskemann.

> The political importance of the Munich Agreement was immense. It was rather as if the Central Powers had won the First World War twenty years later. For Hitler now controlled the old Austrian territory, the core of the Pan-Germans' Mitteleuropa; the Czech interior of Bohemia and Moravia lay at his mercy and he was ready for his much heralded expansion far to the East. The French had broken their long standing treaty with the Czechs and lost their European standing.

Source C

Here is the front page of the British newspaper the *Daily Express*, 30 September 1938.

1. What is the message of Source A?
2. In what ways can Source A help a historian understand the view of the Munich Agreement in the USSR?
3. What, according Source B, was the impact of the Munich Agreement on international relations?
4. To what extent does Source C support the views held in Sources A and B?

Was the Munich Agreement a failure?

What happened at Munich could be interpreted as an attempt by the European powers to gain time to prepare for war against Germany. Certainly, Britain and France needed to increase armament production but this was not a popular policy. Citizens were unwilling to see their taxes raised to finance rearmament and, above all, to enter a war. The fact that Chamberlain and Daladier were welcomed back from Munich as heroes seems to support this view. Additionally, in the case of Britain, events in the Far East, with the rising challenges from Japan, were seen as more threatening to national interests than Austria or Czechoslovakia.

On the other hand, it might have been better if Britain and France had confronted Germany in 1938. The German army was not as prepared for a European war as the British and French had been led to believe. In fact, Hitler faced a certain level of domestic dissent as some of his advisors and generals had become increasingly worried at the prospect of war.

As for the Soviets, whether they would have supported a war against Nazi Germany in 1938 in defence of Czechoslovakia is uncertain. Although they were allies to Czechoslovakia, it was unlikely that they would have been allowed into Polish and Romanian territory to defend Czechoslovakia from Germany. Moreover, weakened by Stalin's purges, the Soviet Army in 1938 was not considered a reliable support by Britain and France.

Activity 5   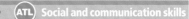 **Social and communication skills**

1. In groups, discuss the extent to which the Munich Conference constituted a victory for Hitler. Do you think Hitler would have preferred a military triumph rather than a diplomatic one?

2. Debate the motion: 'The policy of appeasement alone increased the likelihood of war'. Divide the class into two groups. One group should find documents and arguments to support this idea. The other group should think of reasons to demonstrate why such a policy by itself would not have increased the likelihood of war.

This is a 1938 propaganda card showing the incorporation into the Third Reich of the Czech Sudetenland, the French Saarland, and the Austrian Republic. It reads 'One People, One Empire, One Führer'.

Chamberlain's vision of peace did not last long. In March 1939, in a clear violation of the terms of the Munich Conference, German troops occupied the west of Czechoslovakia and, soon after, Hitler took the Lithuanian port of Memel.

The Polish crisis and the outbreak of war

Key
- Germany (borders established 1919)
- Rhineland (reoccupied in March 1936)
- Austria (annexed in March 1938)
- Sudetenland (occupied in October 1938)
- Czechoslovakia (occupied in March 1939)

Map showing the extent of German expansion by March 1939.

After World War I, an independent Poland was created from former German, Russian, and Austro-Hungarian territories. As you can see in the map above, Poland was given an outlet to the sea via the Polish Corridor, which divided German East Prussia from the rest of Germany. At the mouth of the corridor, the port of Danzig (now renamed Gdańsk) became an international city under the mandate of the League of Nations. Over 800,000 Germans were living under Polish rule in the interwar period.

Germany resented the creation of Poland and was unwilling to see the settlement that had carved out the country and divided it into two as permanent. In previous sections of this case study, you have read about the 10-year German–Polish Non-Aggression Pact that Hitler signed in 1934. So why did war break out between Germany and Poland only five years later?

After Munich, Hitler began to demand the restoration of Danzig as well as the construction of roads and railways through the Polish Corridor to connect East Prussia and Germany. In exchange, he offered to renew the 1934 Non-Aggression Pact with Poland. The Polish leaders, having seen the fate of Czechoslovakia, rejected the German demands. In response, Hitler dissolved the pact and ordered plans for an invasion of Poland. As a warning to Hitler, Britain and France announced that they would guarantee Poland's independence.

The following cartoon from 1939 is entitled 'News Item: Hitler and Mussolini now Wear Glasses'. It shows Chamberlain asking Hitler and Mussolini the question: 'Is it clearer now, gentlemen?'

1. What is the message conveyed by this source?

Student answer – Marcia

The cartoon shows that Chamberlain wants Mussolini and Hitler to know that Britain will fight. It also shows Mussolini and Hitler as allies.

Examiner's comments

Marcia has identified two relevant messages. However, she could have improved the answer by supporting each message with reference to the source. For example, what elements in the cartoon do you think can be used to support the idea that Hitler and Mussolini were allies?

Even though Britain and France had guaranteed the *independence* of Poland, in reality it meant that territorial changes affecting Poland's *integrity* could still be made. In other words, negotiations with Hitler had not necessarily been terminated: the matter surrounding his claims on Danzig, based on the grounds of German nationals living outside the borders, was still open to discussion. Moreover, after the Munich Conference, Poland had occupied Teschen (see map on page 138) and was therefore viewed with a certain amount of suspicion in Europe.

Furious at these diplomatic developments, Hitler ordered military preparations to invade Poland. But peace was not only being threatened by German aggression. In April 1939, Mussolini moved into Albania, breaking the 1937 Gentlemen's Agreement with Britain (page 108). One month later, he proposed a military alliance with Hitler.

German–Italian relations and the outbreak of war

By mid-1939 it was evident that Germany had established itself as the dominant force in Europe. In May 1939, Germany and Italy signed the Pact of Friendship and Alliance, which Mussolini referred to as the Pact of Steel. Under the terms of the pact, both countries pledged to support one another in case of attack. They were also supposed to coordinate their military plans, though this was harder to achieve in reality: German and Italian commanders would not have wanted to share plans with one another, while Hitler and Mussolini themselves certainly would not have informed each other of their foreign policy plans.

Despite being an Axis power, Italy was not ready to fight a war in Europe. The cost of fighting in Abyssinia and in the Spanish Civil War (known as the 'Spanish ulcer' among the Italians) meant the Italian economy was ill-prepared for a full-scale European war. This became evident when, at the outbreak of World War II, Italy declared itself **non-belligerent.**

Here is a joke about the relationship between Hitler and Mussolini, taken from *Underground Humour in Nazi Germany* by FKM Hillenbrand:

> *Hitler and Mussolini discuss whether Berlin or Rome should be the world capital after the war. As there is no agreement between them Mussolini says, 'None other than the Almighty has declared Rome to be the "Eternal City"—therefore Rome should be the world capital.' To this Hitler replies, 'When did I say that?'*

FKM Hillenbrand, *Underground Humour in Nazi Germany, 1933–1945*, Routledge, 1995, p. 17

CHALLENGE YOURSELF

Thinking and communication skills

What does this joke reveal about the nature of Hitler and Mussolini's relationship? In what ways can political jokes be useful to historians?

Activity 7

ATL **Thinking and communication skills**

Source A

This is a cartoon by John Collins entitled 'Straining the Axis', published in 1939.

Source B

Stephanie Hodgson was a university student when she wrote an article entitled 'Hitler and Mussolini: A comparative analysis of the Rome–Berlin Axis 1936–1940' (2011). Below is an extract from her article.

❝ *On paper, one would think that Nazi Germany and Italian fascism should complement each other; however this theory failed to transpire into reality. After thorough research of this topic one gets a sense of that the Rome-Berlin Axis was an alliance based on mistrust, animosity and suspicion of each other's motives. Each power flirted with the enemy as a means to maximise their own interests, and this was seen most potently with the German signing of the Nazi-Soviet Pact and equally with the Italian signing of the Anglo-Italian agreement. Mussolini and Hitler, although [they] held [the] same leadership principles and begrudgingly respected each other's achievements, never gauged a true friendship.*

1. What is the message conveyed by Source A?
2. According to Source B, what were the challenges faced by the alliance between Germany and Italy?
3. To what extent can the 1937 Anglo-Italian Agreement (Gentlemen's Agreement) mentioned in Source B be interpreted as a 'flirtation with the enemy'?

The Nazi-Soviet Pact

Hitler concluded negotiations with the Soviet Union by signing the Nazi-Soviet Pact on 23 August 1939. In Case Study 1 you have read about how this non-aggression pact came as a surprise to the world (see Chapter 3, page 62), not least given Nazi Germany's views on communism and its participation in the Anti-Comintern Pact.

By the terms of the Nazi-Soviet Pact, Germany and the Soviet Union pledged to each other a 10-year non-aggression period during which they agreed not to support any third power that might attack the other member, not to join in any alliance that could threaten the other party, and to solve their disputes diplomatically. The pact was important to Hitler for two reasons: it gave Germany Soviet neutrality in case of a German–Polish war, and it prevented the Soviet Union from concluding negotiations with Britain and France that might result in a war on two fronts for Germany.

The Nazi-Soviet Pact ended Soviet diplomatic isolation and postponed a confrontation with Germany. Had Stalin entered an alliance with France and Britain to protect Poland, one that made more sense from an ideological point of view, he would have had to enter a war against Germany. An alliance with Germany therefore offered the Soviet Union time to prepare better for war.

Activity 8   **ATL** **Thinking and communication skills**

Source A

Entitled 'Safety first', this is a cartoon by Bernard Partridge. It was published in *Punch*, 30 August 1939.

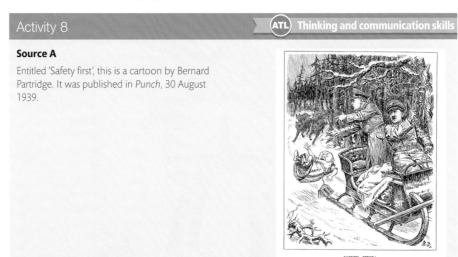

SAFETY FIRST !

This cartoon appeared in the British newspaper the *Daily Mirror*, published on 21 September 1939.

"GERMANY SHALL NEVER BE ENCIRCLED."

Source C

Below is an extract from *Poland, 1918–1945: An Interpretive and Documentary History of the Second Republic*, a book by British historian Peter D Stachura.

> No Polish leader can be blamed for not envisaging the nightmare scenario where Nazi Germany and the Communist Soviet Union, ideological opposites who had been conducting violent propaganda wars against each other since 1933, came together in a formal alliance in August 1939. In that context, there was no Polish foreign policy, military or political strategy that could have prevented or repulsed the combined onslaught that ensued.
>
> In face of the German invasion on 1 September and of the Soviet invasion on 17 September, Poland stood alone. Britain and France declared war on Germany, but confined their action to diplomatic protests and radio broadcasts to Poland – empty, futile gestures. True to historical tradition and the national temperament, the Polish armed forces fought heroically and well against overwhelming odds. The final outcome, however, could never have been in doubt.

Peter D Stachura, Poland, 1918–1945: An Interpretive and Documentary History of the Second Republic, Routledge, 2004, p. 117

1. What is the message of Source A?
2. What is the message of Source B?
3. What, according to Source C, was the significance of the Nazi-Soviet Pact for the events of September 1939?
4. To what extent do you agree with the author of Source C in that 'the final outcome could have never have been in doubt'?

6.2 International response between September 1939 and May 1940

On 1 September 1939, Nazi troops entered Poland. Two days later Britain and France sent ultimatums demanding that Germany withdraw from Poland. When these expired, the Polish crisis officially became a European war.

By the end of September, Poland was overrun and divided between Germany and the Soviet Union. One of the reasons for the quick defeat of Poland was the German **blitzkrieg** (lightning war), which combined air warfare with the use of tanks (*panzers*). The German Luftwaffe destroyed the Polish railways and air force. Although the Polish resisted bravely, they were unable to repel the German attack.

This photograph shows Warsaw in the aftermath of the German blitzkrieg.

Activity 9

ATL Thinking and communication skills

The following extract comes from historian Marian Kamil Dziewanowski's book *Poland in the Twentieth Century*. The author had taken part in the defence of Poland during the German invasion.

> *The fact that in those tragic September days England and France abandoned Poland to face German aggression alone could have been no surprise to Hitler. He had no fear of Poland's Western allies when he launched his attack and withdrew his troops and military equipment from Germany's western borders, leaving them almost unguarded [...] Germany in September 1939 had barely twenty poorly prepared combat divisions on its western frontier. All the better troops, all tanks, and practically the entire air force had been thrown against Poland. Facing these meager German forces in the west were more than ninety French divisions, about 2,500 tanks, 10,000 guns, and 3,000 French and British aircraft, which were soon joined by a dozen British divisions with several thousand tanks and guns. None of this great force was used to mount an offensive. All the allies of Poland managed to do was to send a few patrols and reconnaissance flights and drop an occasional pacifistic proclamation.*

Marian Kamil Dziewanowski, *Poland in the Twentieth Century*, Columbia University Press, 1977, p. 108

1. What does this source reveal about the British and the French response to Nazi aggression?
2. With reference to its origin, purpose, and content analyse the value and limitations of this source for a historian studying the international response to Nazi aggression against Poland.

To successfully answer Question 2, it is important that you use the information in the source attribution in your answer. In this case, what impact does your knowledge of the author (that he helped to defend Poland during the German invasion) have on your interpretation of his account?

The response of the United States

During the interwar period, US diplomacy supported neutrality towards conflicts in Europe. The United States was not a member of the League of Nations and, as tensions mounted in both Europe and Asia throughout the 1930s, it increased the efforts to maintain neutrality. You have already analysed the significance of the US Neutrality Acts in Case Study 1 (see Chapter 3, page 68).

When war broke out in Europe, the United States declared neutrality. However, in November 1939 President Franklin Roosevelt lifted the embargo and modified the terms of the Neutrality Act to allow belligerent nations to buy materials from the United States and transport them in their own ships.

War in Europe, September 1939 to May 1940

Following the surrender and partition of Poland, as stated in the Nazi-Soviet Pact, Stalin took over the Baltic States and invaded Finland. However, little happened in the West between the start of the war and April 1940. These months were known as the **Phoney War**, which ended only when Germany took over Denmark and Norway in an attempt to secure access to Swedish iron ore through Norway. These victories also guaranteed Hitler a sea corridor from Denmark to southern Norway. The overrunning of Denmark and Norway contributed to major changes in British politics. Chamberlain resigned as prime minister and was replaced by Winston Churchill. If before May 1940 Hitler had hopes of negotiating with Britain, Churchill's appointment put a definitive end to them.

At the same time, Germany launched blitzkrieg attacks on Holland and Belgium; it had also unexpectedly entered France through the Ardennes (a mountain range covered by vast forests and uneven land), bypassing the French defence fortifications. It was not long before Holland and Belgium surrendered. The British and French troops, who had been mobilized into these countries for defence, became trapped by the Germans along the English Channel in Dunkirk. The operation to evacuate them was codenamed Operation Dynamo.

'The Withdrawal from Dunkirk' (1940) by British painter Charles Cundall.

CHALLENGE YOURSELF

Research and social skills

In groups, use a map to locate Dunkirk and explain the significance of the evacuation. Was Operation Dynamo a military defeat or a moral victory for the Allies?

Thinking and research skills

This speech by Churchill inspired many British citizens to make sacrifices to defend their nation at a time of war. Can you think of other historical examples in which a leader motivated the people to support their country in difficult times? What are the similarities and differences in the ways leaders motivate their nations across different cultures?

Thinking and communication skills

TOK

In ToK, we are required to reflect on the role of *faith* – or *trust* – as a way of knowing. In what ways did Churchill appeal to the *trust* of British citizens in his speech? How significant do you think it was for Churchill to obtain their trust? In what ways was trusting Churchill important for the British people at the time?

Activity 10

ATL Communication and thinking skills

Source A

This cartoon was published in Punch Magazine in 1940.

READING THE SKIES.

"I have conquered all Gaul. How long will it take to conquer all Britain?"
"Wait a moment, Leader, while I look at the omens of the air."

Source B

Below is an extract from a BBC radio broadcast by Winston Churchill, 19 May 1940

" *Our task is not only to win the battle – but to win the war. After this battle in France abates its force, there will come the battle for our Island – for all that Britain is, and all the Britain means. That will be the struggle. In that supreme emergency we shall not hesitate to take every step, even the most drastic, to call forth from our people the last ounce and the last inch of effort of which they are capable. The interests of property, the hours of labor, are nothing compared to the struggle for life and honor, for right and freedom, to which we have vowed ourselves [...]*

[...] I have formed an Administration of men and women of every Party and of almost every point of view. We have differed and quarreled in the past, but now one bond unites us all: to wage war until victory is won, and never to surrender ourselves to servitude and shame, whatever the cost and the agony may be. [...] Behind the Armies and Fleets of Britain and France, gather a group of shattered States and bludgeoned races: the Czechs, the Poles, the Norwegians, the Danes, the Dutch, the Belgians – upon all of whom the long night of barbarism will descend, unbroken even by a star of hope, unless we conquer, as conquer we must, as conquer we shall.

1. What is the message conveyed by Source A?
2. What does Source B reveal about the British response to international aggression?
3. With reference to its origins, purpose, and content, analyse the value and limitations of Source B for a historian studying the changes in the British response to international aggression between 1938 and 1940.

The Fall of France

Despite attempts to halt the German advance, the French surrendered on 22 June 1940. The Germans had taken direct control of the northern part of the country, which gave them access to submarine bases on the coastline along the Atlantic. A puppet government (headed by Marshal Philippe Pétain) was set up under German supervision to run what was now called the French State (also known as the Vichy Republic). During this period, General Charles De Gaulle, from his exile in London, led the 'Free French' movement and encouraged French citizens to resist the German occupation.

Here is a photograph of Hitler in Paris, taken on 23 June 1940.

1. What is the significance of this source?
2. In groups, find out the reasons why France was defeated in June 1940. Consider the domestic political tensions as well as the military factors.
3. Find information on the response of the United States and Britain to the news of the Fall of France.

Italy's entry into the war

Although Hitler and Mussolini shared a determination for war, their countries' capacity to fight it was clearly different, as Italian unwillingness to declare war in 1939 demonstrated. However, on 10 June 1940, when France was about to fall, Mussolini declared war on the Allies. He was certain that the war would be over soon. Professor Julian Jackson suggests that Mussolini did not enter the war to honour his alliances with Hitler but as part of his plan to keep pace with him and avoid being Hitler's 'junior partner' (*Europe 1900–1945*, OUP, 2002). In September 1940, Mussolini attacked Egypt from the Italian colony of Libya. The following month, he attacked Greece.

Source A

Martin Kitchen is a British–Canadian historian specializing in European history. The following extract is taken from his book *A World in Flames: A Short History of the Second World War in Europe and Asia, 1939–1945* (Wiley-Blackwell, 1990, p. 51).

> Germany's relatively cautious policy in the Balkans was placed in serious jeopardy when Italy attacked Greece on 28 October 1940. German military experts estimated that the Italians would find it exceedingly difficult to defeat the Greeks. This raised the unwelcome possibility of British intervention in the Balkans, something which Hitler was determined to avoid. The German military estimated that the British would send at least three divisions to Greece. Indeed, Britain had given Greece a guarantee of support in April 1940 and Minister President Metaxas immediately requested assistance… Churchill insisted that the fall of Greece would have a 'deadly effect' on Turkey. Churchill persuaded the Chiefs of Staff that aid for Greece was essential, and Wavell was ordered to give 'the greatest possible material and moral support' to Greece 'at the earliest possible moment'.

Source B

This is a cartoon entitled 'Haunted'. It was published in the British magazine *Punch* in December 1940.

1. What is the message conveyed by Source B?
2. According to Source A, what was the international response to Italy's invasion of Greece?

However, Mussolini was unsuccessful in both Egypt and Greece: Britain rapidly drove him out of Egypt and into Libya, sunk part of the Italian fleet, and occupied Crete. Greece drove the Italians out and marched into Albania. The campaigns demonstrated that Italy was ill-prepared to fight a war of such scale. Hitler implored Mussolini to accept support from German forces. But it was not just Italian prestige that was damaged in the Balkans. Germany's involvement also delayed other military plans, such as Operation Barbarossa (the invasion of the Soviet Union), with catastrophic effects.

The Battle of Britain

With Britain being the only power standing against Germany in Europe, the German Luftwaffe launched a preliminary bombing campaign to destroy the British Royal Air Force (RAF) between July and September 1940. The aim was to gain air superiority by destroying the RAF along with its airfields and radar bases so that Germany could control the English Channel. This would either allow an invasion of Britain or force it to surrender. However, Hitler could neither invade Britain nor force a peace negotiation. Later, the German bombings targeted major British cities to destroy the country's industrial capacity and infrastructure as well as people's morale, but they also failed to achieve these aims.

CHALLENGE YOURSELF

Thinking skills

The failure of Nazi Germany to invade Britain in the summer of 1940 was a pivotal moment in the war, as this was the first time since 1933 that Hitler had been checked. What do you think the significance of this was on the international community?

Activity 13 — ATL Thinking and research skills

Although the Battle of Britain failed, by the end of 1940, Hitler dominated vast areas of Europe. Look at this map of Europe and answer the following questions.

KEY
1. Poland had been divided between Hitler and Stalin by end of September 1939.
2. Over 200 Allied ships had been sunk (mostly by German U-boats and mines) between September and December 1939.
3. Phoney War (October 1939 to March 1940); Germany invaded Denmark and Norway on 11 April 1940.
4. Netherlands, Belgium, Luxembourg, and France were conquered by Germany between 11 May and 22 June 1940.
5. Allied troops were rescued from Dunkirk between the end of May and start of June 1940.
6. Italy declared war on Britain and France on 10 June 1940.
7. Battle of Britain took place over the summer of 1940. Germany called off invasion.
8. Italy occupied British Somaliland by August 1940 and invaded Egypt by September 1940.

1. Which territories had Germany and Italy gained before the outbreak of war in September 1939?

2. Which territories did they invade between 1939–40? What was the international response to each campaign?

3. To what extent did the failure of the Italian campaigns up to 1940 interfere with the Germany's successes?

4. Go back to Source B in Activity 7 (page 146). To what extent do you agree with the views its author, Stephanie Hodgson, expressed about German–Italian relations? Support your views with reference to specific examples drawn from this section.

6.3 Historiography – different interpretations of the outbreak of war

Many reasons have been suggested to explain the outbreak of World War II in Europe. They include the following:

- Nazism, with its aggressive foreign policy, was solely responsible for the outbreak of a large-scale war – one that had been planned by Hitler from the start.
- Hitler did not plan a global war. The expansion of Germany was more a result of Hitler opportunistically taking advantage of circumstances as they made themselves available than a calculated plan.
- It was not only for territorial ambitions that Hitler pursued an aggressive foreign policy. He had a relatively unstable power base in Germany, which forced him to look for successes in foreign policy to strengthen his rule and maintain public support.
- Appeasement was to blame for the outbreak of war because the negotiations with Hitler encouraged him to continue to take risks.

Below are the views of a number of historians regarding the main factors of war during this period:

- **Hugh Trevor-Roper** was a British specialist on Nazi Germany who argued that Hitler had a master plan of expansion that could be traced back to *Mein Kampf*. More recently, the view that World War II was caused by Hitler's determination to achieve *Lebensraum* and defeat Bolshevism was echoed by Canadian military historians **BJC McKercher** and **Roch Legault**.
- **AJP Taylor** was a British historian who argued that Hitler's foreign policy was not based on a calculated plan, but rather that Hitler was an opportunist. He also claimed that the Nazi foreign policy was not too different from German foreign policy before World War I.
- **Richard Overy**, a British historian, also sees Hitler as opportunistic. He claims that, although Hitler wanted war, World War II broke out because by 1939 Britain and France were determined to stop him after the invasion of Poland.
- **Martin Broszat** was a German historian who specialized in modern German history. He placed more importance on the structure of the Nazi state than on Hitler. He argued internal tensions and competitions within the Nazi state made Hitler more radical in his policies as he looked for opportunities to increase his support.
- **Winston Churchill**, who served as British prime minister during World War II, wrote a detailed account of British foreign policy in the 1930s in *The Gathering Storm*. Churchill was highly critical of the policy of appeasement, both at the time as well as in his later writings. He claimed that not standing against German aggression before 1939 had made war more likely. In his own words: 'An appeaser is one who feeds a crocodile hoping it will eat him last' (from an address to the House of Commons, January 1940).
- **Keith Eubank** was an American history professor who believed the seeds of World War II were planted in the peace treaties of 1919, which created grievances among the Germans. Although Hitler took advantage of appeasement to revoke some of the terms of the treaty, Eubank did not place the main responsibility for the outbreak of war on appeasement. He claimed that, although it was a rational approach to the diplomatic problems of the interwar years, the fact that Hitler wanted a war meant that the policy of appeasement would not have succeeded.
- **Adam Tooze**, a British specialist in economic history, puts emphasis on the German economic limitations that led Hitler to believe that the sooner there was a war, the better. Tooze argues that with Britain and France getting closer, Hitler wanted war

CHALLENGE YOURSELF

 Thinking and research skills

Read both lists above. See if you can match up the historians' interpretations (list two) with the reasons given for the outbreak of war (list one).

to break out quickly, even if the German economy and armed forces were not fully prepared in 1939.

A review of Chapter 6

This chapter focused on events in Europe between 1938 and 1940. It first analysed the role of German Nazism and Italian Fascism in the outbreak of World War II in Europe, by focusing on the events in Austria, Czechoslovakia, and Poland, and how these contributed to the outbreak of war in September 1939. These events were not only the result of increasing aggression on the part of the Axis powers but also of the international response to them, such as the policy of appeasement and the changes in the diplomatic alignments in Europe that led to the Nazi-Soviet Pact of August 1939.

It also focused on the war in Europe in 1939 and 1940 by evaluating Nazi strategies during that period, including the Fall of France and the Battle of Britain. It assessed the contribution of Hitler's initial victories to Mussolini's decision to enter the war and evaluated Italy's involvement in the course of the war.

Finally, it provided assessments of different historical interpretations both of the causes of the outbreak of war in 1939 and the question of the extent to which Hitler had planned such a conflict before its outbreak.

This chapter concludes the case study on the causes of expansion, the key events, and the international response to Italian and German aggression between 1933 and 1940.

Activity 14   **(ATL) Thinking, research, self-management, and communication skills**

Now that you have read through this chapter, answer the following question:

Using the sources and your own knowledge, evaluate the contributions of Hitler's foreign policy to the move to global war between 1938 and 1939.

This question is typical of the fourth question you will get in the Paper 1 exam. You can check back to the end of the previous chapters to see the suggestions for how best to approach this kind of mini essay. Don't forget: although it may be tempting to answer this question first (because it carries the most marks), you are better off working through each question in order as this will help you think about what may or may not be relevant for the fourth question. As long as it isn't during the five-minute reading time, you could also highlight possible quotations as you come across them in the various sources.

Don't forget that the question asks you to include references to the material in the sources as well as your own knowledge. To write a good answer, you need to include references to all the sources (there are always four sources included in the exam), and use your own knowledge as well as the sources to support your argument. You can use your own knowledge to either support the message of a particular source, to argue against it, or even to start a new argument. For this particular question, consider the following points:

- Hitler's aims in foreign policy
- his military actions between 1938 and 1939
- Nazi diplomacy between 1938 and 1939
- other contributing factors, such as specific alliances and treaties, the role of appeasement, economic pressures, or events surrounding the invasion of Poland.

What other factors could you add to this list? For each argument, find some supporting evidence from the sources and/or your own knowledge. Finally, write a brief introduction that shows that you have understood the demands of the question and a focused conclusion to summarize your answer.

 To access websites relevant to this chapter, go to www.pearsonhotlinks. com, search for the book title or ISBN, and click on 'Chapter 6'.

Theory of Knowledge

Introduction

The Theory of Knowledge (ToK) course is part of the core of the IB Diploma Programme and, along with the subject-specific courses, counts towards the Diploma. History is both one of the subject-specific courses in the IB Diploma and an area of knowledge in ToK. This chapter aims to discuss the key concepts of ToK, showing the interaction between the History course and its function as an area of knowledge within ToK.

There is a substantial overlap between history and ToK as both emphasize the importance of critical thinking. Both ask the question, 'How do we know?' Both want you to understand that your cultural identity is rooted in the past.

ToK uses knowledge frameworks as a concept to differentiate between areas of knowledge. This table helps you see how a knowledge framework could apply to IB History.

Scope/ applications	• It is the study of the recorded past. • It helps us to understand that our cultural identities are rooted in the past.
Concepts/ language	• It discusses change and continuity. • It explores causation and consequences. • It recognizes the power of language in influencing thoughts and actions.
Methodology	• It has a clear, strong, and demanding methodology. • It has recognized ways of collecting evidence, questioning sources, and constructing theories. • It tests significance. • It asks, 'How do we know?'
Historical development	• It recognizes that current values affect our views of the past. • It changes over time in subject matter and interpretations.
Links to personal knowledge	• It acknowledges the influence of individual historians on shared knowledge. • It allows for a range of perspectives. • It recognizes the importance of a shared history on a person's identity.

You will find that an understanding of ToK will help you to evaluate sources in your History course. It will

also help you to complete the reflection section of the Internal Assessment component of the History course.

You may also find that an understanding of history is useful in your ToK course. It will help you to analyse the real-life issue in your ToK presentation and will provide a strong area of knowledge, with great examples, to refer to in your ToK essay.

Ways of knowing

Both ToK and history ask the question, 'How do we know?' ToK answers this question by identifying eight possible ways of knowing. Your knowledge must come from somewhere, and by analysing where it comes from, you are able to assess its reliability.

ToK identifies the eight ways of knowing as:

- Language
- Perception
- Reason
- Emotion
- Memory
- Intuition
- Imagination
- Faith

You can use these concepts in ToK to assist in:

- checking the reliability of first-hand testimony
- analysing the way emotions influence the witness and the interviewer
- determining the possible bias in the language used
- assessing the fallibility of memory
- analysing the desire to see a rational explanation for events.

You can also use them in history to assist in establishing the origin, purpose, and content of sources, in order to assess their value and limitations.

Language is one of the key ways of knowing, so here is a case study exploring the use of language in the accumulation and communication of knowledge in history.

Case study: It's all in the name

Below are two maps. The first is of Europe in 1919 and the second is of Europe in 1940.

Source A

This is a map of Europe in 1919.

Source B

This is a map of Europe in 1940.

Source C

The following quotation is taken from *The New Doublespeak: Why No One Knows What Anyone is Saying Anymore* (1996) by William Lutz, an American linguist.

> *Naming things – using language – is a very high level abstraction, and when we name something we 'freeze' it by placing it in a category and making a 'thing' out of it.*

Some of the political changes reflected in the maps you have used in this book demanded that the new countries changed their official language. Official languages have a special legal status. They are used in government communications, in courts, at school. However, official languages are not necessarily the language people speak in their everyday life. Foreign words, dialects, all contribute to the ways in which we transform and use language to communicate.

Source D

This is an extract from an article by psychologist Gianluca Schiavo entitled 'Language and National Identity: The "Revolution" of Italian Neorealism' in the journal *Fu Jen Studies: Literature & Linguistics*, 45, 2012.

> *During the Fascist period the nationalism of the regime considered dialects and particularly foreign languages as real obstacles to the process of nation building, which, according to Mussolini and many other party officials, required a strict linguistic uniformity. A very drastic campaign was carried out against the ethnic minorities, which suffered a brutal process of Italianisation, and the usage of foreign words in the Italian language (including its literature) was also strongly discouraged.*

Activity 1

1. Study the maps of Europe in 1919 and 1940 (Sources A and B). Consider the impact of the territorial changes on European citizens between 1919 and 1940. Think, for example, of the people living in Eastern Europe who, throughout this period, became subjects of different states. Identify two specific territories that experienced such political changes. What different names were given to them?

2. Now, find a contemporary map of Africa and study it. Can you find Abyssinia on it? What is the name given to this territory nowadays? What are the implications of the word *Abyssinia* being used only on historical rather than political maps? What does this suggest about the value and limitations of maps as physical representations of reality?

3. With reference to Source C, to what extent, in your opinion, do the names given to countries help or hinder the national identity of the groups that live in them? For example, do you think the Germans in the Polish Corridor or the Austrians in South Tyrol felt Polish or Italian as a result of the postwar territorial changes?

4. Why do some groups reject the national identity of the larger community they live in? Can you think of other contemporary examples?

5. Find out the differences between an 'official language' and a 'national language'. Why aren't they necessarily the same? What does this reveal about language as an instrument of power?

Areas of knowledge

History is one of the eight areas of knowledge identified by the ToK course. A full list of the areas of knowledge is:

- Mathematics
- Natural sciences
- Human sciences
- History
- The arts
- Ethics
- Religious knowledge systems
- Indigenous knowledge systems

You can use these areas of knowledge to understand why we approach different types of knowledge in different ways. We recognize that a work of art is not the same as a chemical formula or a historical interpretation. We test them using subject-specific criteria, recognizing that a historical fact cannot be verified in the same way as a natural science fact. History uses a rigorous methodology to test its facts, but it is not the same method as used in the natural sciences.

History and the arts

There is an interesting interplay between history and the arts. In one sense, the arts reflect the historical forces at play in society, but in another sense, the arts influence history. Here are a couple of examples exploring the complex relationship between them.

Case study: Remembering a war through film

World War II has been a popular source of material for commercial films; in turn, these have also influenced the way that the War is remembered and written about. One example is *Pearl Harbor*, a film that was released in 2001. On the whole, the film was not well received by film critics and there was also criticism that it was not entirely accurate.

Source A

This quotation is taken from a film review by military historian Lawrence Suid.

 [for] most historians the liberties the filmmakers took with the facts render Pearl Harbor useless as a tool to teach students about the Japanese attack.

Source B

The following is taken from a review of "Tora! Tora! Tora!" that appeared in the *Turner Classic Movies (TCM)* website.

 There was little tolerance in some quarters [in the United States] for anything portraying the Imperial military as anything but barbaric, and any interest in seeing the conflict from the Japanese side was eclipsed by feelings of discomfort. On a psychological level, seeing Asians cheering 'Banzai' as they defeat Americans didn't feel right, especially if one had a loved one fighting in Vietnam. Timing is everything but it's possible that there would never have been an optimal time for Tora! Tora! Tora! in America. On the other hand, it's obvious why the movie was a breakout success in Japan. It even ends with a respectful shot of the Imperial Naval commander Yamamoto.

Both Sources C and D are taken from an article by Marie Thorsten and Geoffrey M White entitled 'Binational Pearl Harbor? *Tora! Tora! Tora!* and the Fate of (Trans)national Memory' from the *Asia-Pacific Journal*, 8/52, No. 2, 27 December 2010.

Source C

❝ *Perhaps the most scathing [critical] denunciation of Tora! Tora! Tora! was delivered by critic Satake Shigeru in Eiga Geijutsu in 1970. Cynically denouncing Tora! Tora! Tora! as an 'enlargement of truth' (shinjitsu no bōdai),… he assailed the film's implications of conflicted innocence on the part of the emperor and Admiral Yamamoto. In the film, diplomats speculate on the emperor's anti-war stance by his reading of the poem (actually written by his grandfather, Emperor Meiji, and delivered on September 6, 1941): 'Methinks all the people of the world are brethren. Then why are the waves and the winds so unsettled today?' By denying the emperor's culpability, and by agreeing to a security alliance that merely remoulded the emperor as a living being rather than a deity, the mentality of Tora! Tora! Tora!, Satake felt, acquitted the imperialism of both America and Japan…. [Satake] claimed that Tora! Tora! Tora! missed the basic point of why Japan lost the war: it wasn't a matter of might, but rather that the war was basically inhuman: 'Tora! Tora! Tora! rehashes [repeats] the "enormously false myths" over and over again; ergo [therefore], Japan-US relations are peaceful.'*

Source D

❝ *Reviews and commentaries of these films inevitably became opportunities for characterizing the other's subjectivity (and, by implication, historical sensibility). Americans especially wondered, 'Just how does Japan remember the war?' But this attitude consistently overlooked internal Japanese protest against that country's America-led (re)militarization, and the painful irony of America's own collusion with Japanese war amnesia in the project to build an anti-Communist stronghold in Asia. The most uninformed critics often assumed that Tora! Tora! Tora! presaged [anticipated] Japan's resurgent national pride. One US politician stated that the Japanese would probably cut Tora! in half and rename it 'The good old days.'*

Source E

The following extract is taken from an article in the *Financial Times*, 15 February 2015, by the British historian Simon Schama. The article is entitled 'What historians think of historical novels'.

❝ *Invention may compromise authority but then we don't go to great historical fiction or feature films for hard documentary truth. What they deliver, instead, is an imaginative impression but when that impression emerges from rich research it is often capable of delivering a much more vivid sense of the past than an arrangement of unimpeachable data.*

Activity 2 Thinking, research, self-management, communication, and social skills

1. How far, do you think, do we watch films about historical events (like *Pearl Harbor* and "Tora! Tora! Tora!") for information and knowledge?

2. What do these reviews tell us about how war films may be used for political ends?

3. Carry out a survey among your classmates asking them to name one war film they have seen and how far it has influenced their knowledge of that event.

4. How far, do you think, do commercial films influence how history is taught in the classroom?

5. Are we more likely, do you think, to uncritically assume the accuracy of a recently made war film as opposed to one that was made shortly after World War II? Give reasons for your answer.

6. According to Alexander Pope, an 18th-century English poet, 'a little learning is a dangerous thing'. Bearing this in mind, how far would you agree with the view in Source E?

7. What, do you think, are a) the benefits and b) the risks of making history entertaining?

Historical development

Historical development is one of the criteria on the knowledge framework that ToK uses to differentiate between the areas of knowledge. Historical development is part of all the areas of knowledge, recognizing that our knowledge and the way we approach that knowledge changes through time. For instance, the way we approach natural sciences and what we know about them today is quite different from a hundred years ago.

You can use this concept to explore how our approach to history changes, i.e. what subjects we study in history, how our views change as more information comes into the public domain, and how our current values influence our view of the past. Historians use reason to construct a logical interpretation of the past based upon the available information. Sometimes there is so much information that it is difficult to find a single thread of cause and effect in it. Sometimes there is too little information. Occasionally new information becomes known, as official documents are released or research is completed.

Historians are human beings with roots in their own time, place, and background. Their interpretations have an emotional and cultural context, so it is not surprising that the interpretations change over time, as society's values change.

Here are two case studies exploring how history and our view of history can change.

Case study: Dr Seuss and the war

In pairs, study the cartoon below and discuss its meaning.

"Gimme some kerosene, some excelsior and a blow torch. Ma wants to bake a cake."

When you have finished discussing it, consider the following information:

- The cartoon was published in the American newspaper *PM* on 11 November 1941. It was created by a political cartoonist called Theodor Seuss Geisel (1904–91), who was perhaps better known as Dr Seuss, the children's book author.
- Before the United States entered World War II, Geisel's political cartoons focused on showing why the country should abandon isolationism. When his country entered the war, Geisel produced a set of cartoons to encourage American citizens to buy bonds to finance the war effort.
- During the war he supported the internment of the Japanese living in the United States in camps. He visited Japan after the war and, horrified at the effects of the atomic bombs, changed his anti-Japanese views.

The only way we can know about the past is by studying and interpreting sources. However, interpretations of events change with time. In the case of Geisel, he changed his views on Japan after he visited the country at the end of the war. Why do you think this might have happened? What does it say about the nature of historical knowledge?

Activity 3

(ATL) Thinking, communication, and social skills

1. Has your interpretation of the cartoon been affected by the information on the background of Geisel and his time? If so, in what ways? If not, explain why.

2. Which of the facts above have you found most useful in assisting your interpretation of the cartoon? Which ones have you found the least helpful? Discuss the answers with your group.

Case study: Interpretations of war

Now, consider the following interpretations of the outbreak of World War II:

- Intentionalist historians (such as Allan Bullock and Hugh Trevor Roper) claim that Hitler's foreign policy was planned and intended for war from the onset.

- Structuralist historians (such as Martin Brozat) claim that Hitler was an opportunist with no long-term plans. They stress the importance of internal pressures and external factors in shaping Hitler's foreign policy. In their view, opportunism would be a better description of Nazi aggression.

1. In groups, consider the following facts. Write **I** or **S** next to each one, depending on whether you consider it to be supporting evidence for the intentionalist (I) or the structuralist (S) interpretations.

   a. *Mein Kampf*

   b. The murder of Dollfuss

   c. The reoccupation of the Rhineland

   d. The Hossbach Memorandum

   e. The Anschluss

   f. The Munich Conference

2. Compare your answers with the rest of the class. Have you had disagreements in your classification? What do they reveal about the way historians interpret evidence?

3. Discuss the following questions:

   a. What constitutes a good interpretation?

   b. How do we determine whether one historical interpretation is more valuable than another?

   c. Can this change through time?

4. How significant is it to know about the time and place in which historical knowledge is produced?

Personal and shared knowledge

ToK is interested in the links between shared knowledge and personal knowledge as it relates to history. You can use this concept to explore the role of key historians in shaping our shared knowledge, but you can also use it to investigate how our shared knowledge helps shape our own identities. One of the key concepts of IB History is that multiple interpretations are possible, and one of the key concepts of ToK is that individuals should be encouraged to think critically for themselves.

You can use the ToK concept of memory as a way into this topic. On a personal level, memory is important in creating our personalities; on a cultural level, collective memory is important in uniting, but also in dividing, people. Here is a case study exploring memory in history.

Case study: Shaping our collective memory of World War II

Source A

President Bill Clinton (C) at Felix De Weldon's Iwo Jima memorial during the ceremony commemorating the 50th anniversary of the WWII US Marine landing at Iwo Jima. Feb 19th 1995.

Source C

Museums are an important source of historical knowledge and, at Kure in Japan, one of the main attractions in its maritime museum is a model of the battleship, *Yamato*, the largest ever built. It was sunk in 1945 while attempting to defend Okinawa.

Below is a description of the ship from the Yamato Museum website.

> *The one-tenth scale model of the battleship Yamato (length: 26.3m) is duplicated as accurately as possible, based on original drawings, photos, and underwater images done by submersible surveys. As the centerpiece of the Yamato Museum, this one-tenth scale model of the battleship Yamato conveys the importance of peace and the potential of industrial technology to future generations.*

Source B

A group of imperial envoys leave the controversial Yasukuni shrine in Tokyo as Japanese Emperor Akihito presents an offering at the shrine's autumn festival on 18 October 2014. Two Japanese ministers visited this controversial Tokyo war shrine, becoming the first cabinet-level ministers to join a pilgrimage by 100 lawmakers to the spot condemned by China and Korea as a symbol of Japan's wartime aggression.

Source D

On 2 September 1945, Japan signed the formal declaration of surrender aboard the USS *Missouri*. The battleship is now part of a series of memorial sites to Pearl Harbor that can be visited in Hawaii.

Activity 5

ATL Thinking, research, and communication skills

1. Study Sources A and B. How do these two photographs reflect present-day perceptions of World War II?

2. Which photo, do you think, is more controversial? Give reasons for your answer.

3. Do some research to find out the significance of the battleship *Yamato* and why it is considered so important for how World War II is remembered in Japan.

4. How do places like museums and memorials (Sources C and D) help to shape a collective memory of World War II?

Conclusion

There is a considerable overlap between history and ToK. The concepts of change, continuity, significance, causation, consequence, and perspectives are included in the IB History syllabus and they fit well into the knowledge framework in ToK.

You can use skills you develop in history to add depth and meaning to your ToK presentations and essays. You can use skills developed in ToK to help you evaluate sources and to write the reflection section of your historical investigation. You can use the methodology of history to address the real-life issues that you discuss in ToK. By collecting evidence, weighing the value and limitations of sources, and building a logical, consistent interpretation of the facts you will be able to construct sound, well-supported arguments. History is one of the key areas of knowledge in ToK.

For further information about the ToK course, consult *Pearson Baccalaureate: Theory of Knowledge, 2nd edition*.

Case Study 1

Best, Antony, *Britain, Japan and Pearl Harbor: Avoiding War in East Asia, 1936–41*, Oxford: Routledge, 2001

Buruma, Ian, *Inventing Japan 1853–1964*, New York: Modern Library, 2004

Chang, Iris, *The Rape of Nanking*, UK: Penguin, 1997

Cheng, Per-kai, Lestz, Michael, Spence, Jonathan (eds), *The Search for Modern China: A Documentary Collection*, New York: WW Norton, 1999

Chickering, Roger and Forster, Stig (eds), *The Shadows of Total War*, New York: Cambridge UP, 2007

Costello, John, *The Pacific War*, Brattleboro: Rawson Wade, 1981

Crozier, Andrew J, *The Causes of the Second World War*, Oxford: Blackwell, 1997

Dallek, Robert, *Franklin Roosevelt and American Foreign Policy 1932–45*, New York: Oxford UP, 1981

Duus, Peter, (ed.), *The Cambridge History of Japan, Volume 6: The Twentieth Century*, UK: Cambridge UP, 1995

Fenby, Jonathan, *The Penguin History of Modern China: The Fall and Rise of a Great Power*, UK: Penguin, 2009

Ferguson, Niall, *The War of the World*, UK: Allen Lane, 2006

Hane, Mikiso, *Japan, A Short History*, UK: Oneworld Publications, 2015

Hsu, Immanuel CY, *The Rise of Modern China*, Hong Kong: Oxford UP, 1995

Hunter, Janet E, *Concise Dictionary of Modern Japanese History*, Los Angeles: U of California Press, Los Angeles, 1984

Hotta, Eri, *Japan 1941*, USA: Vintage Books, 2014

Iriye, Akire, *The Origins of the Second World War in Asia and the Pacific*, UK: Longman, 1995

Jones, Maldwyn A, *The Limits of Liberty, American History 1607–1992*, New York: Oxford UP, 1995

Lawrance, Alan, *China since 1919: Reform and Revolution*, UK: Routledge, 2004

Livingston, J, Moore, J, Oldfather, F (eds), *Imperial Japan 1800–1945*, New York: Pantheon, 1973

Lynch, Michael, *China from Empire to People's Republic 1900–1949*, UK: Hodder & Stoughton, 2003

Macmillan, Margaret, *Paris 1919*, New York: Random House, 2003

Mowat, Charles L, *Britain between the Wars 1918–1940*, London: Methuen & Co., 1976

Mitter, Rana, *China's War with Japan 1937–1945*, UK: Penguin, 2014

Pantsov, Alexander V and Levine, Steven, *Deng Xiaoping, A Revolutionary Life*, New York: Oxford UP, 2015

Stone, Oliver and Kuznick, Peter, *The Untold History of the United States*, UK: Random House, 2013

Taylor, AJP, *The Origins of the Second World War*, London: Hamish Hamilton, 1962

Tooze, Adam, *The Deluge: The Great War and the Remaking of Global Order*, UK: Penguin, 2014

Yu, Maochun, *The Dragon's War: Allied Operations and the Fate of China, 1937–1947*, Maryland: Naval Institute Press, 2013

http://afe.easia.columbia.edu/tps/1900_jp.htm#ww2 (Asia for Educators)

http://japanfocus.org/-Christopher-Gerteis/4159/article.html (Political protest in inter-war Japan)

Case Study 2

Adamthwaite, AP, *The Making of the Second World War*, London: Routledge, 1989

Boyce, Robert, (ed.), *French Foreign and Defence Policy, 1918–1940: The Decline and Fall of a Great Power*, London: Routledge, 1998

Bullock, Alan, *Hitler: A Study in Tyranny*, New York: Harper & Row, 1962

Calvocoressi, Peter et al., *Total War: The Causes and Course of the Second World War*, Vol. 1, London: Penguin, 1989

Churchill, Winston, *The Gathering Storm*, Boston: Houghton Mifflin, 1948

Cowan, Laing Gray, *France and the Saar, 1680–1948*, New York: Columbia UP, 1950

Duggan, Christopher, *Fascist Voices: An Intimate History of Mussolini's Italy*, 2012

Dziewanowski, MK, *Poland in the Twentieth Century*, New York: Columbia UP, 1977

Ebenstein, William, Fascist Italy, New York: American Book, 1939

Eubank, Keith (ed.), *The Origins of World War II*, 3rd ed., Wheeling, IL: Harlan Davidson, 2004

Fischer, Conan, Europe between Democracy and Dictatorship, 1900–1945, Malden, MA: Wiley-Blackwell, 2011

Herb, Guntram Henrik, *Under the Map of Germany: Nationalism and Propaganda, 1918–1945*, London: Routledge, 1997

Hibbert, Christopher, *Il Duce: The Life of Benito Mussolini*, Boston: Little, Brown, 1962

Hitler, Adolf, *Mein Kampf*, New York: Reynal & Hitchcock, 1939

Jackson, Julian, *Europe 1900–1945*, New York: Oxford UP, 2002

Kershaw, Ian, *Hitler 1936–1945, Nemesis*, New York: WW Norton, 2000

Kitchen, Martin, *A History of Modern Germany, 1800 to the Present*, 2nd ed., Malden, MA: Wiley-Blackwell, 2012

Lee, Stephen, *Aspects of European History 1789–1980*, London: Routledge, 1992

Lukes, Igor, *Czechoslovakia between Stalin and Hitler: The Diplomacy of Edvard Beneš in the 1930s*, New York: Oxford UP, 1996

Mavrikis, Peter (ed.), *History of World War II*, Vol. 1, New York: Marshall Cavendish, 2005

McElwee, William, *Britain's Locust Years: 1918–1940*, London: Faber & Faber, 1962

Morgan, JH, and MacDonogh, GMW, *Assize of Arms: The Disarmament of Germany and Her Rearmament (1919–1939)*, New York: Oxford UP, 1946

Offner, Arnold A, *American Appeasement: United States Foreign Policy and Germany, 1933–1938*, Cambridge, MA: Belknap Press of Harvard UP, 1969

Passant, EJA, *Short History of Germany, 1815–1945*, Cambridge, England: Cambridge UP, 1959

Perlmutter, Amos, *Making the World Safe for Democracy: A Century of Wilsonianism and Its Totalitarian Challengers*, Chapel Hill, NC: U of North Carolina, 1997

Rich, Norman, *Hitler's War Aims: Ideology, the Nazi State, and the Course of Expansion*, Vol. 1, New York: WW Norton, 1973

Rich, Norman, *Hitler's War Aims: The Establishment of the New Order*, Vol. 2, New York: WW Norton, 1974

Scheck, Raffael, *Germany, 1871–1945: A Concise History*, New York: Berg, 2008

Stachura, Peter D, *Poland, 1918–1945: An Interpretive and Documentary History of the Second Republic*, New York: Routledge, 2004

Taylor, AJP, *The Origins of the Second World War*, London: Penguin, 1991

Zalampas, Michael, *Adolf Hitler and the Third Reich in American Magazines, 1923–1939*, Bowling Green, OH: Bowling Green State U Popular Press, 1989

Allies: Great Britain, France, USA (as of 1917), Russia (up to 1917) and their allies.

Anschluss: The annexation of Austria by Germany in 1938.

Anti-Comintern Pact: An international communist organization that sought to end communism across the world.

autarky: a country that is economically independent.

Axis powers: One of the alliances which fought World War II. It was formed by Germany, Italy, and Japan. These countries mutually recognized their spheres of influence. For Germany, it was domination over most of continental Europe. Italy's sphere of influence included control of the Mediterranean Sea. Japan sought control over East Asia and the Pacific.

bakufu: Often referred to as Tokugawa bakufu, this term was used to describe the system of military government associated with the Tokugawa shogunate. In 1603, the Tokugawa made up the largest group of landowners of the period; from this group the shogun (military commander) was appointed by the emperor. The system remained in place until 1868. Also known as the period of 'centralized feudalism' when daimyo were given land and retainers in return for loyalty. The shogun and the daimyo always came from the samurai class.

blank cheque: A cheque bearing a signature but no amount, therefore allowing the recipient to withdraw as much as they like.

blitzkrieg: The German term for 'lightning war'; an intense military campaign intended to bring about a swift victory.

Bolshevism: A majority faction of the Russian Social Democratic Labour Party, which seized power in the October Revolution of 1917.

Blackshirts: The name given to members of the Italian Fascist paramilitary organisation MVSN (Milizia Volontaria per la Sicurezza Nazionale; Voluntary Militia for National Security) established in 1919. The name derived from their uniform, which included the use of black shirts.

Blue Shirts Society: The name given to a group within the GMD in China.

Brownshirts: The name given to members of the Nazi SA (*Sturmabteilung*: storm detachment or assault division) paramilitary organization. The name derived from their uniform, which included the use of brown shirts.

Bushido: 'The way of the warrior', Bushido was a code that outlined such virtues as living a frugal, honourable life and complete loyalty to one's lord, even to death. It was believed that dying for one's lord was the ultimate expression of loyalty and there were many instances of samurai committing *hara kiri*, or ritual self-disembowelment, when their lord died or was killed in combat.

capitalism: An economic system where a great deal of trade and industry is privately owned and runs to make a profit.

capital ships: This was a term used to describe the biggest ships of the naval fleet. Before the outbreak of World War II, these would have been Dreadnought-class battleships and battle cruisers.

Central Powers: Germany, Austro-Hungary, Turkey, and their allies.

collective security: Alliances between states with the aim of defending each other from aggression on the principle that an attack on one member is an attack on all its allies.

Comintern: The abbreviation for the Communist International. This organization was set up in Moscow in March 1919 and its task was to coordinate communist parties all over the world, helping the spread of global communism.

Communist Party of China (CPC): The ruling political party of the People's Republic of China, founded in 1921. In 1949 it defeated the Guomindang and has been in power since.

Conference of Ambassadors: Created after World War I to contribute to the enforcement of peace treaties and to solve the conflicts arising from their application.

conscription: Compulsory enlistment in the armed forces.

deification: To be given a god-like status.

embargo: An official ban on trade or other commercial activity with a specific country.

Fascism: A political ideology that favours limited freedom of people, nationalism, use of violence to achieve ends, and an aggressive foreign policy. Power is in the hands of an elite leader or leadership. Italian Fascism (Fascism for short) was the name given by Mussolini to his movement from 1922.

feudalism: This is a term used to describe European society in the Middle Ages when monarchs allocated land to their knights, in return for their services in time of conflict. The knights owned not only the land on their estates but also the results of the labour performed by the people who farmed them. In return for labour these peasants were given plots of land that were used for subsistence farming. In Japan the system was a little different but there was a similar exchange of land for loyalty and military support between the daimyo and the shogun.

Freikorps: Different right-wing paramilitary groups who claimed they protected Germany from Bolshevism. The government often resorted to using these groups to help restore order.

Great Depression: An economic crisis that began in the USA in 1929 with the collapse of the stock market; it led to the financial ruin of banks in Europe and the USA, and impacted on economies worldwide during the 1930s.

Guomindang (GMD): The Nationalist party, led by Jiang Jieshi, which fought against the Communists in the Chinese Civil War. After it lost to Mao Zedong's Communists in the Civil War, it set up the Chinese Nationalist government on the island of Taiwan (also known as the Republic of China).

historiography: The study of the writing of history and of written histories.

hyperinflation: Extreme or excessive rise of prices which leads to a decline in both purchasing power as well as in the value of the currency.

interior minister: The minister responsible for internal security.

jingoism: Propaganda linked specifically to promoting imperialism among the population of Britain, in particular.

League of Nations: An international organization set up after World War I, intended to maintain peace and encourage disarmament.

May Fourth Movement: A student-led movement that sprang up, in May 1919, in response to the treatment of China at the Paris Peace Conference and the Chinese government's acceptance of Japan's demands.

mandate: A commission from the League of Nations to a member state to administer a territory.

Marxism: A political ideology based on the works of Karl Marx and Friedrich Engels, the main belief of which is that the workers rise up against the middle and upper classes to create a society where all resources are shared.

non-belligerent: The state of not fighting a war. It differs from neutral in that a non-belligerent state may still be supporting one side of the conflict.

passive resistance: Opposition to a government or occupying force by refusing to comply with orders.

Phoney War: This term is used to refer to the period between September 1939 and April 1940 when no major hostilities took place in Western Europe. It is also known by the name given to it by Winston Churchill, the Twilight War.

plebiscite: A plebiscite is a process in which voters are given the opportunity to express their support of or opposition to a single issue.

protectionism: Government policies that inhibit international trade to encourage the development of national industries and to protect the economy from foreign competition. Protectionist policies include import tariffs, restrictive import quotas, and subsidies to national businesses.

Qing dynasty: A dynasty established by the Manchus, which ruled China from 1644 to 1911.

self-determination: The process that enables a country to determine its own statehood and form its own government.

Shintoism: The 'indigenous' religion of Japan that was traditionally animistic and held the view that there were sacred spirits within both animate and inanimate objects. In terms of political power, it also believed that the imperial family were descended from the Sun Goddess.

shogunate: This refers to the rule of the shogun, who was the military deputy of the emperor. In practice, the shogun ruled Japan with the emperor secluded at the imperial court in Kyoto. In 1603, Tokugawa Ieyasu was named shogun and this began the period of the Tokugawa shogunate (see also **bakufu**) that, in effect, ruled Japan until the Meiji Restoration in 1868.

socialism: A political theory of social organization stressing shared or state ownership of production, industry, land, etc.

Stresa Front: An agreement signed in April 1935 between Italy, Britain, and France to act collectively to resist a German challenge to the Treaty of Versailles. It broke down two months later, when Britain and Germany signed the Anglo-German Naval Agreement.

'strike north': This was a strategy, popular with the Japanese army, that favoured preparing for war against the Soviet Union.

'strike south': This strategy was the one adopted in 1941 when the IJA (Imperial Japanese Army) headed south into Indochina, Malaya, and the Dutch East Indies and the IJN (Imperial Japanese Navy) headed into the Pacific.

Treaty of Versailles: Peace treaty concluded in 1919 between the Allies and Germany. It contained controversial clauses relating to the payment of reparations, war guilt, territorial losses, and the loss of all of Germany's colonies. The United States Congress rejected this treaty as it contained the covenant of the League of Nations. Congress ratified a later version (without the covenant) known as the Treaty of Berlin.

Treaty of St Germain: Peace treaty concluded in 1919 between the Allies and the Austrian Republic which ended the Austro–Hungarian Empire, distributed parts of its territory, and forbade Austria to unite with Germany.

Twenty-One Demands: A set of Japanese demands made in 1915 that would have given Japan significant control over China.

warlordism: Used to describe the period after 1911 in China, when the Qing dynasty had been overthrown but there was no strong central government. Regions fell under the sole authority of independent leaders with their own armies.

Wilson's Fourteen Points: Guidelines proposed by US President Woodrow Wilson in 1918. They included respect for the principle of self-determination, the pursuit of open diplomacy, the reduction of national armaments, and the establishment of a League of Nations to settle international disputes.

zaibatsu: Large financial and industrial conglomerates in Japan.

Italic page numbers indicate an illustration, be it a picture, table or map. Bold page numbers indicate an interesting fact box.

Improve your learning

Take a look at some of the interactive tools on your
History: The Move to Global War eText.
Note that the examples below may be from a different title, but you will find
topic-appropriate resources on your eText.

Worksheets

A variety of research activities
with questions for you to
work on together outside the
classroom, giving you practice
of essay-writing skills.

ACCALAUREATE

The Move to Global War

Change in Japan 1853–1890

Read through the first section of Chapter 1 up to the subheading 'Fir

Work with a classmate in order to:

1. Identify external factors that stimulated change in Japan

2. Identify internal factors that stimulated change

   Decide which was the most significant and justify your deci

   See how much you agree or disagree with each other's

   vity will help you focus on key concepts such as
   t your analysis with factual evidence. It
   in this case: What factors

Chapter 8: Cross-Regional War: The Second World

Put the following developments in chronol

Drag and drop the events into the correct order and then click Submit.

Hitler's armies reverse the defeats of the Italians i

Italy enters the Second W

The British sink half the

Revision Quizzes

These include a variety of
exercise types e.g. check
whether you can put events
in the correct order.
Get immediate feedback:
great for revision practice.

...er 1 Example question 3: Com...
...r violence by Japanese soldiers. [6 m...

Work through the stages of planning an answer to this...

Exam Practice Activities

Practice with source analysis helps to get you ready for the exam.

Sources

Source 1

Inventing Japan 1853–1964 (2004) by Ian Buruma

For years, the Japanese had been told that the
Chinese were inferior and the Japanese a d...
race. Contempt for the Chinese goes ba...
Meiji prints in which the Japanese are...
vigorous and the Chinese are coweri...
...tins; Government propaganda, p...
...tic Japanese press, told sold...
...ly war.

...correct answers.

...is is a typical example of Question 1b in Paper
...question is asking you to do?

☐ Demonstrate understanding of the source's message...

☐ Consider the successes and failures of Mussolini's fore...

☐ Give an account of the similarities and differences bet...
expressed in the source and your own knowledge on...
foreign policy.

...ook at Source 1. What event is it referring to?

...lini's declaration of aims for f...

HITLER

1889–1945

Adolf Hitler (1889–1945): Austrian-born German politician and
leader of the Nazi Party. As Chancellor and dictator of Germany,
his expansionist regime led to World War Two, one of the most
deadly conflicts in the history of humanity. Hitler's political and foreign
policy aims were outlined in his book *Mein Kampf (My Struggle)*, which
included strong anti-Semitic views. His aggressive foreign policy,
which sought to find 'lebensraum' or living space for Germans, caused
the outbreak of the Second World War. Hitler's war also led to the
Holocaust, where millions of Jewish people were killed.

Biographies

To help you remember who the key figures are, these posters include the significant facts on each person.